# Triggs

Paul Howard is a former Irish Sports Journalist of the Year, a two-time Irish Book Award winner and the creator of the cult character, Ross O'Carroll-Kelly.

# Triggs

The Autobiography of Roy Keane's Dog

HACHETTE
BOOKS
IRELAND

First published in 2012 by Hachette Books Ireland
Copyright © 2012 Paul Howard

1

The right of Paul Howard to be identified as the Author of the Work has
been asserted by him in accordance with the Copyright, Designs
and Patents Act 1988.

A CIP catalogue record for this title is available from the British Library.

ISBN 978 1 444 74299 2

Typeset in Berling Antiqua and Myriad Pro
by Bookends Publishing Services

Printed and bound in Great Britain by Mackays of Chatham Ltd, Kent

Hachette Books Ireland policy is to use papers that are natural,
renewable and recyclable products and made from wood grown
in sustainable forests. The logging and manufacturing processes
are expected to conform to the environmental regulations
of the country of origin.

Hachette Books Ireland
8 Castlecourt Centre
Castleknock
Dublin 15, Ireland
A division of Hachette UK Ltd
338 Euston Road
London NW1 3BH

www.hachette.ie

# Contents

# Acknowledgements

I would like to thank my agent, Faith O'Grady, as well as Breda Purdue, Ciara Considine and everyone at Hachette Books Ireland for their support and enthusiasm for this book. Thank you to Ciara and to Rachel Pierce for a wonderful editing job. Also, thank you to Mary McCarthy, Dion Fanning, Declan Lynch, Mark McGuinness, Ian Whittle, John Boyne and Vincent Howard for your kind help, encouragement and advice.

# Prologue

A HAZY AFTERNOON IN MID-SEPTEMBER ELIDES into a cool, ambrosial evening. I'm stretched to my full length on the patio, in a paling wash of sunlight, eyes gently closed, ears alive to the sounds of birds fossicking for food scraps in the B&Q rock-effect water feature. I've been lying here most of the day, pondering the undeniable finiteness of life.

I love the south of England, which is not to say that I love the north any less. How could I? All of our memories are there. But staring out each morning at the vast, undulating tableland of the Suffolk countryside has helped me to adjust to the new metre of my life. You could say I've eased into old age as into a warm bath.

It said in one of the morning newspapers that I was dead. Which, I can assure you I'm not, even though my list of infirmities lengthens by the week – my failing eyesight and complaining hips an ever-present reminder that while time is as generous as a drunken uncle when we are young, so does it claim its forfeit in the end.

It's a year since I began to feel it – the slow creep of age. Arthritis has insinuated its way into my joints. I'm missing a tooth or two. I can clear a room in short time with my flatulence. And there are days when sounds come at me muffled, as if through a closed door. None of which is a surprise to me. I'm old. It's the way of things. Still, I can't tell you how much reading your obituary in the morning paper is liable to piss you off for the day.

Journalists have been known to get things wrong, of course. They've got *him* wrong, after all. I'm talking about the caricature with which you're no doubt familiar. The monster. The permanently angry man. The brooding depressive with no friends. He's none of those things. Take it from me – the dog who's been at his side for the last thirteen years, the dog I once saw described as 'the most terrified-looking pet in England' – that they are wrong, wrong, wrong.

Wrong about Roy Keane. Wrong about me. You'd think that on the day the national press decided to kill and bury me they could have got right the one fact that should be obvious to the human eye and is not exactly irrelevant in the context of an obituary.

I'm a girl.

Yes, I know what you thought, but you were wrong.

I will confess that fulfilling the role of best friend to the most alpha male footballer of his generation has meant sublimating my true feminine nature into a kind sort of blokeish androgyny. But I'm not a he. Never was.

As misassumptions go, though, it's not quite as bad as the headline, 'Keane's Beloved Triggs Is Dead', which stared at me from the front page of this morning's *Sun*. That was the real doozy, the one that's had me lying here since eleven o'clock this morning, sadly contemplating death's imminence.

The photographs used to illustrate the story only served to compound the feeling that has hung over me all day – that my better years belong to a fast receding past. Nonetheless, they did take me back. They were taken in 2002. That silly summer when we opened the door each morning to face the bruit of the encamped paparazzi and walked through them like they were invisible to us.

Oh, happy days.

Roy, sporting a round-neck sweater, jeans and trainers, looked like a joyrider. I'd forgotten that. His occasional derelictions in taste – especially in the areas of fashion and music – were a source of good-humoured discord between us. As for me, God, I looked young. I *was* young. My nose was wet, my coat as smooth as a trout's scales and my eyes sparked with the assuredness of a dog in the prime of her optimistic youth.

Many times I've been asked to tell my story. To give my account of the role I played in the life of the most compelling and misunderstood footballer of his generation – with particular focus, of course, on what happened that crazy May, pushing on for a decade ago now, when Roy was sent home from the World Cup for calling Mick McCarthy, among other things, a useless wanker, and images of us out walking were catapulted on to the front pages of newspapers in India and Pakistan at the same time as the two countries were threatening each other with nuclear annihilation.

The money, I was told, would be good. Not that money has ever been a motivation for me. There was a rumour once that Harry Redknapp's bulldog had nearly two hundred thousand pounds stashed in a bank account in Monaco. Good luck to her. Me, I've never had much use for the stuff.

On the subject of telling my story, I always demurred, preferring to put it off until some distant future date, which I've realised, thanks to this morning's papers – another headline was 'GRRR.I.P. Triggsy' – may not exist for me. Which is why I've decided, finally, to have it committed to print, as my life's final reckoning, if you like.

I should mention at the outset, seeing as I'm contributing to the canon, how much I loathe football autobiographies. *And* how shamed I am by the large number of them I've read. There were dozens of them lying around the house when I was growing up and all I can offer in my defence is that I didn't buy any of them. But I did read them – perhaps in an effort to better understand Roy and the world in which he moved.

Oh, yes – all those hysterical tales of practical jokes that involved shaving foam and hotel beds and expensive designer shoes! All those bare footballers' bottoms hilariously borne in public bars! All those speeding and drink-driving offences indulgently excused on the grounds of youthful immaturity! All those Christmas party incidents that admittedly got a bit out of hand and – *between one fing and anuver* – the police ended up being called and then, of course, the papers went and had a field day!

All those exclamation marks!!!

No, I want this book to be an honest rendering of the role I played in the life of Roy Keane. The publisher might well adorn the jacket with dramatic adjectives, such as 'Sensational!', 'Shocking!' and 'Explosive!', and I don't doubt that the story, in parts, is all of those things. But what I am more interested in – despite the threats of super-injunctions from one or two individuals – is producing an account that is truthful, uncomfortable as it may be for some people to read.

This isn't some saccharine-sweet story of a love affair between a man and his beloved pet. I'm no Marley. And, God knows, Roy is no John Grogan. (For what it's worth, we both read the book and agreed that the dog's essential problem was too much handling in the neonatal phase.)

It's not my intention to cast myself as the heroine of this story. That is not to say that I am not the heroine. In fact, while I was known throughout the world as Roy Keane's best friend, I think he himself always considered me his genius.

Humility forbids me to say it, but it does make me sad to think about how he'll cope when he no longer has me at his side. Especially at this time of year – the first few weeks of a new football season. Ipswich Town, the team he now manages, lost to Queen's Park Rangers the other night. It was their first defeat of the season, but a heavy one (3–0), and he's been vague and distracted ever since.

This is a huge year for Ipswich Town Football Club. How

many times did I hear him say that over the course of the summer? The supporters are demanding nothing less than promotion to the Premier League and there are days when the weight of that becomes too great for even his broad shoulders to bear.

I'm listening to him now, flapping around the kitchen like a bird trapped indoors. 'Where is it?' he asks in his Cork sing-song. 'I was only after been listening to it this morning.'

I have a good idea what he's looking for, but I don't stir. Soon, he joins me on the patio. 'Can't find my Bob Dylan CD,' he says. '*Blonde On Blonde*, to be fair. It was in the CD player this morning?'

I stare off into the mid-distance, all innocence.

He takes a breath, then he crouches down and playfully knuckles the back of my neck. I've always liked that. He laughs. 'What *am* I like?' he says, because there are times when he's a mystery even to himself.

'It's just . . . I don't know, I look at our players, Triggs, and – I've spoke about it before – they've got their huge watches and their mansions and obviously their high-performance cars. You're on about championship players! Jesus! Nineteen, twenty years of age! And they've got it all. And I can't help but think, you know, at the end of the day, what can *I* say to motivate them?'

I get up silently and I make my way back towards the house. He follows me inside. I pad through the hallway to the front door, where I stop and look back over my shoulder at him. He laughs. He says, 'Good idea.'

Humans, I can tell you from long experience, are the most wonderful company. But this much is also true – and isn't it the story of my life? – they do need to be walked.

*Triggs*
*September, 2010*

'Unlike humans,
dogs don't talk shit.'

Roy Keane, 2002

# 1.

# 'I Was Roy Keane's Dog. What the Hell Was Wrong with That?'

IT WAS ONLY IN RARE MOMENTS OF MELANCHOLY that Roy could bring himself to talk about the day that was to be the tipping point in both our lives – the beginning of the little intrigue he enjoyed with that splendid *bon vivant* and highly decorated football genius, Alf-Inge Haaland.

It happened very early on in our acquaintance, in the autumn of 1997. I didn't see it at the time. In my defence, I was only a few months old and the height of my ambition – much as it embarrasses me now – was to pull the washing from the rotating clothes line in the garden or drink the blue water from the downstairs toilet bowl.

But since then I've watched it dozens of times, from beginning to end. The two of them haring after the ball with all the dumb excitement of Chris Kamara watching a couple of midtable Npower League Two teams play out a scoreless draw on a Monday night in January. Alfie reaching it first. Roy collapsing suddenly, in the manner of a detonated building. Then Haaland standing above him, loudly damning him for his theatrics.

I was never certain what, in fact, caused Roy the most

distress – that he was accused of feigning injury by a fellow professional or that the player who rushed in to defend his honour was David Beckham.

'I was lying there on the turf,' he told me years later, 'and I was thinking, "Kill the fucker, Becksy! Kill him!" And he came steaming in, in fairness to the lad. But then he stopped. Do you know what he said to him, Triggs? He said, "You leave him alone!" Jesus! Like your mother would say if she was pulling a bully off you in the playground after school. And in that fucking voice of his – as I've said in the past, like two pieces of polystyrene being rubbed together.'

It wouldn't be long, of course, before Beckham was pillaging his wife's knicker drawer and cruising the Mediterranean coast in a skirt.

I think Roy's alpha malehood suffered a grievous blow that day. But if there was one moment that determined the course of our lives together, then that unfortunate afternoon's business with Alfie Haaland was it.

If they seem like a lifetime ago now, those early, innocent days of our friendship, it's because they were. I was just a pup when I entered Roy's life and, well, I suppose quite a few people would have said the same thing about him.

Much as it offends the narrative conventions of the traditional animal-buddy story, I don't recall the precise moment of our first meeting. I'd love to tell you that our eyes locked through the latticework fence of an animal rescue shelter in Salford or Stockport and we both understood immediately that our finding each other was fate. Or that I performed some endearing little trick that singled me out from the rest of the litter in the kitchen of some breeder's home in Crumpsall or Altringham or Higher Blackley.

But I can't.

All I've ever had was Roy's account of how we came to be in each other's lives. And it was as sober and colourless a story as you'd expect from a man who's always made a virtue of keeping his emotions on a tight chokelead. He saw an ad somewhere – it might have been the *South Manchester Reporter*. He visited a house, but he couldn't say exactly where. It was some time in the spring of 1997, but he couldn't remember exactly when. There were six pups, he did remember that, in the corner of a converted garage. He nodded – and he always told this part of the story with a cool, unfocussed stare – and said, 'Any one of them will do.'

I'm not hurt by it. Not at all. What I will admit is that I always found it curious, that need of Roy's to talk things down. Despite all the very terrible and very wrong things that were said about him over the course of his career, I often thought that to accuse him of being a sentimentalist would be the grossest libel you could commit against his character.

I saw him on television once talking about his excellent work with the Irish Guide Dogs for the Blind. Someone from the press wondered what it was about that particular charity that made it worthy of his patronage. Now, asked the same question, Niall Quinn, say, would have had some carefully thought-out position paper on the matter – something about having been fortunate enough to be blessed with the gift of vision and what an unimaginable living purgatory it would be not to be able to properly appreciate flowers and birds and all of God's wonders. But then that's Niall for you. Football's questionable gain was Christian country music's undoubted loss.

Anyway, not for the first time in my life, I found myself silently pleading with him through an inch of television glass: 'Play the game, Roy! Just this once, play the game!'

Roy just said he liked the dogs.

I love television, by the way. I've been an avid watcher ever since the day that Roy – at least in my imagination – carried me across the threshold, swaddled in an old car blanket, then laid me down on the sofa, whining and fretting for my mother, in front of his then state-of-the-art Nordmende set, which incidentally weighed the equivalent of a small family car.

I've always experienced television in a way that's different from other dogs, most of whom will just stand there watching the moving colours with a look of utter bewilderment on their faces. The same way that Laurent Blanc used to defend during his years at Old Trafford.

Forgive me. I should stop myself. I sometimes think that the only concession to my feminine nature left is my occasional tendency towards bitchiness. I'll admit that I'm like Marley – that unthinking, fur-covered lump of protoplasm – in just one way. I'm beyond reform.

But let me get this out of the way at the beginning: I've always regarded professional footballers as, frankly, an intellectually inferior breed. Roy is a happy exception. The rest – well, you really would have to wonder sometimes what, if anything, is going on between their auditory canals. This is a world, remember, in which David James is considered an intellectual because he begins sentences with the word 'ironically' instead of the word 'obviously. (Just as a footnote, I have never heard David James use the word 'ironically' in its correct context. Is that an irony in and of itself? I don't know. But certainly don't ask him!)

A memory suddenly pops up at me from out of the recent past. It was one afternoon in Roy's last full season as a Manchester United player and he telephoned Wayne Rooney at home to talk about, oh, some team matter or other.

'Can you phone me back later?' Wayne asked him. 'It's just I'm reading at the moment.'

I remember the surprised smile that was suddenly slashed across Roy's face. 'What are you reading?' he wondered, always happy to hear about a teammate making the effort to improve his mind.

'Ceefax,' came the reply.

I always liked Wayne.

He was easy company and a great lover of dogs. And anyone expecting a cheap joke here about hookers, young or old, is going to be disappointed. He was, as they say in the parlance, a smashing lad and a top, top player. Yet whenever I think about Wayne, I always think of his mind turning over at the same rate it takes for those teletext pages to refresh themselves.

I'm off the point again.

I have little or no memory of the first few weeks of our relationship. According to Roy, we fell into a kind of rhythm early on. He would switch on the television for me every morning before he left the house for training. Always the History, Discovery or National Geographic channels, which, he noticed right from the beginning, seemed to hold my gaze in a peculiar kind of way. Later, when he returned home, I would apparently hold forth – no doubt in a show-offish manner – on all the extraordinary things I had learned during the day, while he grinned a rictus and picked up whatever little piles I'd left about the place, or chased puddles of my piss around the laminate flooring with fistfuls of ill-absorbent kitchen roll.

I was only a few weeks old, and therefore still not housebroken.

Roy loved listening to these stories – or so he told me – about subjects as varied as the Battle of Austerlitz, the life of Jesse James and the sinking of the US aircraft carrier, the USS *Lexington*. There was nothing I didn't know, it seemed, about Prince Eugene of Savoy, the seventeenth-century military commander who led the Austrian Hapsburgs to victory in the Battle of Zenta with the Ottomans rattling the gates of Vienna. And I could prattle on for hours, apparently, about Simón Bolívar, the brilliant revolutionary leader who loosed Spain's grip on Latin America forever and whose famous *Decreto de Guerra a Muerte* I had – much as it embarrasses me to say it – committed to memory.

Yes, it seems that I was a precocious pup.


I don't have a first memory as such, although I was dimly aware from very early on – perhaps the late spring of 1997 – that Roy made his living by kicking a ball around for the entertainment of others. I do remember, that first summer together, watching a documentary on the History Channel about the writing of the original rulebook of association football. I also remember Roy telling me, around the same time, that he'd been awarded the captaincy of Manchester United. And while knowing little about football beyond the story of its codification, I understood that the game was part of the collective consciousness of just about every country on Earth and that being captain of Manchester United, the world's best-known club, was, in human terms, a very, very big deal indeed.

It was during that summer that Roy and I fell into our happy habit of walking everywhere together, though mostly across the chequerboard dales and along the leafy, private security-patrolled laneways of Hale and Altrincham, where the palaces of many great footballers stood. As June turned into July, I noticed that Roy had begun to walk discernibly taller. Dogs pick up on these things. With his chest thrust out like a bantam, he would talk about his antecedents as though he was part of some royal lineage, and of course to many millions of humans he was.

'Denis Law, Bobby Charlton, Martin Buchan,' he would say, rhyming off the names of the men who'd worn the captain's armband before him. 'We spoke about Ray Wilkins. Bryan Robson. Brucie, to give him his due. Then, obviously, Eric. It's the biggest honour in the game. Jesus, can you not stay out of the fucking puddles, Triggs?'

He took to leadership, as everyone knows, like a man who owned the patent on it.

'In this world,' he told me one morning, 'a man must be either an anvil or a hammer.'

I remember thinking, where did he pick that up? But at the same time, okay, he's going to be the boss in this relationship.

I recall another conversation we had the day after United beat Coventry City early in the 1997/8 season. Roy scored one of United's three goals and he still had quite the air about him the following morning. I was in the kitchen – I remember it like it happened yesterday – sniffing at a dishwasher tablet that had fallen, only partially dissolved, from the drawer of the new Bosch, trying to decide whether to eat it or not.

'I've an unbelievably good feeling about this year,' he said.

We were only getting to know each other – still defining the contours of our relationship, you could say – but I think even then, in those early days, it struck me as unusual to hear him express himself in such effusive terms.

'Really?' I said.

I had decided not to eat the dishwasher tablet after all.

'Well, obviously, no one's getting too carried away,' he said, picking my lead off the hook under the stairs where it always hung. I immediately headed for the front door. The rattle of the chain, the jangle of keys – it was all about picking up on the little social cues.

'As I've said before, you don't win trophies in August – except, obviously, the Charity Shield. But listen, we've got good players at the football club. We spoke about the young lads. Fergie's Fledglings, blah, blah, fucking blah. Scholesy, who's obviously done tremendously well. Becks, we all know the quality he has as a footballer. Obviously, the Nevilles. Giggsy, when he's on song and fully fit, can do things that can maybe take your breath away. Andy Cole, who'll get you a lot of goals in a season, always lurking with intent . . .'

To me, it was a laundry list of meaningless names, which seems extraordinary to me now, in the light of later events.

'Teddy Sheringham. Teddy should have been at a big club years ago – for me, as I've said before, he's always been a top, top player, even though – as I've said in the past – we're never going to be bosom buddies. That's documented. Listen, we've a good team this year. For me, we should be maybe starting to think in terms of winning obviously the European Cup . . .'

The man could talk. I was learning that. 'Are we going out or not?' I said.

Roy laughed. There was a cheekiness about me as a pup that I think reminded him of himself as a younger man.

As it turned out, this happy form – both Roy's and United's – continued until the middle of September, when the team experienced what was, by the standards that Roy was determined to set for them, a minor catastrophe. First, a goalless draw with – from memory – Bolton Wanderers, then a 2–2 draw with Chelsea, a match from which, I remember Roy saying repeatedly, they were fortunate to come away with even a point.

It was the morning after the Chelsea game that I first became aware of the unforgiving pressure that he exerted on himself and his teammates to win every single match, regardless of its importance. I emerged from the laundry room, where I'd taken to sleeping some nights, to find him pacing the kitchen floor, muttering about teammates who, as he saw it, had been sated and made soft by success.

(I know others were often cowed by his fierceness, but to me, Roy's occasional flashes of anger always had a slightly comic edge, especially the way the pitch of his voice tended to ascend to a register commensurate with his level of outrage. Years later, when he told Mick McCarthy, in the final act of their hierarchal dispute in a Chinese restaurant in the middle of the Pacific, to shove the World Cup up his arse, or his hole, or his bollocks – depending on which account you read – I couldn't figure out how the other players managed to keep in their laughter.)

'They're paying these fellas,' Roy said, travelling up through the keys, 'as I've said in the past, twenty, thirty grand a week?' This was in the days, remember, when twenty or thirty grand a week was considered a lot of money for a footballer. 'It's no wonder these lads have no hunger! Listen, a lot of them are going to have to start asking themselves some serious fucking questions.'

The following Saturday, I remember, dawned dark and unpleasant – a perfect correlative for what was to happen that day. The team was travelling to Leeds, a city for which I've never heard him profess any great love. Manchester United and Leeds United supporters, I learned much later, hated each other with a meanness of spirit that transcended football. I heard someone describe it once as an enmity as old as the ages, with its historical roots in the War of the Roses. It might have been one of those ridiculously overwrought Sky Sports Super Sunday trailers – in fact, yes, when I close my eyes now, I can hear Richard Keys saying the words. From what Roy told me, it was more likely down to the fact that the Leeds supporters liked to sing a song celebrating the deaths of eight Manchester United players in the Munich air disaster of 1958.

Whatever it was, Roy always set off for Leeds with the mien of a man going to war. The last thing he said to me before he left the house that morning was, 'Tomorrow, we'll do a really long walk – maybe two miles.' Then he delivered a final rebuke, 'And keep your nose out of the fucking toilet, will you?', because whatever chemicals he was using to keep the bowl clean and pearly white, were playing havoc with my lower digestive system. 'Shitting custard' was the rather choice phrase I heard him use a couple of days earlier during my very first visit to the vet. Roy was the one having to pick up after me, I suppose.

The day passed slowly. Or perhaps that's just how I remember it. As usual, Roy had put on the television before he left and I watched biographies of George Harrison, Chairman Mao and Crazy Horse and documentaries about Lorenzo de' Medici, the Beekeepers of Wadi Du'an and the plot to steal Abraham Lincoln's body. I also took several naps in the laundry room, which I had decided would be my permanent den. It was in there that I would later do some of my best thinking. From watching Roy, I had learned how to open the spin dryer at the end of a cycle, and there were few pleasures I enjoyed more than popping the door of the machine and making a bed for myself inside its soft belly, especially if the Egyptian cotton towels were in there. It was another of my puppyish habits that drove Roy to distraction.

'Jesus Christ, I'm going to have to put them through another fucking wash cycle,' he'd fume. But then, a moment later, I'd catch him shaking his head while smiling indulgently. He had a similar relationship, I think, with Jason McAteer, whose nickname, incidentally, was Trigger, and after whom I came to mistakenly believe I was named. Jason drove him mad at times, but I think he always loved – and maybe even envied – the lightness in his soul.

Roy never had it in him to stay annoyed with me beyond the time it took him to transfer the towels back to the washing machine, pour fabric conditioner into the drawer, pop a biological tablet into the little string bag and throw it into the barrel, set the temperature control and press the on button again.

Anyway, I was nestled in the spin dryer when I woke up at some point deep into the evening – I know now that it was well after midnight – with that leaden feeling you get when you know that something is wrong. Dogs are extraordinarily intuitive. Roy wasn't home. I knew it without even needing to check. It was in the early hours of the morning that I became aware of a commotion outside in the front driveway. It was *his* voice that I heard first. Being still an infant in human terms, I must admit that it came as a huge relief to me.

'Yeah, just leave me here,' he said.

I sprinted into the living room and observed the scene through the window. There were two cars outside – the Bentley, which belonged to Roy, and some form of German car, which may or may not have been an Audi. At the wheel of the Bentley was a boy of five, maybe six years old, who immediately noticed me staring at him from the window.

From the moment our eyes locked I felt the anxiety rise in me, for the boy had quite the look of the brat about him. I had sudden flashes of agonising tail-pulling and ear-twisting tortures to come – or, worse, being pressed into service as some kind of pack animal, forced to carry the grinning little monster around the house on my back, with him cruelly beating my flanks with a rolled-up back issue of one of Roy's *Autosport* magazines.

My urge to flee was stopped short by the sight of Roy making a clumsy effort to negotiate his way out of the front passenger seat. First, he swung his two feet out onto the cobblelock of the driveway. Then he gripped the roof of the car with one hand and the top of the door with the other, attempting to render himself vertical.

It's a terrible slur on his character, but I did speculate that this awkward ballet had its roots somehow in alcohol. At that moment, the most plausible explanation for this little scene was that he had taken the circuitous route home, via The Bleeding Wolf – his 'local' – and enjoyed the hospitality there, to the extent that it was considered safest all round if the landlord's five-year-old son drove him and his car back to Hale.

Like I said, a terrible slur.

When he eventually managed to persuade himself out of the car and upright, I could see rather more clearly that it was something other than alcohol that had waylaid him. His leg was sheathed in plaster from ankle to hip.

On his good leg, he hopped to the back of the car, retrieving from the boot a pair of metal crutches, which he then used to pick a path for himself to the door. The boy, to my considerable relief, climbed into the Audi next to a man who I took to be his father. Soon, the little rug rat was gone, though not before rolling down the window and shouting, 'Don't fucking bother saying thanks, then,' at Roy's departing back.

It's rare that I'm wrong in my judgments of people.

I stepped into the hallway. I heard Roy's key rattle in the lock, then the front door opened to the full. I don't recall if I asked what happened, but when he spoke, it was with a sad tremor in his voice. He said, 'Triggs,' the name he'd only recently taken to calling me, 'I've only gone and done my cruciate.'

The word meant nothing to me. I expect he could see that because he chose to elaborate. 'My career could be over. Twenty-six years of age. Jesus! Done!'

To try to take his mind off what had happened, I dragged some of my toys from the kitchen into the living room – a rubber chicken, a pull-rope, a squeaky hotdog with the smiling face of a Schnauzer on it – but he was in no mood to play that night. So I jumped up onto the sofa beside him and we sat in silence, side by side, neither of us saying anything.

You might not be surprised to learn that Roy wasn't given to unnecessary displays of affection. I'm not saying he was withholding or anything like that. His love was just something you earned over time. It was like when Dwight Yorke turned up to train with his United teammates for the first time and Roy larded every pass he played to him with just that little bit of extra weight. Yes, you had to work for Roy's affection, no matter who you were. But when you felt his fingers in your coat, well, I can tell you that there is no greater feeling in the world.

So there we were, sitting side by side, in the early hours.

'I can't *do* anything else,' I remember him saying, his voice rising and falling as it was wont to do. 'No trade. No exams. Jesus, I failed me fucking Inter. At the end of the day, all I *have* is – as I've said in the past – football.'

Unfortunately, I had no answers for him. I was only six months old, or five years in human terms. All I could do was sit and listen to him recount, over and over, the events of the day: chasing after a pass from Ryan Giggs that maybe asked a little bit much of him, flicking a thoughtless boot at Alfie Haaland, who ran across his flightpath, then experiencing the most excruciating pain shooting up his lower leg.

'I tried to play on,' he said, 'like the lad we spoke about last week – who was that fucking lunatic, Triggs, who wouldn't die?'

'Rasputin,' I said.

I was watching sometimes fourteen hours of television a day.

'That's the lad. But as I said, I knew. I knew straight away what it was. Fucking cruciate. Be nearly the worst injury that a player can get – it's well documented.'

He was staring absently at my snout. He knew I'd had my head in the toilet bowl again. The stubby little hairs around my nose were stained blue and I smelt generally of detergent. Yet he didn't make an issue of it. That's how upset he was.

I didn't know what to say. But then, I didn't have to say anything. It was always the case with Roy that talking matters through, even to himself, helped him see things in a more reasonable light. We sat there for the entire night, just the two of us, considering all the various contingencies, until the first light of dawn fingered the blinds and Roy said he was going to bed. By that time he had managed to conjure up the names of a number of other footballers who had successfully recovered from the same injury.

'Gazza,' he said. 'And obviously the lad Shearer.'

I remember he stopped in the hallway on his way towards the stairs, frowned importantly and said, 'I have this tendency to maybe focus on the negative sometimes.'

In time, I would discover the truth of that. For Roy, the joy of the highs never lasted as long as the torment of the lows. Isn't that always the way with driven people?

'Anyway,' he said wearily, 'thanks for listening to me. Helps to – as I've said in the past – hear myself think these things out loud.'

Then, with his knuckles whitening on the handles of his crutches, he levered himself slowly up the stairs – each one seeming to cost him enormous effort.

Of course I had something on my mind, too.

'The boy,' I said. I just blurted it out like that. 'Who is he?'

Roy stuck his head over the top banister, his little features bunched in confusion. 'Boy?' he said. 'What are you talking about, Triggs?'

'The boy who drove you home tonight,' I said. 'With the blond hair.'

He turned his head both ways, as if looking around for someone to share this moment with. 'Triggs,' he said, 'that's Ole Gunnar Solskjær.'

I looked at him blankly. Admittedly, I'd never heard of him. Roy laughed. 'He scored nineteen goals for us last season, a lot of them coming on as a second-half substitute. For me, he's done phenomenally well since coming in. Kind of player who only needs a yard, and evidence, in fairness, of obviously our strength in depth.'

'But he's just a boy,' I said.

'Triggs, he's twenty-fucking-three!'

'Twenty-three?'

'At least.'

I must confess, I was terribly confused.

'So Peter fucking Schmeichel in the other car,' Roy said, 'who did you think he was?'

'I thought it might be his father.'

'His father?'

'That's what I thought.'

This prompted an explosion of laughter so loud and sustained that I feared a herniated intestine would be added to whatever misfortune had befallen his leg.

'His father!' he repeated, between gasps for air.

I could hear him still laughing through the ceiling an hour after he'd dragged his damaged limb upstairs to bed. Indeed, he laughed for a good deal of the following day, too.

His sense of *bien-être* didn't last long into the following week, though. Tuesday was the day the club doctor confirmed the worst – it *was* his cruciate – and he placed the injury at the serious end of the spectrum. It would require an operation that would keep him out of football for possibly up to a year.

I don't think Roy would consider it too gross an exaggeration to say that the light dimmed in his eyes that day. In fact, a darkness seemed to descend over the house during the weeks that followed. Most days he slept late and when he did finally get up, he just pottered about sullenly in his dressing gown.

'Hard,' he said, by way of explanation, 'to put any kind of trouser on over the cast, at the end of the day.'

He was quiet a lot of the time. We exchanged courtesies, of course, usually when he fixed us something to eat. More often that not it was chips for him and textured soya protein, or something of that order, for me. (I was – and remain to this day – repulsed by the idea of eating meat.)

Then it was, 'There you are, Triggs,' and, 'Thank you, Roy,' and that, frankly, was about the measure of it.

Even my little infantile transgressions around the house went unchecked. My face was never out of the toilet, yet nothing was said. I did my business, as Roy called it, indoors, leaving little masala-coloured patties all over the good laminate floors. He cleaned them up without so much as a word of reproach. He didn't seem to care at all when I wrestled the kitchen bin to the floor in search of the potato peelings to which I was rather partial. There wasn't even an admonishment when I chewed my way through the pairs of trainers that he was careless enough to leave within my reach.

Look, I'm not going to deny it – it was a difficult time for me. As it happened, I had my own aches and pains to contend with, too. My bones were growing at a faster rate than my musculature. I was now approximately twenty-four inches long – I measured myself against the Nordmende and I was almost half the size of it, from nose to rump – and I was experiencing dull, arthritic-like symptoms in my legs and back. Growing pains, as they're known, although I did, for a time, suspect it was panosteitis, a common bone disease that can cause lameness in young dogs. Still, I resolved to suffer it with the quiet stoicism that is the Labrador Retriever way.

The weeks fell off the calendar. Roy did a lot of his brooding in front of the television – or rather, one of the many we had in the house. He listened to various medical experts on Sky News speculating about the extent of his injury and the chances of him ever playing football again. I remember the phrase 'long road back' being used quite a lot. These prognoses he always took to heart. He stopped shaving, as he's still known to do from time to time. Within two weeks, a thick scrub covered the lower half of his face.

Watching football brought him little or no happiness. Everything that happened had a negative implication. Manchester United drew 2–2 with Derby County and he tutted and harrumphed about it for hours. 'Not being disrespectful,' I remember him saying, 'but you don't win Premier Leagues by struggling to put away teams like obviously Derby.'

Yet when United scored thirteen goals in their next two games – against Barnsley and Sheffield Wednesday – it didn't exactly send him into great transports of delight either. In fact, this was when he seemed at his lowest ebb, since it appeared to him that he wasn't missed at all.

For a while, I was at a loss as to what to do. But Labradors, more than any other dog breed, have a highly developed sense of their calling. It was in October or November of 1997 – around the time I reached my ninth human month – that I gained a sudden awareness of what was to be my role in life.

I remember I was lying in my basket in the laundry room one afternoon, waiting for the dryer to finish its perfunctory business so I could pop the door and get inside. I was still small enough to fit, though only just. I was feeling more than a little sorry for myself. Was I depressed? Looking back, perhaps. What I do know is that, like Roy, I was having an existentialist crisis of my own. Believe me, it's a sad pass indeed when you find yourself, still some way short of your first birthday, thinking about all the things you could have done with your life.

But that's what was going through my mind.

I could have been searching for lost mountaineers in the freezing fog of the Swiss Alps. I could have been sniffing out explosives bound for the cargo hold of a commercial airliner. Looking back, I could have been shitting on John Grogan's floor on the way to selling six million books worldwide and the rights to a box office smash starring Owen Wilson and Jennifer Aniston.

But that's when I had a sudden moment of clarity. It came out of nowhere. It hit me like . . . well, like Roy oh so very nearly hit Alan Shearer in 2001, until Gary Neville – why did he have to get involved? – interrupted the trajectory of the punch and denied Shearer the split lip that was coming to him his entire career.

As the machine performed its final rotations, I realised, with a sudden insight that was in fact way beyond my tender years, that this *was* my calling. I was to be a friend, confidant, sister, brother, walking companion, teacher, sidekick, sounding board, gentleman's gentleman and, yes, emotional crutch to a man I'd heard several times described as the best footballer in England. And what the hell was wrong with that?

If I could pinpoint the moment when my dumb puppy phase ended and my more thoughtful adolescent years began, then that was it. I resolved to be more of a help in Roy's life and less of a hindrance. I made a firm promise to myself right there to stop doing my famous 'business' in the house. By then, I'd kind of grasped the whole indoors bad, outdoors good trope anyway. My difficulty was persuading my still developing bowel and bladder to hold onto their contents. But I would try twice as hard.

I swore that I would keep my head out of the toilet bowl. Roy had switched to a new lavatory germicide infused with a pine fragrance that made me nauseous, which made it easier for me to keep my promise.

I also made a solemn vow to try to control myself around the kitchen bin. Although there would be occasional slip-ups, I would say in my defence that no human will ever know the torture of having a nose as sensitive as that of a Labrador Retriever.

In short, you could say I decided it was time I grew up.


It was with a new sense of purpose that I talked to Roy in the living room early that evening. He was watching *Home and Away*, I remember, already dressed for bed.

'Hey, Triggsy,' he said when I walked into the room. Footballers, I was learning, liked to tag a Y or an O onto the end of names for reasons of euphony. Scholesy. Keano. Giggsy.

Coley. You picked it up. 'Do you want the television? This is the same episode I watched at lunchtime.'

'Maybe later,' I said. In fact, one of the Baldwins was narrating a documentary about the migratory habits of the albatross, which I was interested in seeing. 'I just wondered whether you wanted to talk.'

This was the new me.

'Talk?' he said.

I watched his teeth flash through the cinnamon thicket of his beard.

'Yeah,' I said. 'You said it helped, didn't you?'

'I don't know, Triggs.'

'Come on,' I said, attempting to chivy him along. I was really warming to my role. 'Not all doom and gloom. United are top of the Premier League, aren't they?'

That was when his face took on a yonderly aspect. 'You're too young to remember Incey,' he said

It was true. At that point in my life, I'd never heard the name.

'As I said before, you're too young. But Incey – obviously Paul Ince – he was top dog, it's been well-documented, until I came to the football club. And before Incey, you'd have to say Bryan Robson was top dog. Captain Fantastic – obviously colossally influential. And now the lad Butty's doing ever so well in midfield. Been immense. You're on about how the team's winning football matches. So what if the gaffer decides to make Butty obviously the fulcrum of the team?'

Being still a young dog with no real interest in football, I had no ready answers for him. But then he didn't expect them from me. Like a lot of humans, I think he just needed to give voice to his worst fears, as a kind of charm against them coming true.

Looking back now, I realise that he may have been experiencing flashbacks to his youth in Cork, when he went through something similar. Roy's story was almost unique

in the modern game. He left school without any exams –
although that's clearly not the unique bit – with his heart
set on becoming a professional footballer. But while just
about everybody who was earning a living from the game
had been signed up by the age of fifteen, Roy was passed
over. Too small was the consensus, then later, too old. At
eighteen, he found himself mired in that grim half-world that
young unemployed males often inhabit, rolling out of bed at
lunchtime to watch *Neighbours* and contemplate the future,
if he could bear it.

It's only now I can appreciate the fear he must have felt.
He'd become a professional footballer against the odds, now
all these years later, he was back where he began – it was only
his choice of Australian soap opera that had changed.

I could understand why he went through a period of almost
luxuriating in his misery.

Again, much later, I discovered that he'd talked to a sports
psychologist, who told him that his cruciate injury was a
type of death – honestly! – and should be grieved as such.
His advice was that Roy should allow himself to experience
every emotion in the range. Which was easy for him to say, of
course – he didn't have to live with him.

If melancholy was the first order, then anger was the second,
for it was shortly after our conversation about Paul Ince that
he began railing against the terrible injustice – as he saw it
– that had been done to him. Any TV pundit who dared to
suggest that the injury might have been his own stupid fault
became the focus of his rage.

'A failed player, a failed manager and now a failed pundit!' I'd
hear him scoff about . . . well, take your pick.

It was no surprise either that Alfie Haaland was the target
of many of these broadsides. Roy found endless things about
him to fixate on: one day, his haircut ('What is he, making
his Communion or something?'); another day, his journeyman

career ('He's been fucking nowhere and he's going fucking nowhere'). Another day – not long before Roy went under the knife that November to have his damaged ligament repaired – it was the soft Yorkshire ripples that striated Haaland's Scandinavian accent. ('*Jesus! I'm all for having will tit win, but end tit day, problem wiy Roy is, he has to realise he's not always gonna be first tit ball.*')

'Where's this fucking muppet even from,' I remember Roy saying. 'Norway or fucking *Emmerdale*? Jesus, he's only in Leeds a wet day and he's forgotten how to say the word *the*.'

It was a peculiar inflection, I had to agree. Cartoonish, even.

'*The*!' he shouted at the screen. 'Say it, Alfie! Just once!'

It was during the course of that interview that Alfie suggested that Roy might enjoy a longer career if he learned to curb his temper. Probably thought he was having the last word on the matter as well, the witless idiot. Well, as Martin Tyler is wont to say, there's plenty more to come.

After that, Roy entered a new phase, which those marvellous geniuses, the sports psychologists, would no doubt call acceptance. Not even a defeat by the hated Arsenal the day before he entered hospital for his operation could upset his happy equilibrium. He watched the match at home, with Denis Irwin, who was injured, too. I always liked Denis, even though he was something of a mischief-maker. It was his habit, whenever he and Roy watched football together, to make little asides that were deliberately intended to get Roy's ire up. Playing devil's advocate, it's called.

I was lying in the hallway, chewing a sweet potato that I'd filched from the vegetable tower, when I heard him praise Ray Parlour, a player who I don't think ever measured up to Roy's impression of a world-class midfielder.

'Playing out of his skin,' Denis said, clearly probing for a tender point. 'Lot of nice little flicks and turns. Doing ever so well. Obviously, he's giving Henning Berg a torrid time out there. I think the final whistle will come as obviously a blessed relief.'

Torrid, I was discovering, was one of those words that football people had made almost exclusively their own. You never heard other humans say it. Aplomb: that was another one.

Roy didn't rise to it. From his voice, I could tell that he knew what Denis was up to. 'Ray Parlour,' he said, 'is a player who, in the past, perhaps hasn't done himself too many favours. But he's acquitting himself well out there today. For me, he's having – full credit – maybe his best game of the season so far.'

This answer clearly came as some surprise to Denis. He gave it ten minutes, then tried to come in from a different angle.

'That Patrick Vieira,' he said, 'he's been on a different footballing planet of late. He's done magnificently well again today. Must be the best player in his position in England right now – what do you think, Roy?'

And back came Roy's response. 'What can you say about a player like Vieira? He's pure quality, no doubt about it – possibly even world-class. Obviously it's no secret that he came to Arsenal after an unhappy time with obviously Milan. Perhaps one or two question marks over his attitude as well. But for me, the lad's come in, he's settled down and he's done well, which is the mark of a top, top player – hats off to him.'

Well, I didn't hear Denis speak another word for what remained of the second half. I know he had designs on a TV career when his playing days were finished and hearing Roy speak so fluently in the idioms of football punditry, I think, startled him. I think he knew in that moment that if Roy ever decided to go down the same road, he was going to be living off his crumbs.

Arsenal won the match – 3–2, I'm reasonably certain – thanks to a late goal from David Platt. It was while Andy

Gray was dissecting it to death afterwards that Roy asked Denis if he'd do him a favour. 'Will you look after Triggs,' he said, 'the few days I'm in the hospital?'

'Look after her?' Denis said.

'Yeah, obviously just come in and maybe feed her.'

'Yeah, not a bother,' Denis said. 'Here, you don't want me to talk to her as well, do you?'

It was obvious that he was still smarting from what happened earlier.

'What do you mean?'

'I've heard you, Roy, chatting to her.'

'So fucking what?'

'Chatting away like you think she's going to answer you back.'

'Obviously, it helps me get things straight in my head, as I've said in the past. Are you saying you don't sometimes talk to yours?'

Denis laughed. And he was right to – he kept lurchers, by some distance the stupidest dogs ever domesticated by man. Even if they could be persuaded to speak, they would have little, if anything, to add to the sum of human knowledge.

'Come on,' Roy said, shaking his head, 'I'll show you the stuff,' and he led him to the laundry room, where my food was stored in three large Tupperware boxes.

I followed.

'What the fuck is this?' Denis wondered, peeling the lid from one. It was the smell, I think, that he found disagreeable.

'That one there's soya protein,' Roy said. 'What I usually do, in fairness, is mix it up with obviously a few of the lentils there. Then throw a bit of – as I've said in the past – low salt yeast extract on it, obviously for the flavour . . .'

'What?'

'Then possibly one of the nights, boil up maybe one or two potatoes – they're a good source of carbohydrates and B vitamins. Maybe a bit of scrambled egg. Or a bowl of white rice the odd night.'

'Roy,' I remember Denis saying, 'what kind of a langer are you?'

'What?'

'I said, what kind of a fucking langer are you? My fellas get a tin of fucking Cesar. Iams at Christmas. That's if they're lucky.'

'Triggs can't eat that kind of stuff,' Roy said, his intonation rising. 'As I've said in the past, she's a vegetarian.'

'Oh, a vegetarian, is it?' Denis went up a note or two himself. It was obviously a Cork thing.

'Yeah,' Roy said, 'she's never liked the taste of meat.'

'Never liked the taste of meat? Look, Roy, don't take this the wrong way. I'm saying it as someone who's obviously been keeping dogs his whole life. You've got to show them their place, at the end of the day. Otherwise, they'll end up the boss of you, rather than you being the boss of them – do you get me?'

Like I said, I liked Denis Irwin. How could anyone not? But he was just one of those people who, while accepting that dogs and humans were part of the same evolutionary continuum, refused to believe that they were conscious or self-aware to the same degree. That was his lookout. But he could have learned a lot from reading his Charles Darwin.

'*Senses and intuitions,*' Darwin wrote, '*the various emotions and faculties, such as love, memory, attention, curiosity, imitation, reason, etc. of which man boasts, may be found in incipient or even sometimes in a well developed condition in the "lower"* [my punctuation marks] *animals.*'

Reading between the lines, I'm reasonably certain that Darwin was referring to dogs.

Anyway, Roy stood there, giving Denis the hard, falcon stare, with which you're probably familiar.

Denis shook his head, disappointed. 'Okay,' he said, 'I'll do it – even though it makes me every bit as bad as you.'

When Denis left, I followed Roy into the living room, where he enjoyed the last few nuggets of the post-match analysis. The credits rolled. Platt's headed winner was replayed from various angles against a grinding soundtrack that Roy identified as 'Tubthumping' by – I think – Chumbawumba. 'A good song – hats off to them.'

'You don't seem too upset about the result,' I ventured.

He threw his shoulders, like it meant nothing to him. 'Platty's done well,' he said, 'especially after coming back from injury. As I said before, I thought Arsenal, overall, deserved the points.'

He was so calm that I had to wonder, even if the operation *was* a success, whether he'd ever have the desire to play football again. It was then that I felt a spasm of pain grip me from my withers right down to the tip of my tail. From my pinched expression, Roy knew immediately that something was up.

'Don't worry, Triggs,' he said. 'Denis will come and feed you. And obviously let you out to do your business. This is Denis Irwin we're talking about. Mister fucking Dependable.'

'I know.'

'Eight out of ten. Always. Everything he fucking does.'

'Okay.'

'Wait a minute . . . Triggs, is your back sore?'

'Excuse me?'

'Your back – is it sore?'

'Er, a little bit.'

'How long's it been like that?'

'A few weeks.'

'A few weeks?'

'Look, it's probably just growing pains.'

He placed a tender hand on the back of my neck. Like I said, there was no greater feeling in the world.

'So why didn't you say something?' he said.

'I didn't want to be a burden.'

'You should have said something.'

'You've had other things on your mind.'

'Triggs,' he said, 'in future, you've got to tell me these things.'

There were times, later on, when I think he regretted saying that to me. Roy always felt I had leanings towards hypochondria.

Denis proved to be as good as his word and reputation. He did the job he was asked to do, although not without voicing certain misgivings for once in his life. 'I don't know *what* the fuck is in this stuff,' he said one night as he dished out the food, his face arranged in the attitude of someone handling weapons-grade plutonium, 'but I'd say it nearly smells worse going into you than it does coming out of you.'

He gave generous portions, I'll say that for him. His own dogs, Beamish and Jimmy Barry, passed the time idly sniffing my tender parts to check if I was ovulating – nice of them – and evacuating their bladders against the upright piano in what Roy used to call 'the good room'. These weren't puppies either. Maybe I was being smug, having recently mastered the whole housetraining thing myself, but they were two seriously uncouth animals.

'You know,' Denis said one night, before mercifully taking them away from me, 'sometimes I look at you and I look at Roy and I wonder who's even in charge.'

It wouldn't be the last time I heard that.

From the corner of my eye, I could see Jimmy Barry, in a state of considerable arousal, attempting to mount the clothes horse, until it eventually collapsed under the weight of his panting exertions. Pardon the language, but if I could have spoken to Denis at that moment, I'd have told him to get his own fucking house in order.

Roy arrived home two days later, mid-morning, in a taxi. I waited in the hallway, my stomach sick with expectation. It was the driver who opened the front door and carried Roy's genuine leather-look overnight bag into the kitchen for him. A few seconds later, I watched Roy lever himself into the house on his metal supports.

I waited for a greeting, but there was none.

'Roy?' I said.

He looked miserable. Beyond miserable. He paid the driver, who showed himself out, then he slowly picked his way into the living room. I followed, tentatively, for I suspected that what he really wanted at that moment was to be alone. He stood with his back to me, examining a photograph that he kept in a frame on the mantelpiece of a young boy with a mullet haircut wearing the red shirt of his beloved Rockmount Boys Football Club.

'There are other things you can do,' I said softly. 'Football's not the be-all and end-all.'

This was a line I'd heard him say many times over the years. The paradox, of course, was that he played like it was.

He turned slowly and pinned me with a look. I was on the point of leaving him to his own company when I noticed his lips twitch, then a smile broke out across his face, bookended by the sweetest of dimples. 'It was a success,' he said. 'I'm going to play football again, Triggs.'

For the first time since we'd known each other, we both went with the emotion of the moment. I jumped up on him – my front paws still only reached as high as his lower thigh – and he gave the area of my shoulders, neck and ears a petting that was surprisingly vigorous for a man who'd just undergone major surgery.

'All credit to the lad who did the operation,' he said. This was later that evening. He was stretched out on the sofa, where he'd spent the day snoozing off the effects of the anaesthetic. I was on the floor beneath him, tending to a Granny Smith apple. I've always been rather fond of the sourness. 'For me, the lad's done unbelievably well today.' He really was full of himself that night. 'Said I should make – as I said before – a full recovery.'

'I'm very happy,' I said.

'Six weeks and I can take the plaster off. Could be back in the gym by the end of January. You know something, Triggs, I've got this feeling . . .'

I waited for him to finish the thought, but he didn't.

'Feeling?' I said.

'About me and you,' he said. 'I think we're going to be very good for each other.'

And you know what? I thought precisely the same thing.

## 2.

# The Long Road Back

THE WINTER OF 1997/8 PASSED AS SLOWLY AS, well, Juan Sebastian Veron tracking back to make a tackle. And I make that observation not as a matter of complaint. In fact, some of those days, I think, both Roy and I would number as being amongst our happiest together.

One Saturday, Roy came downstairs and asked me what I knew about Belgium. As it happened, while he'd been napping that afternoon I'd become engrossed in a documentary on the History Channel about Heinz Guderian, the brilliant German general who was responsible for refining the military tactic of *Blitzkrieg*. Excitedly, I described for Roy the bleached-out, black-and-white footage I'd seen of German Panzer divisions beating an irresistible path through the thickly wooded Ardennes. I got the impression that this didn't mean very much to him at all.

'Er, fair enough,' he said, reversing his body onto the sofa and manoeuvring his mummified leg up onto a pouf.

Well, naturally, I was curious. 'Why do you want to know about Belgium?' I wondered.

He took up the television remote. 'Because we're playing them now in a minute.'

*We*, it turned out, meant the Republic of Ireland, the country of his birth and a team he played for, well – I know it's a touchy subject, so I'm going to be careful here – from time to time. The match, he explained, was the second leg of a play-off for a place in the World Cup in France the following year. Roy had targeted the finals for his comeback.

'The first leg finished honours-even,' I remember him telling me, 'which was obviously a huge disappointment, given that it was in Dublin. Giving them an away goal obviously wasn't ideal. But even without the likes of myself and obviously now Denis missing through injury, the lads have got to be going over there thinking they're in with a shout.'

I decided to leave him to it. I wandered out to the kitchen and passed a futile hour trying to retrieve a custard cream from underneath the fridge. It was exhausting work and at some point I drifted off, although my sleep was interrupted by, alternately, groans of anguish, roars of delight and more than a few opprobrious remarks coming from the living room.

When I got up to check up on Roy shortly after ten o'clock, the television was muted and he seemed dazed by some private thought. It was clear to me that it hadn't ended well.

'I take it you won't be going to France next summer?' I said.

'Fucking muppets,' was the long and short of his analysis. 'Every last one of them, Triggs.'

He let me out into the garden to do my business. By now, I may have already mentioned, I had full mastery over that side of things. And that's not meant to sound smug. I was nearly eleven months old, after all.

I stood in the triangle of light cast by the open kitchen door and lifted my leg against a beech sapling. I know what you're thinking, by the way: female dogs don't cock their legs to urinate. Well, an interesting fact here – some do, if they're raised alongside a particularly strong alpha. Look it up.

'It was there to be won,' I remember Roy saying. 'And the Belgians were gone. You could see it in their eyes. Typical fucking us, though. We just don't have it in us to take that next step.'

That would become a theme of Roy's, of course.


It was while he was buttering his breakfast toast the following morning that Roy said a rather curious thing: 'Whiskey.'

I looked at him, my head cocked at an angle. 'Is it not a bit early?'

He looked up from his ministrations. 'Jesus, I'm not suggesting a drink,' he said. 'No, I'm looking at the marmalade there. Irish Marmalade, it says on the label. What do you think it is that makes it Irish, Triggs?'

I had no idea where this conversation was going.

'There's fucking whiskey in it,' he said. 'Irish marmalade is just ordinary marmalade with whiskey in it. Just like Irish mustard is ordinary mustard with whiskey in it. And Irish coffee, at the end of the day, is ordinary coffee with whiskey in it . . .'

Roy noticed things like that. He had that kind of mind — forever questing.

'So is that our contribution to the world, Triggs? Finding things that are already invented and putting fucking whiskey in them?'

I mentioned Irish stew, which I knew he enjoyed. He loved it when they had it on the menu in the Bleeding Wolf.

'That's stew with fucking Guinness in it!' he said. He laughed. 'Do you take my point, Triggs?'

'Well, it certainly *seems* to be a pattern, yes.'

'But is this how we want to be known?' His voice was ascending again. It was like his lungs were filling with helium. 'It's like last night, you know. Belgium were there — as I said before — to be beaten. And the lads bottled it. Mentally, just not up to the job. But you may bet there was some piss-up afterwards. Because, at the end of the day, that's the reputation the Irish have – we might not win, but we'll certainly bring something to the party. And it'll more than likely be triple fucking distilled.'

Roy was no stranger to alcohol himself. He knew his way around the pumps and optics, and I'm not breaking any confidences by telling you that. But I understood the point he was trying to make.

It would be fair to say, I think, that Roy fell in and out of love with football as that season juddered along. Six victories in succession had Manchester United – to use a phrase for which Mark Lawrenson might well hold the licensing rights – looking down on the rest like lords of the manor. But even in the New Year, when their season began to unspool messily, it had little or no effect on his mood. Days slipped by, in fact, without any talk of football at all.

There was one afternoon shortly after Christmas, I remember. We were sitting in front of the television when he took the remote in his hand and asked me what I wanted to watch. He could be terribly chivalrous like that. I told him no, it was his television. I'd heard him mention that United were playing Coventry anyway.

'No, come on,' he said. 'What do *you* want to watch?'

'Well,' I said, 'there *is* a documentary on the History Channel – about the Battle of Manzikert.'

I couldn't get enough of those programmes. I just found human history fascinating.

'Okay,' he said, 'that's what we'll watch so.'

'It was a key moment in the decline of the Byzantine Empire,' I explained and he nodded as if that went without saying.

I underestimated Roy. I was worried that he might be bored. But on the contrary, he was very quickly immersed in the programme, even making astute observations that anticipated the commentary.

'Too many mercenaries on the Byzantine side,' he said, a full five minutes before the mass desertion by hired soldiers on the eve of the battle was revealed. 'Money can't be your only motivation. No disrespect, but look at the likes of obviously Blackburn.'

The enmity between Emperor Romanos IV and his senior commander, Andronikos Doukas, he also foresaw as a key factor in the loss to Alp Arslan's Seljuq forces.

'The problem is that the lad Doukas doesn't respect him,' he said with extraordinary precision. 'At the end of the day, you're not going to take orders from someone you think is obviously a spoofer.'

This he knew from experience. He'd played for Jack Charlton after all.

Anyway, it all went off exactly as he predicted it would.

After that, we watched a documentary about Alan Turing and the cracking of the Enigma Code, then a biography of Percy Bysshe Shelley, before I suggested switching channels to find out the result of the match. United, it turned out, had lost by three goals to two – Andy Gray said that the United players could expect the hairdryer treatment from Alex Ferguson – although the news didn't seem to trouble Roy much.

That happy equanimity continued through the month of January, surviving two more Premier League defeats – to Southampton and Leicester – as United's hold on the league began to look less sure.

It was some time between those two results that Roy had his plaster cast removed. His leg had been extended to the full for so long that he had to learn how to walk all over again. I remember talking him through his first faltering steps in the back garden. He threw the crutches down on the grass rather dramatically and held onto the brick barbecue for support.

'Put your right foot in front of you,' I said. 'Okay, now your left. You're doing it! You're doing it! Now, your right again . . .'

It was the kind of inner dialogue I imagined happening in

Phil Babb's head, later on, when he was going through one of the regular crises of confidence that pockmarked his career.

Of course, Roy yields to no man when it comes to will and determination and it was no time at all before we had resumed the morning and evening walks that had been an all-too-short-lived feature of our lives before his injury.

We began with short distances – to the end of Bankhall Lane and back, or to the post box on Rappax Road – working up gradually to three or four miles daily. The weather never seemed to be a concern for us. We walked under heavy stair-rods of rain that could beat a tattoo into your back and in cold that would freeze you to the very marrow.

I grew to live for our walks. I think Roy felt the same, although I did worry sometimes that I was perhaps projecting my own feelings onto him, as humans are wont to do with dogs, for instance, when they presume that we desire the same foods as humans do. But I do think they were the months when Roy and I began to genuinely bond.

Admittedly, I'd grown up quite a lot by then. I weighed nearly forty pounds – the same as the average footballer's wife – and notwithstanding the occasional relapse involving the kitchen bin, I had generally made good my promise to keep my destructive puppy urges in check. Roy really appreciated it.

It's fair to say that we were beginning to develop more of an adult relationship, which, at least at the beginning, was characterised by Roy doing a lot of talking and me doing a lot of listening. He told me a lot about his life, I remember, his childhood in Ireland and the various twists and turns in the narrative that had brought him to where he was today.

He talked a lot about Cork, which, like a lot of second cities, had a chip on its shoulder about not being a first city. Over the years that followed, there were times when I thought that explained a lot.

He told me about the frustration of being told he was too

slight to make it as a professional footballer. About writing to every club in England, desperately looking for a try-out, while his best years slipped by. He could quote from those rejection letters verbatim. I always thought it accounted for the undercurrent of payback that was a feature of Roy's psychic landscape.

He had all but given up, he told me, resigned to an unfulfilling life of part-time football and casual work, when a scout from Nottingham Forest showed up by chance at a Cobh Ramblers match one night to watch someone else. But it was Roy who turned his head. He sent word back – there's this other guy, bit on the small side, bit on the old side, but he's definitely got something.

And that's how it happened. It still freaked him out, I think, just the random, snakes and ladders aspect of it. What almost never was.

Yes, how I loved those walks. In time, we developed a kinesthetic knowledge of every climb and descent on every road and laneway in the Hale area. And more than that, we each got to know every twist and turn in the other's mental geography. That's what happens when dogs and humans share the kind of time and the kind of intimacies that Roy and I did.

He was smart – and not just by the standards of his profession either. Engaging, too, with a wonderful wit that, like mine, tended towards darkness. And he was kind. Don't get me wrong, he could be a burry old thing – as crotchety, at times, as a bear dragging around a trap, but along with that there was a softer side that the public rarely saw.

He also had this habit, I discovered, of mentally flagellating himself, especially when he talked about his direct rivals – the players he was most often compared with in the popular imagination. He would measure himself against them and decide that he came up short. Typically, he would say something like, 'I don't know why people ever raved about me at all. Look at the likes of Patrick Vieira. Or even the lad Incey, who's proved an exceptional acquisition for obviously Liverpool. You know, when you think about it, I've achieved nothing in the game – absolutely nothing.' That kind of thing. Clearly, it was done as a means of motivating himself. I heard it quite a lot that spring, around the time of his return to the gym. I didn't know it at the time, but he was spending a lot of hours on the exercise bike at the club training ground, as well as in the swimming pool.

Then one morning – I'm almost certain it was late February 1998 – Roy skipped our morning walk without a word of explanation and drove away from the house at an oddly early hour. When he returned, some time around mid-morning, he seemed a little soupy. I picked up on it instantly.

'Something wrong?' I said.

'I remember when they were teenagers with fucking spots,' he said. 'They're *still* teenagers with fucking spots!'

'Who?'

'Ah,' he said, flicking a dismissive hand, 'all of them. Beckham. Scholesy. Butty. Obviously, the Nevilles . . .'

He must have been at the training ground.

'Did someone say something?' I wondered.

I watched his shoulders rise and fall. 'I mean, it's football,' he said. 'End of the day, banter's obviously a major part of it.'

'A sad fact of life,' I said.

From a number of Roy's stories, I already had a good idea of what passed for humour among professional footballers.

'Well, it was just one or two,' he explained. 'You know, it was, "Are you still here?" and "What's that Irish guy's name again?" You know what players are like.'

'They'd humour a dying man,' I said.

'Well, obviously – as I said before – it's all part and parcel. I can dish it out. Oh, no better man. And I can take it as well . . .'

This was Roy attempting to wish an image of himself into reality. All humans do that, in my experience.

'But it's like . . .'

Then, again with the ascendent chord progression, he said, 'Who do they think they are, Triggs? You're on about us being maybe ten points clear – or whatever it is – at the top of the table. Arsenal have how many games in hand on us?'

'I think you said it was three.'

He shook his head, then he laughed dryly. 'Obviously, I hope for their sake that they're still in a position to take the piss at the end of the season.'

Two days later, United were knocked out of the FA Cup by Barnsley – or, as Roy called them, 'Jesus! *Barnsley?*'


After that, I have to say, he began to resemble, more and more, his old self. He became a voracious watcher of football again – any match he could find. At any hour of the day or night I was liable to find him in front of one of the six televisions we had in the house, his face illuminated by the light of events in Milan or Exeter, Dundee or Barcelona, Munich or Aldershot.

During our walks, he began to refer to opposition players in more bilious terms. 'Vicira's getting away with murder,' he'd say. 'We spoke about him being obviously tremendously influential, but no one's fucking putting it up to him,' and this in a tone suggesting it was a state of affairs that wouldn't continue indefinitely. Or he'd say, 'Obviously no disrespect, but Incey's being made to look a lot better than he is at Liverpool.'

In March, Manchester United played Arsenal again, this time at Old Trafford. It was the defining game of the league season.

'Whoever wins,' I remember Roy telling me, 'has their fate in their own hands. Whoever loses is going to be looking for the other team to slip up.'

He decided to go to the match. I think he wanted people to see how fit and healthy he looked, but also to remind 'obviously certain Arsenal players' that they hadn't seen the last of him.

He arrived home late that night. I remember I was rolling around on the Habitat rug in the hallway, trying to reach an itch on my withers, when he walked through the door. From his heavy tread on the wooden floor, I knew immediately that the night had not gone well.

He walked straight past me and into the kitchen. No greeting. He went to the fridge, took out the milk and drank straight from the carton. With the back of his hand, he wiped away the thin, white paintbrush moustache it left on his upper lip.

I waited.

'Lost one-nil,' he eventually said. 'Fucking Overmars.'

'Oh.'

'Gave us a torrid time, especially in the second half.'

'I see.'

'It's Arsenal's to lose now.'

I attempted to put a positive construction on it – that would be very characteristic of the Labrador breed, of course. 'Doesn't sound like you,' I said. 'It's often I've heard you say – what is it? – it's not over until it's over.'

'One point from a possible nine in our last three games, Triggs. No, you'd have to say the momentum is with Arsenal – hats off to them. You know, people laughed at Alan Hansen when he said you win nothing with kids . . .'

He allowed this thought to stay suspended for some time.

'Maybe, long-term, he was right.'

He stewed about the result for weeks afterwards. Even in happy moments, when you thought he'd finally consigned it to the past, he'd become suddenly distracted and shake his head and make some rueful comment under his breath.

'For them to come and do a job on us like that – at *our* place?' or 'Our lads with their, "What's that Irish guy's name again?", I'd say they remember my fucking name now!'

Arsenal won ten successive games to win the Premier League by a solitary point. It was only when it became a fact that Roy reached an accommodation with it.

'They've definitely overtaken us,' I remember him saying. It was a beautiful morning in the middle of May. We were sitting on the deck at the back of the house, listening to the avian chatter, with the whole day yawning ahead of us. I remember Roy's hand spilled over the arm of his deckchair and gently touched the coat on the back of my neck. In that moment, I was in heaven.

'For me, that's down to us being maybe not hungry enough anymore. Maybe one or two of us have become a bit complacent with the success we've had. And I'm including myself in that. We've a lot to learn from a team like Arsenal.'

I was already familiar enough with the routine to know that he didn't mean a word of it.


*I'm curled into a half-shell on the sofa, watching a documentary about the First Battle of El Alamein on the History Channel, but not really following it, my mind abstracted elsewhere – or rather nowhere at all. I'm lost in a daydream.*

*I feel a cold hand on my back and my body leaps three inches off the Kobi Leather.*

*He's full of apologies. 'Didn't mean to scare you,' he says gently.*

*My heartbeat eventually slows to normal again.*

*'Did you not hear me calling you?' he wants to know. 'I shouted your name – six or seven times.'*

*God, I'm becoming as deaf as a piebald Dalmation. Is that another signpost passed?*

*The bottom half of his face is crosshatched with stubble. The beard is obviously making a comeback. 'What's this you're watching?' he asks.*

*Unusually for a footballer, he was always curious about the world beyond Dubai and Quinta do Lago.*

*He continues to stand, staring at the television. It's a documentary about the halt of the Axis advance on Alexandria – a defining moment in the course of the Second World War.*

*'We'd a good result today,' he mentions, just by the by. 'Beat Cardiff,' he says. 'Two-nil.'*

*The screen continues to hold his gaze.*

*'Obviously it's good just to get the win,' he says. 'I was very happy with the workrate today, obviously after the QPR match. Happy with the way the lads responded. That's what good players do. The three points were richly deserved. Maybe a bit disappointed we didn't put maybe one or two more on the scoresheet. Credit to their goalkeeper. We gave him a torrid time, but he pulled off some great saves . . . Here, who's the lad in the hat?'*

*The television answers the question for him.*

*Erwin Rommel.*

*He repeats the name once or twice. He seems to like the way it feels on his lips. 'Anyway, no one's getting too carried away,' he says, picking up the thread again. 'Obviously, I'm as happy as anyone that we got the three points. But, you know, let's not go patting ourselves on the back just yet. It's a long season and – as I've said before – the championship is one of the most difficult divisions to get out of.'*

*He sits down on the sofa beside me then. 'I was going to ask you did you want something to eat?' he says. 'There's bananas in the kitchen. I could maybe mash one or two up . . .'*

*I have no appetite at the moment, which he gauges from my lack of response.*

*'Or I could do you some, obviously, scrambled egg. The highlights will be on in half an hour. For me, the lad Connor Wickham's done fantastically well today. Only seventeen, Triggs. Obviously,*

*mature for his age, both physically and mentally. I've a feeling he's going to be a player. Although, as I said earlier, he's still young and he's achieved absolutely nothing in the game. You'll have to see him.'*

*But my eyelids are heavy and Roy knows as well as I do that I'm fighting a losing battle to stay awake.*

A few weeks after Arsenal won the Premier League, the World Cup finals began in France. Roy made a considerable show of telling me how little interest he had in it, when, of course, the opposite was the case.

'I wouldn't be a great watcher of football,' he told me. He said things like that from time to time. We were on the A34, I remember, stopped at the Gatley Road traffic lights. He must have sensed doubt in my silence.

'I'm serious,' he said. 'I doubt I'll watch a single game.'

Just as I expected, he didn't miss a single game. Most afternoons and evenings found him staring at the television, as if bound by a spell. And of course, I knew he was measuring himself against the players he was watching.

'There's nothing that Zinedine Zidane *can't* do,' he said to me one morning. I was lying in the garden at the back of the house, being chastised by a crow, who, I couldn't help but notice, cleared off the very moment Roy stepped outside. Clever birds, crows. That's why there's so many of them. 'For me, he's the most exciting player I've seen since the lad Maradona.'

Another day, I was waiting for him outside the Hale Barber Shop on Ashley Road – 'Probably the best barber in Greater Manchester' said the sign outside – when Roy emerged through the ribbon door curtain, his hair shorn to the quick, and said to me, apropos of nothing: 'Rivaldo's the real star of that Brazil team. For me, Ronaldo's not even worth his place on current form.'

None of which meant a thing to me at the time, of course. I just looked at him and nodded with as much enthusiasm as I had in me.

One afternoon – it was the day of the quarter-final between England and Argentina in St Etienne – I was lying on my side on the decking when I heard a truck wheeze to a halt on the cobblelock sweep at the front of the house. I was too comfortable where I was, baking nicely in the summer sun, to get up to investigate.

Much later, Roy came outside. I remember the sun glittering wickedly off the lenses of his mirror shades.

'Triggs!' he said – and he did seem excited. 'I've got something to show you.'

I climbed to my feet, yawned and performed some quick stretches, which is something I often did. Like footballers, Labradors are prone to joint trouble. In fact, it was watching me perform my thrice-daily routine of leg and back extensions that sold Roy on the idea of yoga as a means of prolonging his career. And it was Roy who, in turn, introduced Ryan Giggs and Gary Neville to it.

'Come on,' Roy said, 'you're going to love what I'm after buying.'

I followed him into the house.

Nothing could have cushioned the surprise that awaited me in the laundry room. The basket in which I'd slept for the first year of my life had been shunted into a corner and in its place, dominating the room, stood the ugliest and ungainliest piece of hardware I have ever laid eyes on – certainly until Alex Ferguson paid £10.6 million for Jaap Stam.

It was a complicated-looking contraption, made of rubber and buffed tubular steel, but its function was a mystery to me. Roy obviously saw my confusion because he laughed. 'You don't know what it is, Triggs?'

'Er, no,' I said, much as I hated to hurt his feelings.

'It's a treadmill!'

'A treadmill? Where did it come from?'

He shook his head, exasperated by my slowness off the mark. 'I bought it – where do you think it came from? This is to help me get back to obviously match fitness. I'm watching this World Cup – even though, as I've said in the past, I don't like watching football – and the fitness levels of the players are unbelievable, Triggs, even at the end of obviously a long season.'

He stepped onto the rubber belt, pressed some buttons and the machine groaned into life. He started running, at a gentle pace at first, but after a minute or so he made another adjustment and suddenly he was running at full tilt and I felt a sudden pang of something, which I realise now, in sober retrospect, was jealousy.

'It's unbelievable,' he managed to squeeze out between breaths. 'The best exercise . . . you'll ever get!'

I wandered over to my basket and climbed into it.

'Where are you . . . going, Triggs? Come on, get up . . . here with me.'

I made some demurral.

'That's why I bought . . . the bigger one, Triggs, there's room . . . for the two of us . . . up here . . .'

'I'm, er, not feeling too well as it happens.'

'What?'

I had to shout to be heard over the volume of the thing. 'I said I'm not feeling very well.'

'What's up with you?'

'Stomach's a bit upset.'

'Your stomach?'

'I was thinking it might be a touch of bloat.'

He pinned me with a doubtful look. 'Bloat?' He already had me typed as something of a neurotic when it came to matters of health.

'A touch.'

'You haven't got bloat, Triggs. You'd . . . know all about it . . . if you had bloat.'

He'd read about a dozen books on the subject of caring for dogs before he brought me into his life. He was a stickler for preparation. But then, I'm not telling you anything there that you don't already know.

Roy just shook his head, like he thought me endearing. He picked a hand towel from the top of the spin dryer, twisted it into a long shape and hung it around his neck. Then he continued to run until the machine informed him – in an academic monotone that I grew to really despise – that he'd covered six miles. He jumped off and leaned over the safety rail to regather his breath.

'The only drawback with the treadmill,' I heard myself say, 'is that you don't get to enjoy the scenery.'

He looked at me askance. 'Scenery?'

I felt ridiculous for saying it. 'Yes, the scenery.'

'Up and down Bankhall Lane?'

'No, not just Bankhall Lane.'

'What, the first fairway of Hale Golf Course then? Jesus, you've seen one golf course, Triggs, you've seen them all.'

I tried to take this on board with as much good grace as I could. 'Well, I thought you enjoyed our walks,' I said. Again, there was the fear in me that perhaps I'd been merely projecting. 'I thought you found talking to me helpful.'

'Triggs, I can still talk to you while I'm running on this.'

It wasn't the same thing, even if he couldn't see it.

In a fit of pique, while he was watching the England versus Argentina match that night, I dragged my basket from the laundry room into the kitchen. I was still quite immature. You know how girls can be. Sensing my upset, Roy went to considerable efforts to interest me in the match. 'Definitely one for the neutrals,' he called out to me. 'The lad Owen's scored an unbelievable goal. Be a contender for goal of the tournament.'

It wasn't too long afterwards that I heard Roy, in the living room, unship a long, low groan. It turned out that David Beckham had been sent off.

For what it's worth, I watched the incident much later – around the time that I discovered football for myself – and I thought the referee was the real villain. Diego Simeone shellacked Beckham from behind. All Beckham did was flick his boot at him – a typically limp effort at retaliation, if you ask me. And Kim Nielsen – a Scandinavian, surprise, surprise – surrendered to a wrong-headed liberal impulse to punish the victim.

Of course, the following day you couldn't walk down an English street with a television camera on your shoulder without someone waving a burning effigy of Beckham at you.

I had my issues with the man later on, but I can tell you that he didn't deserve that.

What bothered Roy, I suspect, wasn't so much the red card as the wastefulness of it. If you're going to get sent off, his thinking went, you've got to give the other fellow a reason to remember you later on while he's having Deep Heat rubbed into his sore parts. Ask Gareth Southgate. Ask Gus Poyet. Ask Alfie, if you can bear to listen to the clown telling you *ad nauseam* about the long and honour-laden career he would have enjoyed were it not for what Roy did to him at Old Trafford in 2001.

Still, Roy enjoyed the match, which ended – as these occasions invariably do – with England losing on penalty kicks. 'Triggs,' he called out, 'you've got to come in here, just to see the faces on obviously the England players.'

I didn't stir.

A few minutes later he stuck his head around the door to tell me that it was David Batty who had missed the vital kick.

'No tears out of the lad,' he said. 'Unlike the rest of them. For me, he's one of the few England players out there who had any bottle.'

He made no reference to my new sleeping arrangements, other than to say, 'Oh, you're in here now, are you?'

Then, shortly afterwards, I heard the plangent thump of his feet on the running belt of that infernal machine, which had – as I saw it – now replaced me in his life. He ran for thirty minutes.

As the days went by and the summer slowly melted away, he became more and more enamoured with it. I remember his efforts to interest me in its various modes and functions. 'Measures your heart rate,' he said. 'Even the number of obviously calories you've burned.'

I tried to jolly along with it, as is the Labrador Retriever way.

I could not, in all good conscience, argue that the machine didn't work. The weight tumbled off him and by the time he returned to pre-season training in the middle of July, I barely recognised him. The articulation of all that running was plain to see in his sharpened features and the hard torsion of his muscles beneath his shirt.

According to his own account, Alex Ferguson mouthed the words, 'Jesus Christ!' when he first saw him stripped to the waist.

'Should have seen them all staring,' he told me after that first session. I was in the living room watching a documentary on the Discovery Channel about Extreme Fishermen. 'Even Giggsy – and there's more meat in the Vatican on Good Friday than there is on that fucker. I mean, that's documented. But, as I said before, they know now, Triggs. They knew it when they saw me arrive – this lad means business this year.'

'You, er, certainly seem full of resolve,' I said.

He nodded. 'It's not the cry but the flight of the wild duck that leads the flock to follow,' he said, enigmatically.

'Er, very good,' I said.

'I told them this morning – told them all, right in front of the manager – Arsenal will never come here and do that to us again. Not to Manchester United Football Club.'

As well as redundant, for the first time in my young life, I was – yes, I'm ashamed to say it – grossly overweight. Labradors are prone to chubbiness and while Roy had managed to rid himself of his puppy fat, mine had returned with interest. I was carrying at least eight pounds of excess cargo around my midriff and you could have carved a couple of generous Angus strips from my jowls. I resolved to cut back on my food portions. But mired, as I was, in a deep emotional funk, I tended to eat even more. It was – as that great intellectual and noted wit John Terry would no doubt have it – a Catch-52 situation.

My concerns about Roy and his ardour for that exercise machine weren't entirely selfish. Which is to say that it wasn't just my own ever-thickening neck that I was worried about. After all those lonely hours pounding that moving runway, Roy had, just as I predicted, fallen out of the habit of confiding in me. And much as modesty forbids, etcetera, etcetera, he needed someone to talk to as the start of 1998/9 season drew nearer.

I was never more certain of this than in the week of the Charity Shield that August. Roy returned home from training – I think it was the Thursday of that week – with a slightly distrait air about him, and disappeared into his study. Something was wrong.

Later, he placed me in full possession of the facts. What had upset him was an article in *The Guardian* that had questioned whether he would ever be as committed in the challenge again, having had his career almost ended by a reckless tackle.

A short time later, through the closed door, I could hear the familiar crack of a snare drum summoning a Hammond organ into life, and then I heard two voices caterwauling, through two inches of contemporary oak, about mystery tramps and chrome horses and – God help us! – diplomats with Siamese cats.

I realise that I probably need to explain that, so permit me the indulgence of a short detour here.

For years now, a debate has raged among animal behaviour experts on the question of whether or not dogs possess the quality of clairvoyance. I've seen a lot of documentaries on the subject, in which various domestic pets are filmed working themselves up into a merry lather while their owners are on the way – although not yet within sight of – home. To tell you the truth, I'm a firm believer in canine intuition – more of that later – although agnostic on the question of clairvoyance. But this I will say: there have been many, many times over the years when I knew – just knew – that Roy was on his way back to the house, sometimes up to twenty minutes before I heard the electric gates springing open.

It had nothing to do with extra-sensory perception, though. It was because from the moment he took the slip road off the A562, my eardrums were assailed by the God-awful yowling of that miserable curmudgeon who, too often, shared the journey home with him. And no, I'm not talking about either of the Neville brothers. I'm talking about Bob Dylan.

Even now, all these years later and well into my dotage, I live in dread of those days when Roy pronounces himself in the mood for what he breezily calls 'a bit of Bob'. Dylan's nerve-grinding voice represents by no means the full extent of my beef with the man popularly hailed as the laureate of his generation. Worse – far, far, worse – is the awful nonsense verse that passes for wisdom among impressionable listeners.

You may have already discerned by now that if Roy could have been described as having one mortal weakness in those days, it was his predilection for the words of what might be loosely described as wise men. For inspirational quotes from which to winnow little life lessons ('the recipe for happiness – yearning, earning and learning') the man was an open vessel.

Much as I loved him – and love him still – I can tell you that giving him a present of a *Thought for the Day* desk calendar was like placing a gun in the hands of a child. Or, come to think of it, a .22 calibre air rifle in the hands of Ashley Cole.

I know Mick McCarthy thinks he suffered during Roy's Fail To Prepare, Prepare To Fail phase. Well, he can count himself lucky he didn't have to live through 1999's The Dictionary Is The Only Place Where Success Comes Before Work (Mark Twain) and 2003's Failure Is The Opportunity To Begin Again More Intelligently (Henry Ford). To say nothing of 2005's He Who Is Carried Does Not Realise How Far Away The Town Is (Sierra Leone, traditional). These I bore with the cheerful stoicism for which we descendants of Newfoundland are renowned.

But Dylan presented me with problems on a whole other scale. Roy considered him a genius. And no line from any Dylan song was ever too elliptical to be bent to suit a particular situation.

Years later, when Roy appeared on MUTV and publicly denounced his team-mates as being – let's not mince words here – shit, I can tell you for a fact that he had just listened to Dylan non-stop during a seven-hour flight from Dubai. He left the house for his television assignment that day, horribly jet lagged and muttering bleakly lines I recognised from the interminable *Desolation Row*. Roy would probably deny it, but I was sure he'd taken some kind of message from the lyrics. I didn't know who the blind commissioner of the second verse might have been in his interpretation of the song – possibly David Elleray – but I speculated that Einstein dressed as Robin Hood was Alex Ferguson, a brilliant genius who, in Roy's view, had recently begun taking from the rich (the Glazers) and displaying extraordinary munificence to the poor (Rio Ferdinand, Alan Smith, Darren Fletcher, John O'Shea, Kieran Richardson, etcetera, etcetera).

Again, maybe I'm guilty of projecting. But we all know how *that* episode ended.

Roy always insisted that his love of Dylan was harmless fun. It wasn't. I always knew, whenever I heard the man belching out his bad poetry and vandalising the language in the service of rhyme, that trouble was sure to follow.

Anyway, Roy listened to *Highway 61 Revisited* twice in its entirety the night before he left from London for the Charity Shield. I lay in the kitchen, made earmuffs of my paws and endured it as best I could. (Dylan, by the way, once described the song 'Like A Rolling Stone' as a 'long piece of vomit' – true, I thought, although the description could be used to describe his entire life's work.) Then the music suddenly stopped and I heard that cursed machine clunk into life. He was running again. I stood at the door of the laundry room and watched the slow-moving beads of sweat crawl down his face and gather at his chin.

'Vieira!' he said, between sucks of breath. 'World Cup winner . . . Listen . . . No disrespect . . . But let's see . . . how fucking big you are . . . on Sunday.'

Manchester United were playing Arsenal.

I stepped into his line of regard. 'Hey, Triggs,' he said. 'I'm just doing . . . couple of miles . . . You sure you don't . . . want to hop up here with me?'

'No thanks,' I said in a ho-hum kind of way.

'You could do with it.'

'Excuse me?'

He laughed, but not in a cruel way. 'I'm just saying, you could . . . do with maybe losing . . . a bit of weight . . . Obviously no offence.'

I looked at my reflection in the window of the spin dryer.

He was right. I was becoming morbidly obese. 'No,' I said. 'No offence taken.'

He ran his hands up and down his sides, fingering his ribs like they were accordion keys. 'See, you've got to put in . . . the hours.'

'If you say so.'

'I do say so . . . There's nothing good . . . was ever achieved . . . without obviously hard work.'

The album *Another Side of Bob Dylan*, by the way, was recorded in one six-hour session – some of the tracks in a single take. Except I didn't know that then. I didn't do my research on Dylan until he started to really mess with our lives.

'Let's just say,' he added, 'that Vieira . . . Petit . . . the lot of them . . . are going to be . . . put back in their . . . fucking boxes on Sunday.'

I remember advising caution. 'Perhaps you shouldn't expect too much from yourself in your first game back,' I said. 'The time to measure yourself against those players is surely at the end of the season, not at the end of Sunday.'

I knew little or nothing about football at the time, but I would have thought that was just common sense.

He pulled a face. 'Explain . . . that to me, Triggs.'

Happy to be of service again, I searched my mental hard drive for an appropriate historical metaphor for that weekend's game. As it happened, I had just seen a documentary about the Battle of Dunkirk. So while Roy counted off the miles on the console in front of him, I told him the entire story, from Manstein's brilliant flanking of the Allied forces in northern France to the safe evacuation of almost three hundred and forty thousand soldiers to Dover.

His face suggested he was struggling to make sense of it as it related to his own life. Actually, I probably went on a bit.

'A strategic retreat?' he said.

I could tell he didn't like the sound of it.

'Yes,' I said. 'But it's celebrated as a victory in the overall context of the defeat of Nazism. At Dunkirk, the Allies averted almost certain defeat. They saved the army that eventually returned to Europe to win the War.'

I remembered that part of the documentary word for word.

'Okay, Triggs . . . So what you're saying . . . is that avoiding a beating . . . at the end of the day . . . can be a victory in itself?'

'A victory of a kind,' I said. 'Yes.'

He was unappeased. 'Yeah,' he said, a note of condescension in his voice, 'thanks for that, Triggs.'

And then he reached out a bony finger, pressed a button and the machine kicked into a faster gear. I knew he was no longer of a mind to listen.

'Goodnight,' I said.

'Night, Triggs.'

Of course, Manchester United came a smeller at Wembley that weekend, losing 3–0. The popular view – and it gave me no pleasure to hear it – was that Vieira had given Roy the runaround and that Bob Dylan's counsel, whatever the colour of it, appeared to have little or no effect on the outcome.

I wasn't one to say I told you so – that's not in my make-up – which is why I didn't wait up for him.

Some time in the middle of the night I was awoken by a strange, persistent clanking sound, coming from the direction of the laundry room. I went to investigate.

Well, the sight that greeted me sent a shock of excitement through my body – as does the memory of it, all these years later. The treadmill lay in ruins on the floor of the laundry room – like an exploded space station. Roy was on his knees, with his back to me, humming tunelessly and poring through the debris with an Allen key.

He became aware of me standing there, watching him. He half-looked at me over his shoulder. 'Be careful of your feet in here,' he said. 'Obviously, there's a lot of little parts and – as I said – screws lying around.'

'You've . . .' I was in shock. 'You've dismantled it.'

'Ah, yeah,' he said airily. 'You said it yourself, Triggs – you can't beat obviously fresh air.'

I was as happy in that moment as I had ever been in my young life. I could almost taste the yeast of a new beginning.

A few weeks later, I would watch a football match for the very first time and I don't think it would overstating the case to say that neither of our lives would ever be the same again.

He smiled at me thinly. 'Time is it, Triggs?'

'Midnight,' I said. 'Maybe a little bit after.'

He nodded. I was about to return to my basket when he said, 'Not too late for a walk, is it?'

I felt my heart instantly quicken. 'Never is,' I said. 'It never is.'

*I'm in my basket, pawing the sleep from my eyes, when I hear the front door sucked gently shut. Roy is up early. Who is it this week? Scunthorpe away, I think. Not a fixture to set the average man's haemoglobin pumping – but then, who ever accused him of being that?*

*I climb to my feet. It's becoming a job of work these days. My joints grumble their tired protests. I pad along the hallway, then slip through the dog flap and out into the garden, by which time he's already shrinking into the distance.*

*I bark, sharply, three, four times.*

*Roy turns around. He narrows his eyes to get a bead on me. 'Sorry, Triggs,' he shouts. 'Thought I'd leave you sleep. You seemed pretty tired.'*

*My feelings are hurt. It's the first time he's ever walked without me. But I resolve not to show it. It's a Labrador thing. Fortitude in all things, etcetera, etcetera.*

*He waits for me to catch up with him. He's wearing his flat cap and carrying a blackthorn stick. Anyone who followed what Roy sometimes calls our walks series on Sky News will know that he likes occasionally to play the laird. More so since we moved to Suffolk.*

*'I was only nipping out for a quick paper anyway,' he says. 'Even though — as I've said in the past — I don't read them.'*

*I wait outside the shop, staring in through the open doorway, while Roy and the newsagent pass the time of day. 'Obviously,' I hear Roy tell him, 'Scunthorpe's always a difficult place to go to and get a result. As I've said before, they always set out their stall . . .'*

*'Well,' the newsagent rejoins, 'all I'm just saying is that we belong in the top flight. Big club like Ipswich Town. The success we've had. We won the UEFA Cup, you know, back in — when was it again?'*

*Roy, who is as passionate about nostalgia as he is about the idea of a weekend trapped underground with Alan Shearer, cuts him short. 'Means absolutely nothing,' he says. He almost ululates the words. 'You're on about us needing to be in the top division. Listen, I'm not disagreeing with you. I want us to go up as much as anyone. All I'm saying is that it's not going to happen overnight. Obviously, we'd a good result against Cardiff. But we're not as good as everyone was saying after that match. And we're not as bad as everyone was saying after the QPR result . . .'*

*I pick up a scent. The scurf from another dog. Probably a terrier. Lakeland or Airedale, I would say. I follow it over to the front of William Hill and sniff about for a bit. That's when I happen to catch my reflection in the window.*

*It's quite a shock.*

*The hairs around my muzzle and brow have been losing their colour for a while now. I've never been a vain animal, but I do check myself occasionally in the window of the microwave oven.*

*Somehow, those once intermittent hairs have swelled into a great grey conurbation along the T of my forehead and nose.*

*Old age insinuates itself into your life like that. A hundred little changes that occur unnoticed, like mushrooms coming up in the night. You find yourself thinking, when did that happen? Why am I only seeing it now?*

*When he heard that Roy had got himself a Labrador Retriever, Alex Ferguson told him that it was the ideal companion for a footballer. I heard the conversation myself. It was in the kitchen back in Hale.*

*'The average Labrador lives for thirteen point two years,' Ferguson had said. 'The exact same length of time that the average Premier League footballer will spend at the top of his game. Made for the job, I'd say.'*

*I entered Roy's life, of course, when his football career was already well underway. And though he loves my company as much as I love his, there are days like today, when I'm enveloped by the sad sense that all I'm really doing here is seeing out the clock.*

*'Come on, Triggs,' he suddenly calls out to me. I turn around. He's standing at the door of the newsagents, slapping a copy of the* East Anglian Daily Times *against his thigh. And he's smiling. Happy to see me. He's always happy to see me. I take a breath and steel myself for the effort of following him back to the house.*

# 3.

# So This Is Football!

DOGS, YOU PROBABLY ALREADY KNOW, HAVE A hearing capacity far superior to that of humans. I saw an expert on television once who said that if you wanted to build a keyboard capable of reaching the highest note audible to the canine ear, you'd have to add a further forty-eight keys to the right-hand side of a standard piano – the last twenty of which would produce nothing more than silence to even the sharpest human ear.

I can believe that.

Yet such was Roy's annoyance in the early days of the 1998/9 season that he produced sounds of a frequency that was beyond even me.

The source of it, it turned out, was a blunt exchange of views he'd had with Peter Schmeichel over the issue of the captaincy. Schmeichel – who, I understood, had always had an uneasy relationship with Roy – had been handed what they call 'the armband' during United's pre-season tour of Norway and Denmark. It was supposedly understood by all to be a temporary arrangement, to give him the honour of leading the team out on what Roy described as 'obviously his own turf'.

The problem, according to Roy, was that he didn't want to give it back. And he made a point of saying it as well, the big, blond dolt, which threw Roy into one of his righteous rages.

'A fucking goalkeeper!' I remember he said. At the time I was relieving myself against the bus shelter outside Barclays on Ashley Road. I'd brought Roy the leash and suggested we walk to Hale and try to work off his frustration. 'Do you know *how* you end up being a goalkeeper, Triggs?'

I had to stop mid-stream. 'Er, not really,' I said, 'no.'

'Because you can't fucking play, that's how. Like, when you're a kid, obviously, no one wants to go in goal. So it's always someone who can't kick a fucking ball straight. Or someone's little brother whose mother says you have to let him play. So you say, fuck it, stick him in the goal. Then his father buys him a pair of gloves for Christmas – to encourage the lad. So now he's always in fucking goal, because he wants to get the wear out of the fucking gloves. Then when everyone else has packed in playing football – they're away drinking or they're married or whatever – the lad's still playing in goal for some local team. Because they always need goalkeepers – no one wants to fucking do it.'

I have, I think it's fair to say, always endeavoured to see the best in people, naïve as it's made me seem at times. Years later, for instance, when Stan Collymore was caught by one of the penny miserables engaged in something called 'dogging', I was the one who tried to put a charitable interpretation on the whole business.

'Well,' I remember telling Roy 'at least he's an animal-lover.'

Roy nearly ruptured his spleen laughing. It turned out, of course, that Stan didn't even own a dog, which made the entire episode even grubbier in my eyes.

But I'm off the point again. What I'm saying is that I was hardwired, like most dogs, to try to see the good in humankind. You made us that way after all – any paleontologist worth his PhD will tell you that.

Peter Schmeichel, however, was one of the few players who challenged me in this regard. If moaning was an Olympic event, Peter would have won . . . actually, he wouldn't have won anything because he'd have been at home, sitting on his bed, his arms folded sulkily and his bottom lip stuck out like a bulldog's underbite, all because he wasn't allowed to carry the flag at the opening ceremony.

Why did it always have to be about him? 'Typical fucking Peter,' as Roy has said more than once over the years.

Anyway, Roy and I devoured the road to Hale and back that evening, talking it out. And still it wasn't enough. We followed the narrow capillaries between Bankhall Lane and Arthog Road – up Wyngate Road, down Arthog Drive, up Tolland Lane, down Avon Road, up Laburnum Lane, down Nursery Avenue – searching for a better perspective on things.

Roy was as cranky as a spinster's dog. Once or twice, I pulled on the lead and got an earful from him. 'Triggs, do you have to sniff every fucking lamppost we pass?'

I did, as it happens. Incredibly clever I might have been, but I was still a dog – and as helpless a slave to my nose as, well, Mark Bosnich was later on.

By the time we finished walking – and this was resolving itself into a real pattern now – I had persuaded Roy to see Schmeichel's behaviour in a more generous light.

'Obviously, as I've said before, he *is* a great shot-stopper,' he even conceded. 'For me, he's the best in the world, even though I can safely say we're never going to be great mates.'

'And,' I suggested, 'he's showing great desire, isn't he? The kind of desire that you yourself said was missing from the team last year?'

He considered this and decided he liked the fit of it. 'It's obviously a huge honour to captain Manchester United.'

'Which is why he wants to do it.'

'Well, for me, competition is what's needed. I think I've said it in the past – it's the only way anyone improves.'

'Exactly.'

'I'm, er, sorry I shouted at you back there, Triggs – obviously just a bit wound up.'

'Already forgotten,' I said.

The other item of business on the agenda was David Beckham. The whole of England, it seemed, was still in a fine old righteous lather about his sending off against Argentina. I remember a woman with an academic title and a face scored by sadness and concern telling Sky News that it was a reflection of Britain's moral decline. Oh, come on, I remember thinking.

Dogs don't share that human urge to see every action as a product of some wider social phenomenon. Maybe David Beckham kicked Diego Simeone because he thought Diego Simeone deserved a kick. And he did, of course – just a far harder one than he got. But Beckham had somehow emerged from the whole imbroglio as a figure of hate. The crowd booed him like he was a pantomime villain every time he touched the ball during the Charity Shield.

'The big fucking joke,' I remember Roy saying, 'is that it was the rest of the England team that bottled it . . .'

We were on the M56 at the time, on the way to see a veterinary surgeon in Gatley. I was now convinced that the pain in my stomach, which I may have mentioned earlier, was caused by a small piece of bark mulch that I'd inadvertently swallowed and was now struggling to negotiate its way through my digestive tract.

'You're on about people letting the country down. For me, Argentina were out on their feet. Didn't I say that to you at the time, Triggs? Listen, even with the extra man, you could see it in their eyes – the doubt had started to creep in. Same old England, though. Nearly prefer a moral victory to a real one.'

It was actually my suggestion that he invite Beckham over to the house for a chat. I confess I knew nothing about football at that time, but I was still capable of chipping in with valuable common-sense advice.

Beckham popped around a day or two later. He was wearing jeans and a simple shirt, I noticed, rather than the skirt and velvet bustier number I'd recently seen him photographed wearing while on holidays in the south of France. Roy must have had a word. Hale was a respectable area, where people voted Conservative and had their lawns mowed in tonal stripes. It was known as The Stockbroker Belt – and this was back in the days when stockbroking was considered a respectable job.

Beckham acknowledged my presence in the corner of the kitchen with an astute, 'It's a dog', although he didn't pet me, even when I wandered over to him and sniffed the leg of his jeans by way of a hello. Either he had a fear of dogs or he didn't want the smell of me on his buttermilk-moistened hands.

Experience, I suppose, would tend to suggest the latter.

Roy always had a genuine affection for Beckham. I know a lot of people thought otherwise when he was the only United player to skip his big day the following year. But come on – can you really picture Roy on the cover of *OK!* dressed in virginal white, sitting on the floor amid orchids and fairylights, his suppliant eyes looking up at the bride and groom on their ridiculous thrones? Well, he couldn't picture it either, so he went to the Wolf instead.

He liked Beckham, though – he liked him a lot. But they were just from different worlds. Roy was an alpha; Beckham was dating one. That was just how it was.

Roy made tea and told him what was on his mind. 'Obviously,' he said, 'we all know what happened during the summer. As I said at the time, I thought the lad Simeone made a bit of a meal of it – deserved an Oscar! Although I imagine that's scant consolation because you've become obviously a bit of a scapegoat for the media and the fans alike. Targeted mercilessly, blah, blah, blah. But what I want to say to you – as, obviously, the captain of Manchester United Football Club – is that once you cross that white line, you can't let it affect you.'

One thing that always amused me about Beckham was the process of Balkanisation that his face underwent whenever he talked. His eyes always seemed surprised by what was coming out of his mouth and ready to disassociate themselves from it at any moment.

'Obviously, I appreciate you having a word with me,' he said. 'You're obviously someone who I definitely respect, Roy. For me, you've had an unbelievable career so far – I can safely say the stuff of legend – and you're obviously a major part of why we've done so fantastically well over the last few years.'

There isn't a prince in the whole of the Middle East who could beat the average professional footballer for platitudinous blathering.

Next, it was Roy's turn.

'Well, as I've said before, you're obviously going to be a top, top player. You probably already are a top, top player. I think we all know the quality you've got as a footballer. Well documented. But as I've also said in the past, even in relation to myself, the booing is something you've got to get used to at this level – obviously part and parcel. I think I've said that from day one . . . Becks, what the fuck are you doing?'

Beckham had drifted over to the kitchen cupboards and was pulling jars and tins and bottles out, then laying them on the countertop.

'I'm rearranging obviously your food cupboards for you,' he said.

Roy's eyes narrowed until they'd diminished to outraged little slits. 'What?'

At that point, neither of us knew about the obsessive compulsions that drove Beckham and – if you want my opinion – made him the most perfect passer of a football that I've ever seen.

'The first thing I'm going to do,' he said, 'is put your herbs and obviously spices in alphabetical order. I've done the same for Gary Neville. And for Ronny Johnsen, to be fair. Makes it easier, at the end of the day, to find things. So it's, like, basil, cardamom, er, cinnamon, dill, fennel, mint, nutmeg . . . Or is it nutmeg, *then* mint?'

He looked upwards while he ran through the alphabet in his mind, his lips soundlessly forming each letter, while Roy looked at me with an expression that could best be articulated as, *Am I fucking dreaming this?*

'M comes before N,' Beckham eventually announced. 'Go on, Roy, keep talking.'

'Jesus, I'm after forgetting the fucking point I was trying to make. Becks, will you sit down?'

'No, it's fine,' he said, 'I don't mind doing this. It actually relaxes me. You were saying I obviously can't let the booing affect me.'

'Yeah, no, as I said before, it's part and parcel.'

'Thanks, Roy. Look, yeah, obviously I was ever so disappointed to be sent off in the World Cup finals. I thought, if anything, it should have been a yellow rather than a red card. I think people who said I deserved to be sent off were well wide of the mark. But I know I'm going to get stick for it – that's an unfortunate fact of life that I obviously realise.'

'I'm glad you said that.'

'That's why the start of obviously the new season is going to come as such a blessed relief to me. Because the only way I can answer my critics back is obviously on the field. Ask anyone who knows me and they'll tell you that that's where I've always liked to do my talking. And hopefully, by giving a hundred and ten percent there – and a fitting display for the fans – I can hopefully, as I've said before, win people around.'

Look, I had my own issues with David Beckham later on. But I realised that day there was a stupid stubbornness that was an essential strand in the weave of his character. And it told you that he was going to get through this. I think we both stopped worrying about Beckham then – that was, until he was photographed wearing pink nail varnish at the christening of Liz Hurley's baby. But that's a whole other story.

Roy positively bristled at the prospect of the new season. 'We've bought the lad Stam from PSV,' I remember him telling me, as he tried to pick a perforated bag of rice from a pot of boiling water without scalding his fingers. The vet had told him to place me on a strict diet of bland food until the piece of mulch emerged. It never did, by the way. In time, the pain mysteriously went away. 'He's obviously an exceptional acquisition. The manager thinks that him and Ronny could be the new Brucie and Pally. Although obviously that remains to be seen. They've proved nothing yet.

'Then the lad Blomqvist's come in – after obviously a difficult time in Italy. He's supposed to be a player. Again, how many times have we heard that? I'm not a big believer in reputations anyway. For me, it's what you did in the last game that matters . . .'

I nodded. It all made sense, even to a dog who knew nothing about football.

'The manager thinks we're still missing maybe a piece or two. We've never really replaced Eric – obviously, Cantona. He likes the look of the lad Yorkie.'

'Who?' I wondered.

Imagine, I didn't even know that.

'Dwight Yorke,' he said. 'He's a good player. Done tremendously well for Villa. Ruthless finisher when he's on-song and fully fit. Scores goals wherever he goes.'


It's easy to forget that the 1998/9 season – the most successful in Manchester United's history – took a long time to sputter to life. The team's form in the early part of the season was up and down like – well, to be crude, like Dwight Yorke's arse cheeks, if you believe half of what he says he was up to in his modestly titled memoir, *Born To Score*.

Jaap Stam might well have been the most expensive defender in the history of football, but I heard him described so often as a disaster area that the first time I laid eyes on him I expected him to be roped off with traffic cones and hazard tape.

Roy passed no judgment on him that I heard, other than to say, 'Ten point six million? With a price-tag like that, you've obviously got to be doing it week in, week out,' which I suppose, in retrospect, *was* a judgment.

A second 3–0 defeat to Arsenal that September hurt Roy as deeply as any result before or since. It seemed to bear out the popular view that Arsenal had overtaken Manchester United as a force and that Patrick Vieira was now a better player than Roy.

I still wasn't watching football at that stage, but I was aware that Stam had put in a calamitous shift that day. Angry words were cast about in the dressing room, I know. There was a rumour that Stam, in the heat of the moment, said, 'Hey, Roy, why don't you go home and talk to your fucking dog?' although Roy never confirmed this and the fact that Stam can still get around today without the use of a motorised wheelchair suggests that it was probably fiction.

What I can say for certain is that Roy was more frustrated with himself and his slow return to full fitness than he was with Stam or Schmeichel or whoever else was in the frame for the incompetency that characterised United's form in those early weeks of the season. And that, yes, occasionally he brought his frustration home with him.

I remember I was watching a biography of Pol Pot one afternoon when I heard smooching noises coming from the direction of the back garden. I listened for a minute or two before I realised that I was being summoned. I got to my feet and sauntered outside, where Roy was standing on the decking with an aspect of severity about him that I picked up on immediately.

'Jesus, about time,' he said.

In his right hand, I couldn't fail to notice, he had a short stick, perhaps twelve inches in length, which he held in my line of regard for a few seconds, then said, 'Come on, Triggs, we never really play together.'

One of the endearing little ricks in Roy's personality, I would come to learn, was his tendency, in times of stress, to try to put our relationship on what I would call a regular master-and-servant footing. He turned suddenly and, with what Barry Davies would no doubt have called wonderful fluidity of movement, sent the stick spinning through the air. My eyes followed it as best they could, as it described a high arc, then landed, somewhere amongst a small copse of beeches at the far end of the garden.

'Fetch,' he said.

Was he serious? Well, naturally, I didn't move.

He trilled his fingers. 'Triggs,' he said, 'it's down there – did you not see where it went?'

Still I didn't stir.

'Can I remind you,' he said, a sorrowing catch in his voice, 'that you're *supposed* to be a retriever?'

I looked up to meet his cold, hard stare. After a few seconds, he turned on his heel and walked back into the house, pausing in the doorway for a disappointed backwards look at me.

Much later, I discovered that Roy had been reading an article about Clarence Pfaffenberger, a pioneer in the area of training dogs to lead the blind. It was Pfaffenberger's view that a Labrador's willingness to retrieve thrown objects was the best single indicator of whether or not it would grow up to be a good guide dog. It wasn't that I wasn't being lazy or deliberately thick skulled. I just didn't see myself ever going into that line of work.

Anyway, I allowed some time for Roy's anger to pass, then I followed him inside. He was in the kitchen, tidying all around him. I lay on my mat next to the back door and watched him stack the dinner plates in the dishwasher, then wipe down all the countertops. He opened both doors of the double-door fridge-freezer and began examining the labels on various comestibles, discarding everything that was even approaching its sell-by date – an action I guessed was designed to convey a message.

'You're just not doing it,' he said, without looking at me. 'Obviously, I *throw* the stick. But then I'm standing, waiting there and you don't bring it back to me. No disrespect, Triggs, but at the end of the day, you've got to ask yourself obviously, where's the hunger gone?'

'But, Roy,' I said, as reasonably as I could, 'we don't *have* that kind of relationship.'

A silence of some considerable length followed. He continued pottering around the kitchen, while I lay there and studied him in profile. Roy could never stay mad at me for long. After a few minutes I watched the hard lines of his features soften. He stopped what he was doing and came over to me, hunkered down to my level and started combing my coat with loving strokes of his bony fingers.

'They destroyed us,' he said. He was referring to Arsenal, I knew. 'Tore us apart.'

'You've lost football matches before,' I said.

'Not like this, Triggs. I mean, take a bow, Arsenal – they richly deserved it. They were better than us in every single position on the park.'

'Is that not an exaggeration?'

He stuck out his bottom lip, shook his head. 'I don't think it is. For me, I don't think we're even in the top five teams in England at the moment – as I said before, on current form.'

He *was* exaggerating. I think we both knew it.

'It's only September,' I said. It was often I'd heard him mention that it was a long season.

He smiled tightly. 'I'm maybe asking a bit too much of myself, coming back from, obviously, injury – that's what the manager said. It's something I've possibly been guilty of in the past – not having enough patience.'

'Your frustration is understandable – you were injured for such a long time.'

He nodded. Then his face was configured to say something – I sensed a faint embarrassment about him.

'Listen,' he said, his eyes fluttering around the kitchen like a bee in a field of blooms. 'I didn't mean it. What I said about you not doing anything. Not having any desire. You've been phenomenal for me over the past obviously twelve months or so. When I was coming back from injury, as I've said in the past, I wouldn't have been able to do it without you. You've really helped me keep my head together.'

The man was really opening up to me. Showing me genuine affection. And what I did I have to go and say?

'Socrates regarded dogs as the true philosophers.'

I cringe when I think about it now. And so I should. It was something I'd heard on television. Channel 4 was doing a season of documentaries on ancient Greece. But when did I become so pretentious?

Roy stood up again. He didn't even respond to my line about Socrates, other than to say, 'Anyway – thanks, Triggs.'


It's a fact that most humans who have an emotional attachment to Manchester United also have a Pavlovian hatred for Liverpool. I always felt, though, that Roy's feelings about Liverpool were a moral choice more than a moral reflex. By that I mean he didn't hate them for who they were. He hated them for who they weren't.

His relationship with Arsenal, then, later on, Chelsea, was different. Don't get me wrong, he treasured up a whole lifetime's worth of resentments against them, their players and their personnel. But he also respected them. Not so Liverpool.

'Listen,' he told me once, 'over the last few years they've had Robbie Fowler, Michael Owen and obviously the lad Collymore. You're on about three of the best strikers in the world. And what have they won? Jesus, if they do the double over us in the league, they consider it a good fucking season.'

Secretly, I think Liverpool were everything he feared becoming – self-regarding, underachieving and morally weak. Maybe this fear had its roots in the FA Cup final of 1996, the year before I was born. Roy sometimes talked about it. The Liverpool players showed up at Wembley wearing cream suits with red-and-white candy cane ties. 'Jesus, Triggs,' he told me once, 'they looked like fucking gondoliers.'

And Eric Cantona, he remembered, whispered something suitably mercurial in his ear. 'Know, first, who you are,' I think it was, 'then adorn yourself accordingly.'

I never met Eric, but I hear he was quite the man for the *bon mots*.

In the centre of midfield they had Jamie Redknapp, with his perfect hair and his archer's bow lips. Roy could barely mention him without involuntarily laughing the soft vowel sound in his Christian name. It was always, 'Ja-heh-mie Redknapp.' I think it drove Roy mad the way the press raved about him. He said to me once, 'How long do you think the papers are going to be calling him a future England captain before he manages to get in the England fucking team?'

Alongside him now was Paul Ince. Contrary to popular myth, Roy quite liked Ince. He must have done. He managed to work alongside him for two years without once putting his hands around the annoying idiot's throat. All that, 'Call me

The Guvnor,' carry-on — if I know Roy, he'll have been sorely tempted.

Ince, you just knew, still took his measure from Roy, which was a ridiculous liberty, of course. Alex Ferguson had already settled the argument three years earlier by making Roy the keystone of his team and shipping Ince off to Italy, where he went on to win — as Roy never failed to point out, while in the process of praising him — 'absolutely nothing in the game'. And much as Roy liked him, in his heart he knew that the inclusion of a Manchester United castoff in their midfield was just about the measure of Liverpool's ambition.

Anyway, I'm mentioning all of this as background to the story of United's victory over Liverpool at the end of September 1998, a Thursday night that — and I hope I won't be accused of exaggerating this for dramatic effect — changed the current of both our lives.

I remember a little smile playing on Roy's lips when he left the house that day. 'Off to face the mighty Liverpool,' he said.

What a pivotal night it proved to be. And to think, I was planning to spend the evening watching *After Actium*, the latest in Channel 4's documentary series about Ancient Greece!

The programme wasn't due to start for another twenty minutes and I was mulling over how I might spend the time, torn between snoozing and having another good lick of the sweet spot on the kitchen floor where Roy had earlier spilled a mug of Baxters Vegetable Broth. In the end, I did neither. I switched over to one of the Sky Sports channels. I can't explain why. I've always considered fate to be a silly human conceit. Maybe I was just curious about what it was that made Roy so universally admired.

Manchester United were already winning 1–0, according to the tiny scoreboard in the top left-hand corner of the screen. I watched with only a vague interest at first. I recognised a few faces. Roy's obviously. There was Denis Irwin, my sometime foster father, with that crabbed little expression of his that was so at odds with his personality. David Beckham, who permanently looked like a man trying to remember whether or not he'd locked the car. And, I noticed with a fright that forced me to turn my head away, Ole Gunnar Solskjær, the only human who would ever succeed in bringing the feral animal out of me.

Football was, as Roy had mentioned once or twice in dispatches, a game played between two teams of eleven players on a rectangle of grass using a spherical ball filled with compressed air. The object for both teams was to put the ball inside one of the two wooden frames that were pitched in the middle of the two short ends of the grass rectangle. They attempted to do this generally after a long ritual of pushing the ball around from player to player using their feet or their heads or occasionally their torsos, as I'd seen Roy do many times before in the garden, when he tried to interest me in what he called a kickabout.

The goalkeepers – and I immediately recognised Schmeichel from the time he helped bring Roy home after his cruciate injury and another time when we saw him coming out of Jollyes Petfood Superstore on Birchfields Road but we all pretended not to see each other – were dressed differently from their team-mates and were the only players who were allowed to touch the ball with their hands in general play. Each game or match lasted ninety minutes, with a few more added to the end at the discretion of an impartial referee, who was continuously derided by supporters of both teams as a 'bastard' or 'wanker'. The team that amassed the most goals in the course of a match was deemed the winner, although a draw was declared in the event of a tie.

Listen to me. I've just realised how utterly ludicrous it is, my explaining football to you. If you're human, the chances are you already knew what I gleaned from those first ten minutes

I spent watching the game. Initially, I found it, yes, mildly diverting, although I must confess I struggled to understand why it was that so many people were continually drawn to it as a spectacle. They were just doing the same thing, weren't they, week in, week out? Didn't it ever get old, like tug o' war, or find the treat, or wrestling, or any of the little games that Roy and I played to pass an idle hour?

I yawned, then dropped down off the sofa and puttered across the living room to the door. I was already thinking about that broth stain on the floor of the kitchen. Roy had mopped it up, then run a Flash Wipe over the site, although my scent receptors could still pick up the odour of onions, carrots, celery, potatoes, mushrooms, garlic, bay leaves and soy sauce through the film of linalool, citral, limonene and amphoteric surfactants that Roy had used to try to mask it. Our noses are like that, you see. Dogs can break down smells into their constituent parts.

I don't know why I stopped in the doorway and threw my eyes back at the television. Martin Tyler may have mentioned that Andy Cole was warming up and that Ole Gunnar Solskjær was the man most likely to make way. But look back I did. And that look transformed my life and — I hope it's not stretching matters to say it — set Manchester United on a course of success that had only previously been dreamt about.

I stared at the television for a few seconds. And suddenly, inexplicably, I started to discern a shape and pattern to what was happening. The players weren't just running around headlessly and pinging the ball around in a way that made no sense. Except for Phil Babb, but that was just his thing.

No, the two teams were ranged against each other in a militaristic way in three horizontal lines. Each had a defensive line; a midfield, which appeared to be the base of operations for both teams; then a forward line, whose main function was to score goals. Each player seemed to have a player on the opposition whose job it was to countermand him and the outcome of these private little duels, I understood, would likely have a significant bearing on the outcome of the match.

Passing the ball to a team-mate was the most effective and efficient means of moving it forward in the direction of the opposition goal. The players tended to shuttle forward mostly, though not always, in long corridors of space either on the two flanks or through the middle. And it was in these same channels that they mostly defended when the opposition attacked.

So *this* was football. I moved a little closer to the television, the fasincation gathering in me. I loved it. I mean, I *loved* it. And not only that, I discovered, I *got* it. Right before my eyes – like some silent ephiphany – the players on the screen had resolved themselves into something I understood. I could read a game like a virtuoso can read a five-line staff. By which I mean that it made immediate sense to me, without even the requirement to focus. As I sat and watched, I realised that I could understand the tempo, the beat, the shape of a match. I could perceive subtle changes in tension and course. I could recognise different nuances of style and expression. I could see space, channels, the angles of attack most likely to yield success, the defensive points that were most likely to give way. I *saw* it. That's what I'm telling you. Every time, signature, dynamic and cue.

Roy was right. Liverpool really *were* shit. Okay, it didn't take a genius to see that. I mention it just to make the point that it wasn't all geometry and abstract shapes that I was seeing.

Dogs, I expect you already know, are highly proficient readers of human body language. It's been part of our genetic pre-programming since man took it upon himself to socialise us fourteen thousand years ago. And Labradors can read human signals better than any other dog. I had, I was surprised to discover, an intuitive understanding of the essential character of individual players. From observing the slope of their shoulders, the elevation of their heads, their general carriage, I knew who believed in himself, who doubted himself, who had the heart for the job, who was happier hiding.

Lack of conviction was everywhere in that Liverpool team and there was no better expression of it than the sight of Jamie Redknapp literally bending over backwards to prevent Paul Scholes's goal-bound shot, from damaging his very fetching face. I'm sure Marks & Spencer are delighted today that he did so. Good luck to him. Roy's never been asked to model Blue Harbour stretch denim. But then he won seven Premier Leagues, four FA Cups and a European Champions League.

Of course, what crowned the evening was the realisation that Roy was, by some considerable distance, the best player on the field. My heart well nigh spilled over as all of the clichés I'd heard so blithely tossed about in relation to him – box to box, good engine, colossally influential – were suddenly made manifest before my eyes. He was the game's centre of gravity, as, I'd discover in time, was almost always the case. He was an alpha among betas. There was a wariness of him, you could see it, not only among the opposition players but among his own team-mates. There was a perceptible shift in the energy of the game whenever the ball was at his feet. He tackled ferociously, popped up in little cameos all over the field, passed the ball more cleverly and more efficiently than any other player and seemed to spend an inordinate amount of time shouting at people, most often his own team-mates, demanding more from them. He was a true leader of men. The beating heart of Manchester United. And he was a magnificent sight when he was about his work.

In that moment I gained a sudden, fuller understanding of what I had to offer him, apart from friendship, life advice, a listening ear and the other general benefits that accrue from sharing your home with a dog breed famous for its loyalty, intelligence, even-keeled personality, eagerness to please and all-round clubbiness. I could offer him advice of a highly technical nature about football itself.

From that night onwards, I can honestly say that the game engaged me like nothing else, documentaries included. My mind was still crackling with the excitement of it all when Roy arrived home not long after midnight. He was surprised to find me still up, way beyond my usual bedtime. 'What did you do,' he asked, 'obviously while I was out?'

'I watched the match,' I said.

He laughed. He thought I was joking at first. Then I watched his eyes widen in happy speculation. 'You watched the match? *Our* match?'

'Yes.'

'Did you see Jamie Redknapp,' he said, chuckling mordantly, 'jumping out of the fucking way?'

'I did,' I said. 'I saw it.'

I saw everything.


*Ipswich have drawn 1–1 with Scunthorpe. I hear the result on Gillette Soccer Saturday, some old pro telling Jeff Stelling that it finished honours-even at Glanford Park, although, in truth, Roy Keane's side – shocking in the first half – will be disappointed not to have taken all three points after forcing Scunthorpe to withstand a barrage of second-half chances.*

*I lie down in the hallway and wait to hear his key in the door. At some point I fall asleep, then at some later point – impossible to tell how much later – I wake up to find Roy kneeling beside me.*

*'Bad result tonight,' he says, in a near-whisper.*

*He doesn't seem angry. Not as angry as he used to get when he was a player. He runs his thumb along the crown of my head, then rubs behind my left ear.*

'We're maybe not starting games with enough urgency,' he says, more to himself than to me. 'Although I possibly started with the wrong formation tonight. We'll look at it again next week.'

He stands up, walks to the kitchen. I follow maybe a minute later – as quick as my legs allow. When I get there, I notice a faraway look on his face as he casts his eye over a flyer for a local carpet and upholstery cleaning service that was pushed through the letterbox this afternoon.

'Completely safe and non-toxic,' he says distractedly. 'Most carpets dry in sixty minutes. Full credit.'

But I know what's on his mind. It's only matter of time before the questions are being asked again – the same questions that have followed him here from Sunderland. Does he have the people skills for the job? Is he too unforgiving of human failings to be a boss? Are the same qualities that made him the great player he was – his desire, his unsparing hardness on himself, his refusal to countenance a backward step – going to be his essential failing as a manager?

I wonder myself. I know he does, too.

# 4.

# Genius!

LIKE ANYONE WHO DISCOVERS THEY HAVE AN extraordinary gift, the immediate question for me was, what was I going to do with it? Actually, that's not entirely true. The real dilemma, looking back, was how was I going to break the news of my genius to Roy. God knows, he had a serious aversion to people who thought they knew it all and it was often I'd heard him mutter, 'Fucking spoofer' or, 'How can you live with yourself?' while watching some old pro dispense his questionable wisdom on television.

I know he said once that he wouldn't trust any of the pundits he sees on television to walk his dog. Believe me, it wasn't the first time I'd heard that.

No, the challenge for me, looking back now, was to pass my knowledge on to Roy without seeming as inexplicably pleased with myself as, say, an Alan Hansen or a Garth Crooks. I decided to break it to him slowly, during the course of our twice-daily walks, to try to give him the impression that my football knowledge was something that was flowering over time.

That autumn, as the dark evenings protracted and our breaths fumed on the cold evening air, I began to salt my regular conversation about what I'd seen on television that day with occasional football references. If I was discussing, for instance, a brilliant wartime flanking manoeuvre – the

History Channel had recently shown a documentary about the great Confederate general Stonewall Jackson – I'd mention, by way of analogy, a fullback who had difficulty tackling on his inside. Or if it was, say, a military leader who tended to make wrongheaded decisions in the white heat of battle – Lord Raglan at Balaclava, for example – I'd compare him, all innocent-like, to a goalkeeper who I'd noticed suffered nerves at set-pieces.

Roy would hold his head to one side, the way he does, to consider what he'd just heard, then he'd say, 'Yeah, you could have a point about the lad,' or it'd be, 'Wouldn't be a hundred percent sure you're right there, Triggs.'

Over a period of weeks, I think he came to see that I knew a little of what I was talking about, although my influence, I must admit, yielded its successes slowly. In the months leading up to Christmas, United were a sorry mess – I didn't miss a single televised game – and there was no indication that this was going to be anything other than a very ordinary year.

Aston Villa led the Premier League in December. I mean, the idea of it now.

Even I – new to this game – could see that United's troubles began and ended with Jaap Stam, whose uncertainty of purpose spread like a bacillus through the team that winter, especially the back five. Peter Schmeichel was being made to look like a complete idiot – or rather, more of a complete idiot than was actually the case – while Gary Neville at last had the burden of troubles to go with his miserable, hangdog face.

The penny was a long time dropping for Alex Ferguson, of course. But then, having made Stam the most expensive defender in the history of the game, he was understandably reluctant to tell the club board that it would have been a far savvier piece of business to have simply burned their £10.6 million in a barrel in the car park.

Instead, the lie was allowed to persist that he was a world-class defender who would come good after a period of what those in the know called 'bedding in'. I even heard Roy repeat it once or twice – wishing it was true, I think, if only to see Ferguson's judgment vindicated – but I never revised my opinion of him, even later on when others did. For all the praise he heaped on him, Ferguson bundled him out the door at the first opportunity he got and, believe me, it had nothing whatsoever to do with him calling the Nevilles a couple of 'busy cunts' in his book.

The team was scoring a lot of goals, but they weren't winning matches. I remember that winter they went to Birmingham to play Aston Villa. Roy was of the view that Villa were punching far above their weight – 'like Norwich back in the day' – and that United would give a clear demonstration of the class differential between them. And then they didn't. They were awful. Roy came home and told me the story of the match in a voice that was so desperate in character, I had to pretend I hadn't seen it myself. I just told him I'd slept through it.

'Scholesy opened the scoring,' he said, his voice sad and low, like the bourdon note of a distant thunder. 'Did tremendously well to finish and obviously, you thought, a case of job done. But then the lad Joachim nicked one back at the other end – you'd have to say full credit to him.'

His eyes were lost somewhere in the distance between us. It was really getting to him.

It was the same story in the European Champions League, where United kept somehow managing to draw matches they should really have won. They drew with Barcelona at home and away in the group stage. They drew away against Bayern Munich. As Roy said, they could have had nine points from the three games.

I attempted to jolly him along with words of general encouragement and then, when I thought he was ready to listen to it, advice. I remember the day before the return match against Bayern at Old Trafford. Roy and I walked into Hale under the heavy droop of a battleship-grey sky and I mentioned – as casual as you like – something I'd noticed watching a Bundesliga highlights programme a week or two before. Thomas Struntz didn't like players running at him with the ball.

'It's just an observation,' I said. 'There might be nothing in it. Just thought I'd mention it.'

He didn't say anything, just continued walking, and I wondered whether he'd even heard me. But later, I realised that he must have passed it on because United's goal the following night came as a direct result of Ryan Giggs beating Struntz for pace on the left. And Roy clearly knew what was coming because his run into the penalty box anticipated the cutback and he sent the ball crashing into the net.

United had to win to be absolutely certain of progressing. Bayern, almost inevitably really, equalised, but in the end it didn't matter – events elsewhere meant that United went through to the knockout phase as one of the two best group runners-up.

Not that you'd have known it from Roy's form that night. I turned in not long after ten o'clock, exhilarated by the match, but exhausted from the stress of it. I don't know what time he got home. He opened the door of the laundry room, I remember, throwing a lance of light across the tiled floor and temporarily blinding me.

'Did you watch it?' he wondered.

'I did,' I said.

'One-all.'

I blinked hard, to try to clear the purple Rorschach blots from my vision. 'You, er, took your goal well,' I said.

He cut me off. 'The goal means absolutely nothing to me,' he said in a recitative, matter-of-fact kind of way. I knew the routine well enough by now. 'Obviously, the important thing, as I said earlier, was to get the result that sees us into the next round.'

'Yes, I suppose it is.'

'And anyway,' he said, 'for me, Giggsy's done most of the work. Did ever so well to beat the lad Struntz down the left, showed him a clean pair of heels, then cut it back. You're on about the finish, but all I had to really do was obviously hit the thing. I probably don't score as many goals as I maybe should. The manager's always on at me to possibly shoot a bit more.'

The outcome of the evening, it was clear to me, seemed to bring Roy little joy, which was a mark of the standard he was determined to set for the team.

'For me,' he said, 'we should have put them away. Ronny Johnsen could have made it two. Obviously, he'll be as disappointed as anyone with missing from that kind of distance. It was a chance and he knows it.'

'Hmmm,' I said.

'Then we got caught, as I've said before, ball-watching for the equaliser. A corner! Jesus, when are we going to learn? Full credit to the lad Salihamidžić – he punished us. That's the beauty of playing the game at this level.' He was quiet for a moment, then he said, 'Listen, it was a tough group. No question. Barcelona and Bayern Munich. Two big, big clubs. Two top, top teams. But we didn't beat either of them, Triggs. Four fucking draws.'

'I know.'

'I mean, I'm not asking for miracles. But if we're going to start challenging for the big prizes, we've got to learn to start putting these big teams away. Being straight with you – as I said tonight, to Gary Newborn . . .'

(He always pronounced it 'N*uuu*bon,' stretching the word out to a length commensurate with the level of his annoyance.)

'. . . we might have come through the group, but listen, we've proved absolutely nothing as a team.'

Personally – and this is going to sound a little conceited, I know – I was just thrilled to have had my judgment vindicated. It was a huge night for me and I was now fully convinced that I had a part to play in Roy's football career. At the same time, I decided to proceed with caution. I didn't want him to think I was passing myself off as some kind of expert all of a sudden. So I decided to keep my opinions largely to myself for a while.

Results continued to suffer through the month of December. Poor Gary Neville – clearly unsettled by having Stam near him – got himself sent off against Tottenham, in a match that United looked to have won when they went 2–0 up, but again managed to somehow draw. Tottenham also knocked them out of the Worthington Cup – or the Worth Nothing Cup, as I used to call it, to coax a laugh out of Roy. I mean, that wasn't exactly the end of the world. But what did bother Roy, I think, were the rave notices that David Ginola was collecting that winter, especially for his two performances against United.

Permit me to speak frankly for a moment. To my mind, David Ginola was as big a fraud as ever wore boots and shilled for a shampoo company. And though I can't presume to speak for Roy, I don't think he was exactly his cup of tea either.

I'd noticed that whenever Roy was asked in interviews what team he supported as a boy, he always answered, 'Tottenham,' before adding the qualifier, 'For whatever reason,' like it was some embarrassing detail from his childhood, like a song he was forced to sing at parties, or eczema.

Nowadays, Tottenham were, to Roy, a synonym for underachievement, their fans preferring transient pieces of magic – a back-heel, an overhead kick, a decent run in the Cup

– to genuine and lasting success. Well, if that was what turned them on, then they'd found a man who could give it to them in Ginola.

It wasn't just Tottenham's fans either – the entire game was besotted with him at that time. It was a love affair that reached its moment of consummation when he picked up both Player of the Year awards in a season when Tottenham finished in the bottom half of the table, having won only eleven of their thirty-eight league games.

Pardon my language here, but what a fucking travesty.

I watched, I think, the first of the awards shows on television and it still bothers me all these years later, the memory of him flicking his hair on the way up to the rostrum, while Roy and the other players who went on to create history by winning the European Champions League, the Premier League and the FA Cup in the space of a fortnight had to sit there, grinning like they were being collectively electrocuted.

Roy told me years later that Ginola went into the acting business. I told him he was always in the acting business. He loved that.

Of course, this was all still several months away. As Christmas drew closer, it didn't look like United were going to win anything. A few days after the drawn game with Tottenham, they dropped two more points from a winning position against Chelsea.

I had my views, and strong ones at that, but I decided to keep them to myself, even though I ended up copping some of the backlash. There were more abortive efforts that winter to socialise me. I remember one morning I was stretched out on the sofa, watching a documentary on BBC2 about the poet Sylvia Plath, when I heard two sharp finger-snaps. I looked up.

'Dogs aren't allowed on the furniture,' Roy said.

This was a new one on me.

Another time, I was lying on my front on the cold,

herringbone brickwork at the front of the house, watching a squirrel move concertina-like from one side of the garden to the other. I was trying to make up my mind whether or not to chase the thing when Roy suddenly appeared and in a calm, temperate voice asked me to give him my paw.

I was at a genuine loss, of course.

'The paw,' he said. 'It's a thing that all dogs learn. I say, "Gimme the paw," and you lift it up and obviously put it in my hand.'

'To what end?' I wondered.

He was far from pleased with me. I know some animal behaviorists will interpret all of this as a struggle for primacy in the relationship. All I can say is that, from my point of view, there was never any doubt in my mind that Roy was the master and I was there to serve him. But I was also a pragmatist — another Labrador trait — and I always felt compelled to ask, 'Why am I doing this? Is there a point?'

Some people think dogs are incapable of complex reasoning — well, not this one.

Naturally, it drove Roy to distraction when I disobeyed his commands, just as it did when Paul Scholes or Phil Neville or Jesper Blomqvist did the same thing. There was one day that winter, I remember, when there was a bad air between us over some fetching task involving his slippers that he thought I was simply failing to grasp. Anyway, he went to the lengths of performing a home deafness test on me, standing behind me, out of sight, then repeatedly banging the wok with a metal spoon to check did I prick my ears and turn to the source of the racket. Which I did, obviously. So all was well with my hearing. Roy once again abandoned his efforts to domesticate me and accepted that it was just never going to be like that between us. Or maybe he decided, with everyone playing so badly, that he had bigger fish to fry.

The prospect of Christmas usually excited Roy, but not that

year. As it drew nearer, there was none of the usual seasonal cheer about him. The plastic tree remained in the attic, while the carollers, who were always enthusiastically received at the door ('"*Adeste Fideles*"! A top, top hymn – hats off to it.'), now found nobody home. I remember him saying one night, 'You're on about Christmas, but I don't know why people make such a big deal about it. For me, it's just another day. We really need to start getting a hold of ourselves.'

That was the night before the ignominy of a home defeat to Middlesbrough, which eventually proved to be the turning point in United's season. 'To go three down?' I remember Roy saying. 'At *hooome*? To fucking Middlesbrough?'

He said it couldn't go on and he was right. Something was going to have to change.

Christmas Eve fell that year on a Thursday. Alex Ferguson, who'd been absent for the Middlesbrough game because he was at a funeral, invited all of the players around to his house in Wilmslow that night to discuss the crisis of confidence that had beset the team.

I can't even begin to tell you how madly the excitement boiled in me when Roy asked if I wanted to come along. 'Just for the drive,' he said, although I think the truth of it was that, after the Struntz business, he was interested in what I had to say, or at the very least curious.

Roy drove. That probably goes without saying. The entire way there, he groused like Dickens's Christmas curmudgeon. 'See, if it was up to me,' he said, his seat forward, his shoulders tensed over the wheel, 'I wouldn't even celebrate it. I'd make everyone work, same as every other day.'

Then we arrived at the house. It was some pile of bricks.

The living room, or the lounge, as Ferguson liked to call it – an obeisance to his tenement childhood – was full of voices. When

Roy walked in, a sudden silence descended. I looked around at the faces wainscotting the walls, all of which I recognised from television. I have to admit, I hadn't quite realised, until I heard the vast soundlessness of half-a-dozen conversations stopping at once, the extent to which most of his teammates paid court to him.

Nicky Butt's face bloomed bright red, Paul Scholes's Adam's apple bobbed up and down like a drowning man, while Dwight Yorke fought valiantly to stop himself from smiling, presumably lest Roy take offence. The Nevilles, who were the last to notice us, continued talking about the latest Simply Red release and how it compared to some of their earlier output.

'It's obviously a lot more reflective,' Gary said. 'Pondering, as I've said before, the difficulties that come with love and fame and friendship, to be fair. It's downright amazing. Belting, even. I can safely say that vocally, lyrically, whatever way you want to slice it – for me, it's the best thing they've done. Beyond question.'

Phil seemed unimpressed, though. 'I don't know how you can say that, Gaz. *Stars* is obviously a sublime album.'

'Well, I *am* saying it,' Gary spat back. 'And I'm saying it as someone who's got everything they've ever put out. There's one or two tracks on this album and when I've listened to them, well, all I'll say is that tears were not very far away.'

'Eh, Roy's here,' Nicky Butt observed. And that ended the debate. Such as it was.

Even Ferguson – a far more gregarious man than he came across on television, with his big glasses, red, doughy nose and cheeks that kindled with the glow of a thousand burst capillaries – seemed unusually deferent towards Roy. 'Glad you could come,' he said, chancing to lay a friendly hand on his shoulder. I don't think Roy was a hundred percent comfortable being touched in that way, but he ignored it in the interests of polite form.

No one seemed to notice me much at all.

The atmosphere was as tight as a drum skin. I picked up on the fact that there had recently been some measure of unpleasantness in the dressing room.

'Obviously,' Roy said, 'I said a few things after the Middlesbrough match. And one or two people maybe think I was bit hard on them. The point I was trying to make was that we can't go on defending like we have been. We spoke about giving away silly goals, which we can't keep doing at obviously the top level. And, as I said before, I maybe said one or two things that upset obviously one or two people. But, at the end of the day, all I want is what's best for Manchester United Football Club . . .'

The room was suddenly full of nodding heads.

'Obviously, I do take the point that we shouldn't always be beating ourselves up. We've not been playing well as a team – I think that's been well-documented – and we maybe do need to do something to possibly improve morale . . .'

'Paintballing,' someone said.

There were a few low sniggers. Roy's eyes searched the room. 'Who said paintballing?'

No one owned up. My money was on either Teddy Sheringham or Ryan Giggs, neither of whom showed quite the same servility in front of him as the others and tended to view his outbursts, I always thought, with a kind of bemused detachment.

'Who said paintballing?' Roy asked a second time, his eyes performing a bat dance around the room, looking for somewhere to land.

The tension was almost unbearable. I was too caught up in the moment to notice the figure sitting over my right shoulder, with his back against the wall. It was only when I sensed a hand moving towards me, to touch my coat, that I wheeled around and saw, with a shock that almost stalled my heart, the sardonically grinning face of Ole Gunnar Solskjær.

Well, I skipped the niceties of the usual pre-attack threat gestures — the glazed look, the low rumbling growl, the slow upper lip curl — and tried to take a nip out of his hand, unsuccessfully as it happened. Solskjaer suddenly remembered his manners and recoiled while the rest of the room gasped.

'Well,' Ryan Giggs said — and I'll never forget the pawky look on his face when he said it either — 'she's definitely Keaney's fucking dog, isn't she?'

There was a sudden cloudburst of laughter and, in that moment, the tension was immediately rinsed from the air. Even Roy lightened up.

'Obviously,' he said with a shrug, 'I'm on record as saying that banter's a major part of the game.'

'Stick the dog outside the door,' Alex Ferguson said, with the cold briskness of a man talking about week-old rubbish. Looking back now — remembering the moment when Roy led me out of the room by the collar — I can understand how Jim Leighton must have felt when Ferguson had decided he'd outlived his usefulness. And Lee Sharpe. And Norman Whiteside. And Keith Gillespie. And Paul Ince. And how David Beckham would eventually feel. And Dwight Yorke. And Jaap Stam. And Ruud van Nistelrooy. And, yes, in time — although that night it seemed so remote as to be impossible — how Roy would feel, too.

That's not to say that I wasn't embarrassed and thoroughly ashamed of my behaviour. I was. Especially when I heard Roy apologising to Solskjær on my behalf.

'She's never even growled at anyone before,' he said. 'You *are* a bit funny-looking, in fairness.'

I sat outside in the cold hallway and followed as best I could the eddies of conversation. Ferguson invited them all to help themselves to a drink — 'Only the one, mind!' — and, over the course of the next hour or so, to feel free to say their piece.

Although I was forced to follow the proceedings through a

couple of inches of polished oak, I began to understand that night something of the unique nature of Ferguson's genius. When it came to managing people, Machiavelli could have taken his correspondence course.

'Okay,' he said, 'we've all heard what Roy has to say. And it's good to sometimes get it out in the open like that.'

'Middlesbrough!' I heard Roy say. 'No disrespect, but Brian Deane? Andy Townsend? How fucking old is Andy now?'

Here was the brilliance of Ferguson – and I saw it many times in the years after that. He was content to sit back and let Roy articulate his anger for him. He was kind of like Ferguson's attack dog. It meant that Ferguson could come in afterwards and sound measured and reasonable.

'Quite right,' he said. 'But now we have to start thinking about the future. I think you'd agree with that, Roy – aye? Christmas is the perfect time to put the past behind you and, like I say, move forward.'

Another voice spoke. 'I think Roy was right what he said the other day.' Who was that? Oh. Gary Neville. God, he was a crawler. 'We've maybe all got to ask ourselves, where's the desire gone? Where's the hunger? We've got to take collective responsibility for what's happening. We're all to blame – that's beyond question.'

No, you're not, I thought. It's Jaap Stam's fault. Everything. I could see it and I'd only been following football a matter of weeks. Why couldn't they? Or were they just pretending? Well, speak of the devil, it was *his* voice I heard next. It was unmistakable.

'Uh think you're being a lidda bit unfair to Andy Thownshend, Roy. Heesh enjoying a new leash of laif at de moment. And Brian Deane thish year is shcoring goalsh for – how to shay? – fun?'

What an idiot. I could only imagine the expression on Roy's face.

'Brian Deane is the kind of player who – it's well documented

– only needs a yard.' This was Andy Cole's contribution. 'And, to be fair, he did what all good strikers do. He gambled.'

'He's done ever so well to finish,' Beckham agreed. 'Repaid another massive chunk of that £3.6m transfer fee!'

'He were unlucky,' I think it was Nicky Butt who said, 'not to bag a brace in the end.'

For intellectual cut and thrust, it wasn't exactly *Start the Week* with Melvyn Bragg.

Teddy Sheringham: 'To be fair to Middlesbrough, I genuinely believe they're a better team than their league position would have you believe.'

Phil Neville: 'I think, as well, it were a real cup final for them. And we've not turned up on the day.'

Ryan Giggs: 'They've got good honest pros, like Neil Maddison, then obviously Pally . . .'

Nicky Butt: 'They just wanted it more on the day.'

Denis Irwin: 'I think obviously it's been well-documented that we gave them too much time on the ball. Maybe stood off them a bit, to be fair. Let Dean Gordon get a shot away on his favourite left foot for, I think I'm right in saying, their second goal. Was a tremendous strike, to be fair. Lad did ever so well. But from our point of view, it obviously isn't good enough at this level.'

Gary Neville: 'I can safely say that watching the highlights back isn't something I'd relish. Be a real video nasty, that one! Like I said, I wouldn't relish it.'

Ryan Giggs: 'And Andy Townsend – he's not as young as he was – but he's still a top, top player.'

Gary Neville: 'Vastly talented.'

Paul Scholes: 'Immense.'

Ryan Giggs: 'I mean, they've got a lot of experience in there. And Bryan Robson's done fantastically well – phenomenal, even – with what he has to work with. You know, hats off to him.'

The conversation gyrated around the room like this for what

seemed like forever, until Ferguson performed an exaggerated throat-clearance to bring the inanities to a merciful end.

'Right,' he said, 'I think we all know – as Roy said the other day – what our problems are. You boys have to sort yourselves out at the back. You've not been concentrating. Been sloppy. Giving away joke goals. To be honest with you, I think one or two of you – especially those of you who played in the World Cup – look a wee bit tired. So I'm gonna give you boys a week off after Christmas. Go somewhere. Off to the sun. Get a break in.'

Again, I couldn't see Roy's face, but I suspected it wasn't what he'd have prescribed. I said it to him in the car on the way home – after I'd apologised again for my little aggression display. I said I didn't know what came over me. He was very understanding about it. 'The lad's got to expect it,' he said, 'obviously looking the way he does.'

I waited until we were on the A538 before I brought up the subject of the January holiday. 'Do you think it'll work?' I wondered.

'Listen, at the end of the day, *he's* the manager,' he said. 'Leadership must sometimes wear the harness of compromise.'

'Who said that?' I asked.

'I can't remember.'

Then he chuckled fondly – I realised it was the first time I'd heard him laugh in weeks.

'He always says I possibly give the lads too much stick at times and not enough carrot.'

'You seem more, well, positive than you did earlier this evening.'

'Obviously we've had a bad run of results. Like I keep saying – documented! But I suppose you've got to maybe see the positives sometimes. We're third in the league. Obviously, it's not where we want to be, but we're still in it. We're still in the Champions League. Still in the FA Cup. We've got – I think the manager said it was thirty-three matches at the very most left this season. We're going to make it our priority not to lose one of them.'

As I watched the lights of Wilmslow strobe like tracer rounds past the window, I made it my priority not to keep my opinions to myself anymore.

*I'm lying in the garden at the back of the house, lost in thought, my ears laved by the gentle bubble of a nearby brook. I hear the back door open, then close again. And then I hear his voice.*

*'Can't believe you're still up,' he says. 'It's three o'clock in the morning, Triggs.'*

*He ruffles my hair, then docks himself on the swingchair beside me. He's clearly not tired either. Backwards and forwards he swings, like a metronome, the chains complaining in the quiet stillness of the night.*

*I know that last night's match is being replayed in his head.*

*Ipswich lost 1–0 to Reading. According to the report on the television, they dominated the match but somehow failed to score, and Simon Church bagged the all-important winner for the Royals late on – just twenty seconds after coming on as a substitute.*

*I want to give him the answers. But I don't have them. Not anymore. My gift, such as it was, is gone. My mind now is like this night – just a vast susurration of silence, with the slow creak of a swingchair, like the second hand of a clock, counting down whatever time remains.*

# 5.

# No Surrender

IT WAS 1999. THE FINAL YEAR OF THE HUMAN decade, century and millennium. An historic year in which we were swept along by a rush of events so strong, we were but helpless passengers, taking in the view as the journey took us where it would. At least, that's the impression you'd have got from the ten-year retrospective on United's treble-winning season that I watched recently. Every player they interviewed kept invoking fate.

'It were just our year,' one them said – it might have been Nicky Butt or Paul Scholes. 'Matches we maybe shouldn't have won but did – and you thought, it's meant to be. It were like it were in the stars or summat.'

Take it from me, it wasn't in the stars and it wasn't fate. It was hard bloody work.

After the meeting in Alex Ferguson's house, Roy was fired with a new resolve. As the year turned, he decided that he should be the first player to arrive at the training ground every morning – 'It's obviously up to the captain to set the height of the bar, at the end of the day' – and he became as competitive in this as in all other things.

The problem that drove him to near-despair during the first two weeks of January was that no matter what time he drove through the gates of the training ground, one of the other players was already parked there before him. Roy took this not as a challenge but as an affront to his professionalism and his response was to sacrifice more and more of his sleep time to get there earlier. First, he started getting up half an hour earlier. But when he arrived at The Cliff, a car belonging to one of the other players was already there ahead of his.

He started to get up a whole hour earlier then, but with the same outcome.

A suspicion began to take shape in my mind that Roy was the victim of one of the practical jokes of which footballers seemed so regrettably fond.

My money was on [*name removed on legal advice*], who I'd never much warmed to anyway, always suspecting that a cruel sense of humour lurked behind that carnal smile. Of course, given what I've heard about him since, what lurked behind that carnal smile was probably just carnal thoughts.

At my urging, Roy and I staked out the training ground one Wednesday night. We sat in the shadows in a silver Ford Orion, which Roy rented specially for the job, and passed an hour or two listening to Simply Red. Yes, Roy had succumbed, like the others. I heard somewhere that Mick Hucknall used to hand out his CDs in the players' lounge. I wasn't a fan and blamed his voice for the migraines with which I suffered periodically. One thing I will say for him, though, is that at least he wasn't Bob Dylan. But there did come a point later on when I couldn't listen to his voice anymore and dropped Roy's copy of *Love and the Russian Winter* out of the window at a services stop on the M62, not far from Ainley Top. Roy saw me do it, too, but said nothing.

We waited and waited until eventually, some time afer 11pm, two cars arrived. And it was just as I suspected. [*Name removed on legal advice*] deposited his car in his parking space, then slipped into the passenger seat of Dwight Yorke's Ferrari Maranello, then they drove off, the two of them hacking with laughter.

Oh, what japery!

'Obviously,' Roy said, when he'd had forty-eight hours to reflect on it, 'jokes are – I think I'm on the record as saying it – vital for the morale of the squad. People who don't know me, they maybe look at me and think I take life possibly a bit too seriously. Which obviously isn't true. I like a good laugh as much as the next man,' before adding, in a voice so starchy that it creaked, 'I just hope they're still laughing come the end of May – that's all I'm saying.'

We continued to walk every morning and every evening, treading the seams of the Greater Manchester countryside and talking about everything and anything. By now we were a team. The things I learned from television – especially about the great battles in history – remained a feature of our conversation, but I didn't keep my opinions about football to myself either. And though it might sound like hubris to say it, my words of wisdom began to have a direct effect on Manchester United's results.

While Peter Schmeichel and the other World Cup players repaired to various European duty-free destinations that January (for all their wealth, there are few things in the world that get footballers as excited as cheap gold and discounted after-shave), Roy and the rest of the team trained as usual. Their next match was against Leicester on a day that was borrowed from a Patagonian winter. I remember standing in the shivering cold of the front driveway that morning, our breaths fogging on the rimy air, as Roy tried to scrape the ice from the windscreen of the car. It was ten below zero.

But it was on days like that that we Labradors made our name.

'The Chosin Few would have warmed to a day like this,' I said – this, in reference to a documentary I'd watched on BBC2 a couple of nights before. I was going through that phase that a lot of teenagers do of thinking it was cute to show off my learning.

'The Chosin Few can fucking have it,' came Roy's rather tart reply. Then, a second later, he thought better of it and asked: 'Who are the Chosin Few, Triggs?'

I'd learned to ignore his occasional narkiness, especially in the mornings.

'The Chosin Few,' I said, 'was an army of UN soldiers, mostly American Marines, who pulled off a successful breakout and retreat from the Chinese Army during the Korean winter of 1950 . . .'

'Was that the documentary you were watching obviously the other night?'

'It was, yes.'

'Go on so. I'm listening.'

'Well, China had recently entered the conflict and the People's Volunteer Army had secretly crossed the border into the north of the country, surrounding and entrapping the US X Corps at the Chosin Reservoir . . .'

'How many Americans?' he wanted to know.

'Thirty thousand,' I said.

'What about Chinese?'

'At least twice that number.'

'And, obviously, how cold are we talking?'

'The programme said it was somewhere in the vicinity of minus forty degrees celsius,' I said.

He nodded. He seemed to be tabulating this information. 'Okay, keep going, Triggs.'

'Well' I said, 'the so-called Battle of Chosin Reservoir raged for seventeen days, the main theatre of action being the 120 kilometre road connecting the reservoir to the port of Hungnam. A cold front had recently arrived from Siberia, sending the temperature plummeting and frostbite was soon claiming more casualties than the fighting. There are stories of US Marines who found themselves unable to walk in the morning because their toes had fallen off in the night . . .'

We were both beginning to understand a little of how they felt. Roy had given up trying to scrape the frost from the window and was now attempting to do the job using warm water from the kettle. Except the water kept freezing on contact with the glass. He shook his head.

'Go on, Triggs – I'm listening.'

'Well, the Chinese fared considerably worse,' I said. 'Mao Zedong rushed his troops into action before they could be adequately outfitted to face such conditions. Far more of them died from exposure and starvation than as a result of combat.'

'There's no excuse for bad planning.'

'No.'

'For me, the lad – Zedong, was it? – the lad Zedong has got to know in advance what the weather's going to be like. What time of year did you say this happened, Triggs?'

'It was in November and December – in 1950.'

He laughed bitterly. 'But that's obviously winter!'

'I know.'

'As I said, no excuse for it. By failing to prepare, you're preparing to fail.'

It was the first time I ever heard those words. Three-and-a-half years later, of course, tens of millions of people were quoting the line like it was holy writ. I'm pretty sure he took it from Benjamin Franklin.

'Yes, poor preparation was certainly a factor,' I said. I'm cringing as I recount this, by the way. 'But far more decisive was the adaptability of the US Marines, who, despite their weapons jamming and their vehicles regularly sliding off the road, still managed to break through the Chinese lines while inflicting huge losses on the enemy.'

'So what's your point, Triggs?'

A squall suddenly whipped around the garden. I was glad I was going back inside to a warm house.

'Well, my point is that they were simply better soldiers,' I said. 'The conditions were an irrelevance. It's like Manchester United and Leicester. You have far better players than they have. I mean, Muzzy Izzet, Steve Guppy, Tony Cottee . . .'

The segue was a little clumsy, I have to admit. He stared off into the distance.

'Leicester's still a difficult place to go and get something,' he said. 'That's well-documented. Okay, Tony Cottee's not getting any younger. But they're always a hard team to play against. Set their stall out. I mean, any team that's managed by Martin O'Neill – obviously a top, top manager – has got to be respected.'

I decided to dispense with the historical metaphors. 'They're vulnerable to quick balls played from deep,' I said.

This impression, I admit, was based on just twenty minutes of a game I'd watched over Christmas. But it was enough.

Roy just rolled his eyes. 'We don't play the long ball game,' he said. 'We're happy to leave that to others.'

I would learn all about the long ball game in time, thanks to Gerard Houllier, who would soon have Liverpool playing a style of football that was so dull it almost made your eyes bleed. That big, blond ditz, Sami Hyypia, would launch the ball into the atmosphere for Emile Heskey to head it down into the path of Michael Owen. No one else in the team had any function other than to win the ball and pass it back to Hyypia, in order for the whole jaded process to begin again. Barely a month went by without poor Owen's hamstrings snapping from all those short sprints. Even opposition defenders looked like they wanted to weep for him. It was like watching someone do ninety miles per hour in a vintage Rolls while stuck in third gear.

But there I go, wandering off the point again.

As it happened, I wasn't suggesting that United do what Liverpool later did. It was just an observation that Leicester were quite static at the back. I could see that they played in straight lines. They thought in straight lines, too. Martin

O'Neill had a mind that saw the world in modular terms. It was his legal training, I always believed.

I had noticed, too, the beginnings of the symbiotic relationship between Andy Cole and Dwight Yorke that would make them, for a couple of years at least, the best goal-scoring partnership in the world. They were both fast on their feet. If United could get the ball to them early, not necessarily through long passes as much as clever passes, then they could dispose of Leicester easily enough.

I explained all of this to Roy. I wasn't sure how much of it he took on board until I watched *Match of the Day* that night. Manchester United won 6–2. And to my delight, I saw that Leicester were opened up time and time again by quick passes from deep. Roy was so excited when he returned home in the early hours, he insisted on filling me in on what happened while tidying up my toys.

'A hat-trick for Yorkie,' he said. His teeth were still chattering from the cold. 'He doesn't miss many. Then Andy Cole went and bagged a brace. Then Jaap Stam scored! Can you believe that, Triggs? First goal for the club. You'd have to say full credit. But all the same. Jaap Stam! Jesus.'

Then he said something that almost brought tears to my eyes. 'You know, you were right, Triggs.'

'What?'

'We talked about obviously the quick ball from deep.'

'Well, like I said, it was just an observation.'

'It was a fucking spot-on observation. And the other stuff you were saying about – was it Korea?'

'Er, yes.'

'Made me think. I mean, it was horrible today. Horrible weather, horrible match, horrible everything. We conceded two goals. Which I'm not happy about, by the way – one or two of the lads have still got some serious questions to ask themselves . . .'

He meant one of the lads. And I'm sure I don't need to tell you his name. But just in case, it was Jaap Stam.

'But we dug in. You know, today was one of those matches we might have easily drawn a month ago. I just get the feeling that today was a big, big result for us.'

He was right. United finished the month of January on top of the Premier League. I doubted whether, in all of Hale that night, you'd have found a man more thoroughly pleased with himself.

'As I've said in the past,' he said, 'this is where league titles are won. In the cold of winter. Oh, the sun's always shining in May when you're lifting the trophy. But what the likes of maybe Chelsea and obviously Liverpool have forgotten – and even Arsenal – is that the real work is done on days like today.'

They talk about people clicking. Roy and I just got each other.


It was some time in early February that my dreams – usually such humdrum affairs – took a dark and sinister turn. Actually, I can tell you for certain that the date of my first nightmare was 6 February 1999. I know that because it was the day that United beat Nottingham Forest 8–1 at the City Ground. I remember it well. Forest, I knew, were the first club Roy had played for in England, and he retained a deep affection for not only the club but the town and its people.

'I was pretty homesick when I left Cork,' he told me the day before the match.

We were passing the Pizza Express near the level-crossing in the centre of Hale. I pulled up sharply, I remember, because another dog had urinated over a scent I left on the wall outside only fifteen minutes earlier. I lifted my leg – the alpha female! – and cancelled it out. And Roy allowed me. Didn't tug me away. To be honest, I think he was lost in a bout of reverie.

'Nottingham took me obviously to its heart. And they still give me a good reception. *'There's Only One Keano.'* Full credit . . .'

He seemed to me to be almost full of remorse in advance of the beating that United were about to deal his old club. There was always that conflict with Roy – it was certainly there later, in 2002 – between the heart and the head. The head most often won out.

'Although,' he said after a beat, 'all of that means absolutely nothing to me. I don't want to be repeating myself, but obviously football's a fickle game. You're a hero today, then tomorrow you're out the fucking door.'

The match, as I think he anticipated, was a hopelessly one-sided night's work, memorable only for – deep breath here – Ole Gunnar Solskjær scoring four goals after coming on as a substitute in the second half. It was a record of some description. I don't remember what exactly and that isn't meant to sound churlish. It was after he scored his fourth, then turned away, scratching his nose in an attitude of, I thought, pretend self-effacement, that I heard it – the low and angry drumroll of an animal growl.

I looked around the living room. I was alone. That's when I realised that the noise – ugly and malevolent – had come from me!

I couldn't understand it. I was a Labrador Retriever. We were kindly, outgoing, tractable and keen to please. Sure, I had a sarky mouth on me and I could be a bit full of myself at times, but I was never aggressive, to man or animal. So what was it about this freakish-looking manchild – 'A smashing lad,' Roy always assured me, 'as well as a top, top goalscorer who'll punish any side on his day' – that brought out the savage animal in me?

I tried to pull myself together by forcing myself to sit through his post-match interview. I tried to look at him, to focus on his whorls of innocent blond hair, his confoundingly angled cheekbones, even his puckish little ears, but I could feel my gorge rise and my mouth form itself into a fear grimace.

'Obvioushly,' he said, an awkward smile twitching his lips, 'de game wash already won when I came on de field. The gafoor, he shays to me, "Ole, we don't need any more goalsh. Jusht keep de boll." Of coursh, you know I don't like to hear det!'

Well, I lost it again. I couldn't help it. It was an entirely unconscious action. I backed out of the living-room without once removing my eyes from the screen, snarling like a wild animal in fear of its life. I was still barking a full five minutes after I returned to the laundry room. Then eventually, physically and emotionally wrung out, I fell asleep.

Terrifying penumbral images of Ole Gunnar Solskjær filled my dreams that night. At no point during the course of these nightmares, I should add, did he mistreat me or even speak harshly to me. Instead, his disembodied head just hung there, smiling timorously, saying, *Hello der, Triggsh!*

'Triggs! Triggs! Triggs!'

My head shot up. In fact, I'm sure my entire body did. It was Roy, home from Nottingham. He was kneeling beside me, a calming hand on my ribcage. I could actually feel my heart beating hard in its hollow.

'Jesus, Triggs,' he said, 'you're up to ninety. And you were whimpering there – in your sleep. Were you having a nightmare?'

'A nightmare?' I said. I was still disorientated. It had felt so real. 'I, er, may have been, yes.'

'Are you okay? What was it about?'

'I . . . I don't remember,' I said.

I don't know why I lied.

'Well, you're alright now. Only a bad dream. I'll get you something to eat.'

He stopped in the light of the doorway and turned back to me. I watched his figure told in silhouette. 'We'd a great result tonight. I don't know whether you saw it or not. But a great result.'

*I haven't touched my dinner. He notices. He says, 'Triggs, you haven't eaten any of this,' and that's despite my best efforts to hide the fact. I pushed it all onto one side of the bowl, a trick popular among anorexic teenage girls. Beneath me, I know. But I don't want him worrying.*

*'Listen,' he says, 'you didn't eat your lunch either. And you made a poor enough effort at your breakfast.'*

*Ipswich beat Leeds United 2–1 this afternoon. We should be talking about Tommy Smith's winning goal. About Ipswich moving back up to fifth place. Not my diminishing appetite.*

*'It's no wonder you've no energy anymore, Triggs – especially if you're not getting the right, as I've said in the past, nutrition.'*

*He opens the fridge door and runs his eyes over the shelves. 'What about some stewed apple?' he wonders. ('Steeewed apple?').*

*I can't think of anything I'd like less.*

*'And maybe some of that boiled rice left over from obviously last night?'*

*He takes an apple from the fridge and, using a small knife, pares it with a surgeon's precision. 'We'd a good result today,' he says, throwing a perfect spiral of skin into the bin. 'We gave away a shocking goal for the equaliser, but the players showed tremendous character to bounce back. Possibly could have been a bit more comfortable in the end. We'd the chances. Bit more composure in front of goal and we could have maybe killed the game off. But we'll take the win.'*

*He takes the little silver carton containing the remains of last*

*night's rice from the fridge, then he shrugs – just one shoulder.*
*'But listen,' he says, 'I think we both know the way football is.*
*They're chanting your name today. Tomorrow, they're calling*
*for you to maybe get the sack.'*

*I will eat his stewed apple and rice, I tell myself. Doesn't*
*matter that I have no appetite anymore. I will eat every last*
*mouthful of it.*

'Who was that fella, Triggs, wouldn't give up the war?'

It was late at night. We were passing the little adventure
playground halfway down Bankhall Lane and I had a good idea
what direction the conversation was headed. Late goals were
becoming a theme of Manchester United's season.

'Are you talking about Hiroo Onoda,' I said, 'the Japanese
soldier who continued to prosecute the Second World War
from his jungle hideaway in the Philippines almost thirty
years after his country had surrendered?'

Yes, I blush at the memory of how enamoured I was with
the sound of my own voice. Age couldn't even excuse it. I was
nearly two.

'Exactly,' he said. 'I suppose we're a bit like the lad Onoda.
As I've said before, we just won't accept when we're beaten.'

It would have been truer to say that it was Roy who refused
to accept when they were beaten. In fact, United's progress in
three competitions through January, February and March of
1999 was, more than anything else, down to the sheer force of
his will. He was simply magnificent.

Don't get me wrong, I was doing my bit, chipping in with
observations about players and nuggets of tactical advice. And
though modesty forbids – etcetera, etcetera – I think Roy
would agree that my input was worth at least ten Premier
League points to United that spring.

It wasn't like I was getting carried away with myself – even though, as Roy often pointed out, there was always someone who was prepared to knock you. I'm thinking about something that Teddy Sheringham said one night when Roy and I ran into him on Ashley Road. We were out for a late stroll and Teddy stepped out of the doorway of La Petite Auberge, a new French restaurant in the centre of Hale, straight into our path. It was too late to cross the road and for us all to pretend we hadn't seen each other, so we had to go with it in the interests of civility.

'Alright, Roy?' Teddy said.

'Alright, Teddy.'

There was always an odd constraint between them. It wasn't that they hated each other or anything like that. I think Roy had sized up Teddy when they were at Nottingham Forest together – the Ferrari, the pretty girls, the high cheekbones – and made up his mind that they were never going to be friends.

It was the alpha thing again. You might as well ask two tectonic plates why they can't get along.

'Here,' Teddy said, 'I've just had the most sensational facking meal in there. You a fan of steak, Roy?'

'Yeah, as I've said in the past, it's an important source of iron and obviously protein. Things that are important.'

'You've got try this facking place then. For me, the chef's done ever so well tonight. As I said, the steak was absolute quality. Knife went through it like butter, Roy. And the chips! Facking tremendous. Except they weren't, like, proper chips. They were big facking thick ones. Facking A! With, like, lumps of salt on them and summink else – rosemary or summink like that. Then he's gone and stacked them. You'd have to say, take a bow. Here, is there an ATM on this street?'

'There's one at the top of the road there – next to obviously Asda. I think it's a HSBC, but they take all cards.'

Roy decided this was an appropriate cue on which to part

and we went to move on. That's when Teddy said it. 'Here, do you always let your dog walk ahead of you like that?'

'Excuse me?' Roy said.

I think Roy had already made up his mind to take offence.

'A dog should always be beside you or behind you when you're walking it. Never in front of you. They get ideas, see. They're facking pack animals. It's all about hierarchy. That's well-documented. He'll start to think that *he's* the boss of you.'

'It's a she.'

'Even worse, mate! You know what women are like! Next to the Asda, is that what you said?'

We walked home in silence. Roy seemed nettled by the imputation. I could tell he was thinking about Teddy the entire way. When we reached the house, he turned to me and said, 'Who goes to a French restaurant and orders fucking steak?'

Professional footballers, I thought – that's who.

Roy hardened as the season went on. There's no question of that. He kept demanding more from everyone. Yes, he was difficult to live with at times, but I'm not telling you anything he wouldn't say himself. He walked around the house with moue on him like a Bichon Frise – or the soon-to-be Mrs David Beckham – if he thought his team-mates were giving less of themselves than they had to give.

He brooded at length, I recall, when United failed to beat Arsenal in the league at Old Trafford. In his defence, it was a match they should have won. He knew it and I knew it. I remember Yorke missed a penalty that he should never have been allowed to take. Rolled it apologetically past the post. I could tell from the tension in his shoulders and the doubt in his eyes and the fear in his legs that he was going to miss. I was a dog. I could read the signals. As it happens, so could Roy. In hindsight, he knew he should have pulled the ball out of his hands and taken it himself.

Worse, though, was the goal that gave Arsenal the lead. Worse because it was so wearyingly predictable. I had told Roy to watch Nwankwo Kanu, the night before in the kitchen. Sure, he wasn't exactly blessed with balletic grace, but I knew he was capable of causing a whole world of trouble if he used those big crazy legs of his to run at Jaap Stam. I remember Roy was staring at his till receipt from Waitrose with a belligerent look on his face, convinced, I think, that he'd been overcharged. He satisfied himself that he hadn't, crushed it in his hand, then casually deflected my comment.

'I don't know why you're so hard on Jaap,' was what he said.

I think he'd started to believe the sustaining lie of Stam's career – that he was a world-class player who went through the occasional bad patch, rather than a bad player who went through the occasional world-class patch.

And, let me tell you, it gave me no pleasure to be proven right. Kanu ran at the United defence and Stam responded like a bow-legged woman confronted by a mouse in a cartoon. Honestly, if there'd been a chair nearby, he'd have been up on it. The ball was rolled to Nicholas Anelka, who scored, and it took a header from Andy Cole to retrieve a point from the detritus of a bad afternoon.

'None of us is asking for miracles,' Roy told me the following day. He was cleaning out my ears using a strip of cotton wool and a solution that smelled faintly of alcohol. Labradors are especially prone to ear infections. Goes back to our compulsion to sniff things, which means our ears are forever on the ground. 'But you've got to at least make the goalkeeper work from the spot. In fairness to Yorkie, he stepped up. But at the end of the day, you've got to do more than just have a go.'

In common with many truly great leaders, the men around him – the team – became more and more an expression of Roy's personality as the weeks went by. It hurt them to drop points. You could see it. It hurt them even to concede goals.

Probably because that meant having him melting the wax in their ears with another high-decibel upbraiding about falling standards.

The question about Hiroo Onoda – getting back to it – was in reference to United's FA Cup fourth round victory over Liverpool, which might have been the first time I noticed the imprint of Roy's character on the team. Michael Owen had given Liverpool the lead. (The questions 'Where was the marking?' and 'Where was Jaap Stam?' had come to mean the same thing.) Not long after that, Roy had a header of his own cleared off the line. The fact that it was Paul Ince who denied him a goal – then had the temerity to look, well, a bit too pleased about it – seemed to work Roy up into a rage of effort. In the second half, he had a shot from outside the box deflected wide, then another hit the post.

He was extraordinary that day. You might say that I'm hardly an objective observer, but there you have it anyway.

The other United players responded to his example. As I sat, curled foetally on the sofa, and watched the remaining minutes run out, I remember Andy Gray invoking the F-word. It's probably necessary to add in Andy's case that I'm talking about fate. 'What did I tell you?' he said after another United near-miss. 'It's going to be Liverpool's day.'

The words were still leaving his mouth when Yorke equalised. And, of course, while the Liverpool players were still smarting from the injustice of it and trying to get their jaded minds around the idea of the thirty minutes of extra-time that lay like some terrible purgatory ahead, United put them out of their misery with a second goal, just as the referee was putting the whistle to his lips. It was Solskjær who scored it, which meant I ended up watching the post-match celebrations through the safe embrasure of a parting in the living-room curtains.

Roy was full of himself that night. Not without due cause

either. We both were. We walked the length of Bankhall Lane, mostly in happy silence. I looked up at the deepening navy sky and it was as if the night had cast a spritz of stars across it just for us. That's when Hiroo Onoda's name popped up.

'We just refuse to beaten,' Roy said. 'At the end of the day, that's what it is, Triggs. We just will not lie down – for anyone.'

As the weeks fell off the calendar, Manchester United were on top of the league and still in the two major Cup competitions. Admittedly, Stam was making fewer errors – didn't mean a thing, in my view – while Yorke and Cole were scoring a lot of goals. Roy was playing what he felt was the best football of his career, as were Scholes, Beckham and Giggs – or certainly the best I ever saw them play. There was suddenly talk of a treble, of Premier League, FA Cup and European Champions League victories.

'We could just as easily end up with nothing,' was Roy's response when I mentioned it to him. 'That's what I keep reminding the lads. Obviously, we can't afford to become complacent.'

There was no prospect of that happening, as long as Roy was skewering them with looks or giving them tinnitus with one of his angry diatribes against mediocrity.

'Hard work beats talent when talent doesn't work hard,' was a line he was particularly given to at that time. I don't recall who said it, just that it was his *Thought for the Day* on 8 March 1999. You could see what a leader of men he'd become from the way the other players regarded him, the submissive way they held themselves when they were around him.

They played Southampton, I remember, at the end of February. Roy was supposed to be given the afternoon off. It was only Southampton after all and United had a bigger match, against Inter Milan in the quarter-final of the Champions League, the following week. They laboured and laboured with no success until Ferguson sent Roy on to do the job that the others clearly couldn't. Beckham, as if suddenly stung by Roy's arrival on the field, hung a corner in the air, Yorke laid it back and Roy smashed it into the net with all the frustration that had been building in him watching what had gone before. Then he looked at Yorke as if to say, 'That's what *you're* paid to do,' and Yorke looked at him with suppliant eyes that seemed to say, 'Thank you, oh Great One.'

In that moment, you could have believed they were capable of anything with Roy leading them. And, of course, they were.

It was a Tuesday afternoon towards the end of February. Roy had just returned from training and was standing at the sink in the kitchen, cracking ice cubes from a tray and wrapping them in a red and white checkerboard tea towel to create a compress. A large, ugly bruise, I noticed, was beginning to smart at the top of his leg.

'Scholesy,' he said, which was as much elaboration as was ever required. 'Maybe not the best tackler in the world. Always gives a hundred-and-ten percent, though – even in training.'

It was then, perched on a chromium breakfast stool, cold-dabbing his kipper-coloured bruise, with me at his feet, making short work of a Bartlett pear, that he brought up the subject of Inter Milan. Roy often talked about taking each match as it came. Yes, despite his intelligence, he was as drawn to the clichés of the game as Rio Ferdinand was to mock-Tudor. And also clichés. But I knew this match had been playing on his mind for some time.

'They're a top, top team,' he said, grinning against the cold of the compress. 'They've got genuine class all over the field. Your Djorkaeffs. Your Baggios. Your Zamoranos. Obviously, your Ronaldos, when he's fit. Players who – I think I'm on the record as saying – can genuinely hurt you.'

As it happened, I'd been following the various plot twists

in Inter Milan's season ever since the draw for the Champions League quarter-finals was made the previous December. Forget what you read in *Marley & Me*, Labradors are as strong on initiative as they are on work ethic and intelligence. The more football I was watching, the more tactically astute I was becoming.

Without wishing to underplay the threat that Inter Milan presented, I knew that they were a team with no recent form. As Roy mentioned, Ronaldo, their best player, had been missing for most of the season. Without him, they'd lost five of their previous six matches, were out of the Italian cup and were nowhere in the Italian league. There was a lot of talk, I recall, about wounded animals and the danger that they posed, which, by the way – and I say this as a dog who's genetically hardwired to hunt – is nonsense. Most wounded animals, from foxes to waterfowl, can be finished off without any significant difficulty.

'Players of that class don't become bad players overnight,' Roy told me. The ice cubes had begun to melt and water spilled through his fingers and down his leg. 'Obviously, their fans have been turning against them – they've been maybe letting some of their displeasure be known, which they're entitled to do, at the end of the day. They pay their money. But they're a team with a point to prove and nothing to lose – and they're the ones you have to watch.'

His concern about Inter Milan was, I suspected, a surrogate for another fear – that United might underestimate the job and lose. This, I knew, had happened in the two previous seasons, against Monaco and Borussia Dortmund, and though Roy was innocent of blame (absent through suspension and injury respectively), he feared that the team had some kind of mental block when it came to the Champions League. 'The Holy Grail,' as he often called it.

I decided to keep accentuating the positives. 'You've said it yourself,' I said. 'This Manchester United is a different team from the one they were a year ago, or even two years ago. Scoring a lot more goals. Conceding fewer . . .'

This seemed to bring Roy's eyes back into focus.

'Yeah, obviously,' he said, 'it's important that we're playing well. As you say, we've tightened things up at the back and Coley and Yorkie are obviously banging them in. But we've still proved nothing as a team and it remains to be seen whether we've learned our lesson about obviously conceding silly goals in Europe.'

He was a bit tightly wound. I decided to wait until our walk later that night before sharing with him a little of what I knew about Inter. It was after ten o'clock. We were on the South Downs Road – the B5162 as it's more commonly known these days. It was deserted at that hour. Apart from the occasional teenager in a baseball cap plunging by in a Citroën Saxo, nothing sounded above the gentle splash of our footfall on the wet path.

'Inter are a real mess at the back,' I said – it was apropos of nothing. 'That three-man defence . . .'

Roy cut me off. 'It's probably more four,' he said. 'Diego Simeone plays very deep to protect them at the back. And they've got Giuseppe Bergomi, who's obviously world class. Then Galante and the lad Colonnese can also defend a bit.'

I nodded, just to let him know that I was taking on board what he had to say. I didn't want to point it out, but I had seen a lot more of Inter recently than he had.

'Doesn't matter how good the personnel is if the tactics are wrong,' I said. 'It just struck me, watching some of Inter's last few games, that the unit of three isn't comfortable. They all seem a bit confused about their roles, especially when it comes to defending crosses. Look, it's just an opinion . . .'

He smiled. I think he was really beginning to love the swordplay of our football discussions. 'Go on, Triggs,' he said.

'It strikes me,' I said 'that they've sacrificed stability and balance at the back just to accommodate too many attacking players.'

'Triggs, they've got Djorkaeff, Zamorano and Baggio. And obviously Ronaldo, as I've said in the past, when he's not injured.'

'But three at the back means that the wide midfield players . . .'

'Zanetti and the lad Winter?'

'Yes – they have to work extremely hard to defend. And I'm not sure that Winter, in particular, is that good.'

He rubbed his stippled chin. I think he knew I was talking sense. 'They have been conceding a lot of goals from crosses from the right,' he said. 'I noticed that myself.'

'There you are,' I said. 'The key to stopping Inter scoring, if you want my opinion, is getting on top of Baggio.'

'He's difficult to mark. He floats around as a deep-lying forward, drawing centre-halves out of position, causing obviously mayhem. Unless you deploy – as I've said before – a midfield marker. But that leaves you a bit light elsewhere.'

'I'm just saying, if I was the manager . . .'

'Go on, Triggs.'

'I'd tell Gary Neville, every time you go forward, to forget about overlapping with Beckham, to cut inside instead and pick up Baggio.'

'That's not a bad call.'

'I'd even tell Denis Irwin to do the same with Djorkaeff. I think Beckham is capable of attacking that right wing himself. Provided his mind is on the match, of course.'

The heavy pulse beat of a car stereo approached us from behind. A red Daihatsu Charade with blacked-out windows and a tailfin slowed beside us. A hand appeared out of the front passenger window – thumb and forefinger forming a perfect circle – and gestured to us. 'Keano!' came the shout from the car. 'Fucking wanker.'

This tended to happen from time to time. Roy and I had learned to rise above it.

About twenty yards up ahead, the car slipped out of gear. You could hear the driver press on the accelerator but the car didn't respond, just made a panicked revving sound. I could only imagine how the atmosphere in that little car must have tightened in the seconds before he managed to engage the gears again and – in an anxious scream of rubber on rain-slicked road – speed off in the direction of the A5144.

I was worried that my comment about Beckham might have got lost in the moment. I thought Roy should have another word with him. The media's focus in the lead-up to the match was bound to be on his so-called blood feud with Simeone. It was irrelevant in the context of this match, but I could read Beckham as easily as I could read, say, either of the two autobiographies Michael Owen had authored by the time he was twenty-five. All it was going to take was for someone to mention France '98 and he'd start to believe that the match was all about him and his own personal redemption.

Don't get me wrong. I had a lot of time for Beckham. He was a great footballer. He was a terrific guy. It's just there was no underestimating his egocentricity at that point of his life. This was the man who, years later, turned to his wife in Madrid's Museo del Prado and asked – of Goya's *La Maja Desnuda*, no less – 'How much is this one?' When he was told that none of the paintings was for sale, he shrugged and said, 'What are we doing here then?'

Actually, that's just an urban myth. But do you see how easy it was to believe?

'I'll maybe have another word with Becks,' Roy said.

We'd begun to think very similarly.

'It couldn't hurt,' I said.

To be honest, I don't know how much of what I said Roy passed on to Alex Ferguson. All I know is they discussed tactics before every game. Ferguson was a smart man. I don't doubt he was capable of reaching the same conclusions I did. I'm just making the point that, tactically, I was right. Not only did United win 2–0 at Old Trafford – with Baggio and Djorkaeff largely missing in action – but Yorke headed both goals from Beckham crosses from the right. Roy arrived home, I remember, beside himself with excitement.

'I think we really came of age as a team tonight,' he said. 'And obviously you played your part in it, Triggs.'

Hearing that, my heart swelled like a balloon.

We sat and watched the highlights together, stretched out on the sofa, with Roy's arm wrapped tendril-like around me.

I had recently watched the Biography Channel's excellent documentary on the life of Samuel Johnson, which contained a line by his friend and biographer James Boswell that I had memorised: 'We cannot tell the precise moment when a friendship is formed. As in filling a vessel drop by drop, there is at last a drop which makes it run over; so, in a series of kindnesses, there is at last one which makes the heart run over.'

And that was it. Our moment.

Of course, as was often the way with Roy, the joy didn't last long into the following day. I was still half-asleep the next morning when I heard him padding about the kitchen in his bare feet. It wasn't long after eight o'clock. The dishwasher was already chugging away industriously. I got up. He was cleaning the windows, making a big demonstration of not taking the day off.

'In a way,' he said, without even looking at me, 'it's the worst possible result to take into an away leg. Everyone knows that 2–0 is the worst lead in football.'

It's not, by the way. One-nil is, statistically, the worst lead in football. Two-nil is twice as good as one-nil. Three-nil, three times. Four-nil, four times. And so on. But that's Labradors for you. Logical thinkers. Problem-solvers. Why do you think we make the best guide dogs? It's because we can make sense of things that humans can't see.

Did you really think it was an accident that Roy chose one?

# 6.

# Treble

ROY TOOK ME FOR A DRIVE AROUND MANCHESTER and showed me the sights of the city. The Hacienda Club. The Manchester and Salford Inner Relief Route. The Beetham Tower. The big Debenhams on Market Street. Now we were sitting in the multi-storey carpark of the Arndale Centre and he was filling me in on a little of Manchester United's postwar history. In particular, the plane crash – the one the Leeds United fans liked to sing about – which finished off what was perhaps at that time the best team in the world. Then the rebuilding of the team by Matt Busby, which culminated in the winning of the European Cup ten years later. Then the years of mediocrity that followed – the occasional FA Cup notwithstanding – until Alex Ferguson's arrival in 1986.

It was mostly fascinating stuff, although I must admit I didn't much see the point of the tour.

The thing was, as the prospect of the treble moved ever closer – it was now only ten victories away – there were a lot people giving in to this urge to luxuriate in the past. Nostalgia, humans called it. I'm not knocking it. Without it, let's be honest, there would be no call for me to tell my story. But it was unlike Roy to get sucked in by all that Spirit of Lisbon guff. Hanging around Old Trafford, though, I expect it was difficult to avoid it. I realised that I needed to get Roy focussed more on football and less on the dreamy esoterics.

United had drawn the away leg against Inter Milan to reach

the semi-finals of the Champions League and were to play Juventus for a place in the final. I think it would be fair to say that Juventus held a lot less fear for me than they did for Roy. People who talked about them being the best team in the world tended to rattle off the names of players – Zidane, Davids, Inzaghi – as if each was a winning argument in itself. From what I'd seen of them – and, admittedly, that was only two-and-a-half games – I thought United were a far better team. I told Roy this. And that Edgar Davids was, to my mind, grossly overrated as a midfielder. He laughed at me.

We were still in the carpark of the Arndale Centre.

'There wouldn't be many would agree with that,' he said.

In front of us, a woman was attemping to reverse park a Nissan Pathfinder into a space that didn't seem wide enough. We sat there, both of us momentarily mesmerised by her efforts to defy the laws of space and logic. I often felt the same way watching Ian Harte defend.

'It's just a view,' I said – we were back to talking about Davids. 'All that manic energy. I don't know. He puts himself about the place, yes. I just think sometimes that skews people's judgement of him as a footballer. There are times when he *appears* to be doing a lot. But what's the net result of it?'

He considered this for a moment and decided he liked it.

'Obviously,' he said, 'it's been well documented that he maybe drifts in and out of games. And that he lacks maybe a bit of bottle, especially on the big occasions.'

'I'm not sure,' I said, 'that Zidane is a hundred per cent fit either.'

'Jesus, Triggs. Even a half-fit Zidane . . .' He didn't finish the thought.

The woman had given up her efforts to negotiate the car into the space and had parked in another one further along.

'Juventus have their weaknesses,' I said, 'just like every

other team. Olympiakos destroyed them down the right flank. I'm not entirely convinced by Di Livio's conversion to left-back.'

Roy laughed a little. I think he was more than a little taken aback by the forensic detail of my knowledge.

'The lad Di Livio's done well there,' he said.

'But he's still, by inclination, a right-sided midfielder,' I said. 'I think Beckham could have a lot of success against him.'

Then he drove us home.

The following night, of course, I was proven spectacularly wrong. About everything. What happened at Old Trafford was so at odds with what I'd confidently expected to happen that I had to question whether I was in possession of a gift at all.

Davids was outstanding, full of purposeful running. He bustled and harried and demonstrated extraordinary vision when he had the ball at his feet, which was often. And I was wrong about Zidane, too. He was fit and he was magnificent, using his strength to hold off players with almost regal contempt and popping passes around, long and short, safe and daring – and everything with a flourish.

It wasn't all about those two either. The entire team functioned as fluidly as a new engine. Everything they did, they seemed to have a manpower advantage of two and sometimes three.

Labradors, as you're no doubt aware, make great search dogs. But I combed that field for ninety-something minutes and could provide no information whatsoever as to the whereabouts of Paul Scholes. Roy charged around like a man on fire, but he was as much a helpless witness to what transpired as I was, sitting in front of the TV in the living room, watching the shifting black-and-white kaleidoscope of Juventus's movement until it made me nauseous.

How could I have got it so wrong?

Juventus scored in the first half – Davids's pass to Conte was like some beautiful aria – and how they didn't add the grace note of a second goal was a mystery to everyone, Roy included. Then, in injury time, Ryan Giggs smashed the ball over the line from a corner, an ugly, brutal goal that was almost an offence to the football that had preceded it.

So United escaped with a draw. But you just knew that Roy was going to be kicking the walls of the dressing-room afterwards. It was one of those nights that made you reconsider everything you thought you knew about football.

I loped outside to the back garden and passed an hour or two stripping the bark from a dead sycamore bough that had fallen during the night. It was laborious work, but it helped me think. What was up with Scholes? I wondered. And why had Dwight Yorke and Andy Cole barely touched the ball?

It was a good thing that Roy was in no mood to talk when he arrived home, because I had no answers for him and I doubted if he had any for me. He tramped wearily up the stairs and went to bed. I headed for the laundry room and fell asleep myself, with the match continuing to play out in my subconscious in a confusion of criss-crossing lines and geometric patterns.

How many times has it happened that you've gone to bed utterly flummoxed by a problem only to wake up the following morning with the solution staring you foursquare in the face? It's often been my experience that even a short nap of three or four hours is sufficient to provide a whole new perspective on events. Well, that's what happened. When I woke up, the answer was as clear to me as the first rays of morning light leaking through the gap under the door of the laundry room.

The thing about football is that you can be wrong on any given day but still be essentially right. I *was* wrong when I told Roy that United would beat Juventus, but I was wrong for the right reasons. United *were* a better team – I hadn't changed my opinion on that. They'd just been tactically outmanoeuvred by an inferior opposition. It happens.

And now I understood why.

When I closed my eyes, I could see the match in blueprint detail – how Beckham and Giggs, in their enthusiasm to get forward, had left Keane and Scholes with far too much work to do chasing Davids and Zidane around. They needed to help out more in the middle of the field. When one went forward, I thought, the other should have dropped back – operating a sort of piston effect.

I was congratulating myself on this discovery – and considering what to have for breakfast – when I heard Roy call my name from outside. There was a note of something in his voice, which I thought might have been impatience. And, well, I was right.

I didn't know how long he'd been up, though it must have been some considerable time. In the back garden, he had set out a series of hazards that amounted to a kind of obstacle course. There was a tyre, I remember, swinging from a beech tree, a length of bamboo balanced between two upturned paint tins, a series of traffic cones arrayed like gates on a downhill slalom, as well as various other hurdles. I knew immediately that this was another of Roy's efforts to, if you like, recondition me.

'This again?' I said.

It was, admittedly, a little cheeky. Roy acted as if I hadn't even spoken. He issued one or two general commands, his voice alternating between firm but non-threatening, and enthusiastic and inviting. He also started performing what the training manuals call the basic communication signals – handclaps, whistles, smooching sounds, finger clicks, trying to find the one that would cause me to leap into action and perform.

I wasn't having any of it.

'Do we have any aubergines?' I said casually, then I turned back to the house.

Well, it was a good twenty minutes before he joined me in the kitchen. Even then, he was annoyed beyond expression.

'In the second legs, Beckham and Giggs need to take turns attacking the flanks,' I said, 'while the other drops back and helps out in midfield.'

It suited both of us to forget what had just happened in the garden. Clarence Pfaffenberger, the guide dog guru again, could have told Roy that a dog's willingness to carry out obedience tasks came down to personality factors more than basic intelligence. I'd just missed something in the whole socialisation process. And it was too late to learn it now.

'Listen,' he said – and he said it in a voice that was almost without hope – 'we're not at the same level as the likes of Juventus and obviously Barcelona. I mean, people talk about me in the same breath as maybe Zidane and Davids. Jesus. I'm not even in their class.'

He was talking rubbish, of course.

'An eagle,' he added, cryptically, 'has never been born from a goose's egg, Triggs.'

I decided I'd talk to him again only when he was of a mind to listen.

My ability to read a football match as if it were no more complex than, say, the thoughts that pass through Ashley Cole's mind in a hotel room at one o'clock in the morning with a mobile phone in his hand, was something that Roy struggled with at the beginning. I think he'd admit that himself.

He always put it down to the long hours I spent exposed to the improving channels, especially as a pup – all those documentaries about the great wars, in which battle tactics were discussed in blueprint detail. I'm more inclined to believe it was some mild form of autism, which some experts believe is as prevalent in dogs as it is in humans.

Whatever the truth of it, there was no denying that it was having an effect. Despite the setback of the Champions League semi-final first leg, my advice did continue to yield results as United closed in on three trophies that April. I pointed out, for example, before an FA Cup quarter-final replay against Chelsea, that the opposition's lack of width meant they resorted too often to shots from outside the box. I remember it well. We were taking the path across the golf course in Hale, under a beautiful, tawny, early evening sky, when I told Roy that if they could close down Gianfranco Zola and Roberto Di Matteo, the two best strikers of the ball on the Chelsea team, they could stop them from scoring.

I'm also certain I mentioned, too, that Graeme le Saux, while a reasonable defender and a formidable intellect – at least by the standards of his peers – had a mind that was prone to occasionally wander. Perhaps it went antique shopping – that was the rumour about him that refused to go away, of course.

As it turned out, I was right. Chelsea didn't come close to scoring and le Saux nodded off on the job – 'I'd like to put in an offer for the Victorian mourning bed' – to allow United to score their second goal in a 2–0 win.

And that was how it tended to go. I would make an observation and Roy would either take it on board or brush it aside. But as time went on there was no doubt that he came to trust my opinions more and more.

There was another day when we were in the car, on the A365, approaching the Downing Street Flyover, and I said something that caused him to almost lose control of the Bentley. What I said was that I didn't think Shay Given was a great goalkeeper. Sometimes I pulled these lines from apparently nowhere. I realised this one wasn't a popular view, even before Roy was forced to regather himself and pull us rather heroically out of the hard shoulder.

'No disrespect,' he said, 'but there's very few in the game would agree with you. He'd be regarded as a top, top goalkeeper. For me, he's one of the best net-minders in the business.'

'Yes, he pulls off a lot of spectacular saves,' I said. 'And I doubt if there's a player in history who's won more Man of the Match awards. But at the less – shall we say – televisual business of commanding his penalty area, he's rather less than great. He hates leaving that six-yard box, haven't you noticed?'

He considered this for a moment, then dismissed it with a short little shake of his head. 'I don't think there's any truth in that, Triggs.'

But I always suspected that Roy bounced the idea off one or two of the other United players, because it was shortly afterwards that they beat Newcastle 2–1 in the league. I watched the goals on *Match of the Day* and noted – with all due modesty, you understand – that both United goals came as a result of Given's reluctance to leave his goal line when the situation demanded it.

Roy didn't acknowledge it. Not in words. But the following morning, while I was lying in the back garden, thinking about Juventus again while watching the clouds shift viscously in the giant lava lamp of the sky, he taped a page from his desk calendar to the front of the spin dryer for me to find. I didn't recognise the author, but I still remember the quotation.

'Dogs have given us their absolute all. We are the centre of their universe, we are the focus of their love and faith and trust. They serve us in return for scraps. It is without a doubt the best deal man has ever made.'

Oh, it floored me when I read it. How I'd grown to love the man. I sobbed for an hour.

Bob Dylan nearly killed me. I'm not saying he deliberately set out to do it. I've never had the dubious pleasure of meeting him, though Roy saw him once, I think, at the MEN Arena. But, yes, he did nearly cause my death. It was a few years ago now. The spring of 2004, I think. I was in the kitchen, tending to a bowl of oatmeal and bulgur wheat biscuits while listening to Radio Four, when a well-known academic, with a lucrative sideline in waffling intelligently about popular culture, described Dylan as 'the greatest American poet of the twentieth century'.

The shock of hearing those words caused a biscuit to lodge sideways in my oesophagus. I really believed that my number was up. It took sixty seconds of frenzied hacking to save myself from choking to death.

The myth about Dylan's songwriting abilities grows stronger the longer it endures. I'm telling you, unless something is done about it, he's going to start showing up on school curriculums and that's when the world really will be in trouble.

So I'll go on saying it for as long as there's wind in my lungs. What Dylan produced, even during his so-called golden period, is neither poetry nor even anything approximating it. His lyrics, read flat on the page – try it yourselves – are a cold, thin gruel of willfully oblique images, non sequiturs and gibberish words thrown together in the cause of rhyme, and I challenge any English faculty head to debate me on the subject.

In *My Back Pages* – a random example – he describes crimson flames, tied – *tied!* – to his ears. And don't even get me started on Utopian hermit monks sitting side-saddle on golden calves, or the ghost of electricity howling in the bones of her face, or Cinderella putting her hands in her pockets, Bette Davis style.

You might well wonder why, out of all the bluffers, spoofers and imposters who've crossed our path over the years, Dylan continues to take up so much of my energy. I mean, Jordi Cruyff took a pay packet from Manchester United for four years while the club was pleading poverty in its wage negotiations with Roy. But then poor Jordi – who at least had the good decency not to put the Cruyff family name on the back of his shirt – had as little impression on Roy and I as he did on the club that paid him God-knows-how-much every week.

But Dylan? Dylan was different. He was always there, lurking on the periphery of things, like some troublesome friend from Roy's past that he just couldn't bring himself to jettison.

The draw with Juventus in the first leg of the Champions League semi-final was followed by another draw with Arsenal in the FA Cup semi-final the following weekend. Roy had a perfectly rightful winning goal disallowed for reasons that were never very clear to anyone. He was still furious about it when he got home. I was in the living room, tearing the squeaking mechanism out of a toy duck   I was as frustrated as he was – when he walked in, expletives still spilling from the side of his mouth like untreated sewage. And rightly so. United outplayed Arsenal and all they had to show for it was a replay to add to their already complicated lives. And Roy had another night to look forward to in the company of Patrick Vieira.

Of all the players I heard him mutter unkind thoughts about over the years – opponents *and* teammates, I can tell you – it was Vieira who exercised Roy more than any other. It was never anything as trivial as rivalry, I always thought. It wasn't just that they were the physical reference points of

England's two best teams. They very actively disliked each other. And you didn't need to be a dog to read the signals. Anyone could see it, in the sideways looks they exchanged in the tunnel, the way they bickered off the ball, the murderous abandon with which they threw themselves into tackles.

Most of the so-called vendettas that Roy harboured were mere passing fancies. No, he didn't care much for Alan Shearer or Maurice Setters or Alfie Haaland or Mick McCarthy. Or any of the others I could go on listing – except this is a memoir, not the UK White Pages. But none of those others enjoyed anything like the success that Roy did. That meant, of course, that he could always look at them with an attitude of, well, healthy disdain.

Not Vieira. He was a winner. What's his total now? A World Cup. A European Championship. Three Premier League medals. Four Serie A. Four FA Cups. Two Italian Cups. And he's still going! No, Vieira was his match. And we both knew it.

And here was the other thing. I think most players were, to varying degrees, physically frightened of Roy. Some hid it well, some less so.

Allow me to go back to that business with Shearer in 2001. As I remember it, they were squabbling over the ownership of a throw-in. Words were exchanged. I think Shearer called Roy a prick – *he* was one to talk – and then they squared up to each other, Shearer far less convincingly than Roy. Oh, he made a great affectation of being *prepared* to fight, even pinned his shoulders back in an apparent aggression display. But take it from someone who can read the signals. Shearer was – as Roy rather memorably put it to me later on – shitting himself from the neck up. You could almost hear what he was thinking as Beckham and Wes Brown dragged Roy away: 'That guy would have torn out my Adam's apple and not given a shit how it looked in the referee's report.'

Vieira demonstrated none of that fear. His height was a great advantage, of course. He was tall and lissome, built rather like a welterweight boxer, and with all the agility and grace of one, too. So whenever they had a serious difference of opinion, which seemed to be fifteen or sixteen times during a match, Vieira could make his case from a vantage point of six inches above him. He always looked at Roy down the length of his nose. He had no choice. But I always thought it was this imagined attitude of scorn – remember, Roy was told for years that he was too small to be a footballer – that really got to him.

I always thought, Roy was a better player than Vieira. But I could never relax when they were around each other. One of them was always liable to do something stupid.

Anyway, I shared my thoughts about the replay with Roy the day he left for London. There were some things I needed to say. Much as I rated Gary Neville, anyone could see that his confidence was on the floor. Faced with the trickiness and pace of Marc Overmars, I had a vision of him being sent off. There was also – and wasn't there always? – the question of Jaap Stam. Despite his improvement in form, the fact remained that he was as ponderous in the turn as the USS *Gerald Ford*, and I knew that Roy and Paul Scholes would have to work hard to cut off the supply lines to Nicholas Anelka.

'Obviously,' Roy said, taking this on board, 'stopping the service to Anelka *is* key.'

We had walked as far as the Tesco Express on Ashley Road. He needed one or two things for the trip to London – shaving foam, a book by Jeffery Deaver, batteries for his Discman – and he was tying my lead to the trolley bay outside.

'Overmars,' I told him, 'is the player I'd be most worried about.'

He fixed me with an unblinking look. I expect you know the look I mean.

'I think you and maybe one or two others should have a bit more faith in Gary Neville,' he said. 'You're on about maybe his confidence isn't high at the moment. Yeah, he possibly had maybe one or two problems earlier in the season. Had a torrid time of it, no question. But he's still a top, top defender.'

I wasn't going to get into an argument with him. He could take or leave my ideas as he saw fit. That went with the territory of being his friend and confidant.

It was fifteen minutes later, as he emerged from the supermarket, his purchases swinging in a bag by his side, that I blurted something out.

'Tell Ryan Giggs to run at the Arsenal defence.' It came to me in a wingbeat of inspiration.

'What do you mean, Triggs?' Roy said, as he unknotted my lead.

'He hasn't done it in a long time, has he? Run at people, I mean. Wasn't that always his thing?'

He looked at me, his head cocked at an angle. 'Yeah, obviously,' he said, 'that's well documented,' and then in singsong: 'But he's added a lot more to his game since then. He's worked hard on his passing, Triggs, and on being – as I've said in the past – more of a team player.'

'I know.'

'He's not just a runner, full of tricks but no end product, like maybe one or two others in the past.'

'I know that, too. But it just occurred to me that, yes, he has all of these new dimensions to his game. But he shouldn't forget what it was that made him the player that every defender in England hated playing against.'

I could see him weighing this up. 'Yeah, you could maybe have a point there,' he said,.

So where does Dylan enter the story? Well, just before he

left the house, I noticed him slip *Blood on the Tracks* into his Discman. And Roy noticed that I noticed.

'The one thing you've got to say about Bob,' he said, a slight tincture of sheepishness in his voice, 'is that he didn't take shit from anyone.'

'No,' I said, as quick as John Terry is slow, 'the exchange was usually the other way around.'

He laughed. We had a very similar sense of humour, Roy and I. A few minutes later, I heard the engine of the car catch and then he was gone to London.

Roy had an air about him in that match that I would have considered consistent with prolonged exposure to the disputatious yammering of – ha! – the greatest American poet of the twentieth century. It was the attitude. Roy articulated it well enough himself: take no shit.

I knew it from about the fifth minute, when the camera caught sight of him with that vein in his forehead – *that* vein – pulsing like motorway traffic, the same vein that, a year later, looked like it might burst, sea-monster-like, from his head to choke the life out of Andy D'Urso. I had an idea what way the night was going to end for Roy. And I wasn't wrong. First, he got himself booked, then he got himself sent off, for taking the legs from under Overmars, who, by the way, gave Gary Neville the runaround, just as I had predicted.

Arsenal were much the better team, but the score after ninety minutes somehow remained knotted at 1–1. Denis Bergkamp missed a penalty very late in the game – I could see what he was going to do with it – and the match shambled on into extra-time.

United continued to defend with hard-hat stubbornness. Then Giggs intercepted a scatterbrained pass from Vieira inside his own half and I knew – I just knew – from the confident set of his shoulders when he received the ball that Roy had had a word. He moved quickly up through the gears, winding his way around defenders then cracked the ball past David Seaman as if his real intention had been to decapitate him with it.

It was wonderful. And I won't deny there was an enormous measure of satisfaction in knowing that I had played a part in it.

I had no idea what kind of mood Roy might be in when he returned home in the small hours, the fear being that he would be less pleased for the team than furious with himself. As it turned out, I was to be happily surprised. I heard the car pull into the driveway, then the engine die and I made my way from the laundry room to the hall.

'Did you see it, Triggs?'

They were his first words when he came through the door. And his smile could have been the handiwork of a Beverly Hills surgeon.

'Yes, I watched it,' I said.

'Giggsy's goal?'

'Wonderful.'

'That was you.'

'What?' I said, all innocence. Yes, I probably wanted to hear him say it again. You show me a Labrador who doesn't want to be loved and I'll show you a Labrador-Weimaraner cross.

'I told the lad to maybe start running at defenders again,' he said. 'Like you said.'

'Did I?'

Shameless, I know.

'And the lad scored,' he said, 'with obviously aplomb.'

'You're not upset,' I wondered, 'at being sent off?'

He shook his head. 'No, it's the result that's important and obviously reaching the FA Cup final. As I've said in the past, my personal feelings don't come into it.'

I followed him into the kitchen. He flicked the kettle switch. He was going to make tea.

'So what happened?' I asked him, even though I knew the answer.

He shrugged. 'Just one of those nights,' he said. He was clearly already over it. 'When Overmars is in that kind of form, someone always gets sent off.'

As I made my way back to bed, he said, 'By the way, I threw it out the window, Triggs.'

I turned back.

'The CD,' he said. 'Dylan.'

I nodded. 'The man is a dangerous lunatic,' I said.

He laughed. 'I thought it'd make you happy alright.'


Much has been said and written about the circumstances that kept Roy out of the 1999 Champions League final. What has never been acknowledged until now is that I prophesised it. It was a Sunday night – the night before the team left for Turin, as it happened – and Roy was filling up the Bentley at a service station just off the M56.

We were talking about football, as we almost always were by that time – players we rated, players we thought were getting away with murder – when he told me that he'd come around to my view that Juventus weren't quite the team they looked in Manchester a fortnight earlier. I remember he was unscrewing the fuel cap and reaching for the unleaded Superplus when he said it.

'I wouldn't be so sure about their bottle.'

I marshalled what I hoped was my best look of surprise. 'Oh?' I said. I didn't want him to see how pleased I was with myself, but it was clear that he was really beginning to trust my judgment.

'Obviously, there's got to be a reason why the lad Lippi walked out on them in the middle of the season,' he said. 'It's maybe not the happiest dressing-room in the world.'

He stared at the fuel meter with a look of baleful concentration, watching the numbered reels roll around. One of the little challenges Roy set himself was to let go of the trigger when the amount reached exactly fifty pounds, not a penny more, not a penny less.

'And obviously it's the opposite with us,' he said. 'A happy dressing-room. Jesus, even Gary Neville's happy at the moment. And look at our form since Christmas. We haven't lost a match. How many is it now, Triggs?'

'I think it's twenty-three.'

'Twenty-three matches unbeaten. Then look at Juventus.' His voice travelled upwards, like a gull riding a thermal. 'They're losing every other week. There's obviously something wrong with a team that can play the way they did against us, then lose to – who was it?'

'Perugia,' I said.

I'd been watching a lot of Italian football on Channel 4.

'Perugia!' he said. *Perooogia*! 'No disrespect – but fucking . . .'

The low mechanical drone of the pump stopped abruptly. I looked at the meter. Fifty pounds even. He nodded. Pleased.

'Do you take my point?' he said, returning the fuel gun to its holster. 'I'm not sure there's any real fight in them. I think they're the kind of team who, if you maybe put it up to them, they'll crumble.'

I followed him across the service station forecourt. The ground was sticky with something spilled. 'The most important thing,' I said, 'is not to give Zidane and Davids the kind of room they enjoyed in the first leg.'

'Yeah, no, obviously,' he said, 'that's key. We need more bodies in the centre of midfield, so they don't have it their own way again. As I've said in the past, I think Becks could maybe do a bit more. And obviously the lad Blomqvist.'

Giggs had injured his ankle against Arsenal.

'What was that word you were on about, Triggs?'

'Which one?'

'You remember – one goes forward, the other stays back.'

'A piston action.'

'Piston, that was it.'

Roy went inside to pay. There was a newspaper stand to the right of the door, I remember, and my eyes were drawn to the front page of the *News of the World*.

Oh no, I thought.

The newspaper had – in the language of the game – 'gone and done a number' on Andy Cole and Dwight Yorke with a story about what they'd allegedly been up to at night. The story wasn't even true, as it happens, but my instinct told me that it would be better all round if Roy didn't see it. He did like to play the puritan from time to time. There was a night a year or two later, when we were watching *They Think It's All Over* on BBC1 and Mick McCarthy, who was a panellist on the show, made some crack about hairy kebabs. Well, it sent Roy into a kind of moral hissy fit. He'll tell you the story himself.

'Jesus, Mick,' he implored at the television, 'you're supposed to be the manager of your country.'

It wasn't long after that, of course, that Roy – during their status-anxiety-fuelled falling-out in Saipan – *called* Mick a hairy kebab, or rather a four-letter synonym for it.

But there I go, racing ahead of myself again.

Yes, it would be prudent, I thought, to keep Roy from the story. I could just imagine him shaking his head, all wounded irascibility: 'Jesus Christ, lads, you're playing for Manchester United!'

The last thing any of us needed was for Roy to go upsetting the beautiful chemistry that Cole and Yorke shared by landing on their doorsteps and asking them what the fuck they thought they were doing. Especially when, like I said, the story wasn't even true.

Andy was a sensitive enough soul as it was. He was still giving Teddy Sheringham the silent treatment for not showing him enough respect or something like that. There was a lot of talk of respect among footballers at the time. They were all demanding it and they were looking sulky if they weren't getting it.

Everyone was listening to a lot of rap music.

When he stepped out of the petrol station, I picked up the thread of the conversation again. 'Yes,' I said, 'I have a good feeling about the away leg,' and shepherded him back towards the car.

He opened the back door for me and I jumped up onto the seat. He climbed into the front.

'We've got to start maybe giving ourselves a bit more credit,' he said. 'After the first leg, people were saying, you know, we were totally outclassed and we lost 1–1 – that kind of thing. For me, that's rubbish. Obviously, we felt we maybe didn't do ourselves justice on the day. But we still feel we're good enough to beat any team in the world.'

I watched him pull the seatbelt across his chest. But there was an air of distraction about him, I thought. I wondered was he thinking the same thing as I was. So I said it straight out.

'You do realise,' I said, 'there's a chance that you won't get to play in the final?'

He blew his lips out. He *was* thinking the same thing as I was. And it seemed like a relief to him that it was finally out there.

He was carrying a yellow card into the match after a piece of pointless pushing and shoving with Ivan Zamorano in the first leg against Inter. Another booking and he would miss the final. He knew as well as I did that no player could perform the job he had ahead of him in Turin – stopping the combustible forward momentum of Davids, while denying

Zidane the space to perform his magic – without at least one mistimed tackle, one challenge with a bit too much meat in it.

'I'm trying to think of that quote,' he said. 'I'm pretty sure it was the lad Napoleon.'

'The battlefield is a scene of constant chaos,' I said. 'The winner will be the one who controls that chaos, both his own and the enemy's.'

It was from a History Channel documentary we'd recently watched together.

'A scene of constant chaos,' he repeated. 'The winner is the one who controls that chaos, both his own and the enemy's. It's a great fucking quote.'

'You can't let it affect you,' I said. 'The fact that you're carrying a yellow card.'

'Listen,' he said, 'you won't find *me* hiding, Triggs.'

A car horn sounded, echoing in the hollow of the forecourt. The driver immediately behind us was waiting to use pump four. Roy stared hard at him in the rearview mirror, then he turned the key in the engine and soon we were on the road to Cheadle.

It had become the custom, when he had to be away for more than one night, for Roy to place me with Idina Houseman, a retired *Manchester Evening News* copytaker, who ran a boarding kennels at the back of her dormer home not far from Abney Hall and its wonderful surrounding wetlands. Idina was a porcine-faced but sweet-natured spinster, with a great big shiny pompadour that was a shade of black I had never seen in nature, large Gypsy-style earrrings and a voice coarsened by a forty-a-day cigarette habit. She was from Colwyn Bay in Wales, addressed everyone – men, women and animals – as 'Lover' and seemed to have no friends other than the shifting dramatis personae of dogs and cats with whom she shared her life.

I was very fond of her, just as she was fond of me. Early on, she picked up on the fact that I was more sensitive than other dogs and she treated me like I was her own, allowing me to sleep in her kitchen rather than in the admittedly comfortable and warm kennel accommodations at the back of her home. And being one of those humans who, like Roy, was brilliantly attuned to dogs and their thoughts, she noticed very early on the way my eyes kindled with interest whenever *he* was on the television.

'Look at you,' I remember she said, a John Player Blue smouldering in the V of her fingers. 'You like watching him on the box, Lover, don't you?'

She never let me miss a game after that. So there's a case for saying that Idina Houseman – with her men's shoes and her rouged cheeks and her miner's cough – was the unsung hero of United's treble-winning year.

The second leg unfolded just as I expected it would. I knew that Juventus would score again, which is why I told Roy that, whatever else happened, United should set themselves the target of scoring twice. And I was right. Inzaghi scored two goals in the opening eleven minutes – for years I argued the case that the second should have been credited as an own goal by Stam, although Roy always accused me of being vindictive – but still United didn't panic because the target was still the same. Two goals.

Roy scored the first of those, calibrating his run into the box perfectly to head in Beckham's corner. But it was Yorke's diving header from Cole's cross before half-time that killed Juventus. You could see it. The weaker minds among them just couldn't deal with the cruel, distorted logic of the away goals rule. They had dismembered United at Old Trafford. Then they'd scored twice in Turin while many fans were still looking for their seat numbers. And here they were, approaching half-time and somehow behind on aggregate.

The funhouse mirror mathematics of it all got to them, especially Davids, who just disappeared.

It's often I've heard it described as Roy's greatest ever performance. I'm more inclined towards his own view, which was that he played just okay. He didn't touch the ball as often as you probably think he did. His real contribution that night was in noticing before anyone else that Juventus were starting to doubt themselves, then communicating that to the others, especially Cole and Yorke, who played with the giddy abandon of two Springers off the leash. They even had the effrontery to go and score a winner.

Roy copped a lot of praise for taking his booking so well. I think that image of Paul Gascoigne back in 1990 – I'd seen it once or twice on television, the tears leaking out of him like a burst radiator – had so seared itself into the English consciousness that anyone in a similar situation who reacted in any way differently was deemed to be almost superhuman. I know Roy was embarrassed by the elevation of his performance in that match – he always believed in that very Calvinistic principle that no man deserves praise for doing the right thing.

That said, the booking was a silly piece of nothing. A pointless trip on Zidane that another referee on another night might have just let go. At least Paul Scholes deserved *his* card – and every card of every colour that was ever flashed before his face. But not Roy. Even Zidane looked at the referee in an attitude that seemed to say, 'Booking him for that demeans us all.'

Stoic is the word I heard used most often to describe Roy's attitude towards missing the final. And it's true, he put on a hard front. You should have seen him at home. He even vacuumed stoically. But I knew that under that protective outer carapace, the man was hurting.

'Often in history the leader who masterminds a great

victory isn't around to see what he inspired,' I said to him the day that he arrived home from Turin. He was washing me with the hand-held shower in the bath in the ensuite. Much as I liked Idina, her endless smoking – using the dying light of one cigarette to bring the next one to life – meant I always came home from Cheadle smelling like a Parisienne brothel.

Roy asked me what leaders I was referring to, although all I could come up with in that moment, as Roy kneaded the shampoo into a lather, was Moses.

It was weak, I know.

'Listen,' he said, 'as I said before, the most important thing is obviously the result. Through to the final. My feelings are unimportant.'

But I think he believed that with less and less conviction as the weeks went by.


I barely had a moment to myself. United were still in two cup competitions and were just a point behind Arsenal in the league, having played one game fewer. But they were tiring. I could see it. The demands of chasing three trophies – all those energy-sapping midweek flights across Europe – told in their slowing tread. Mediocre teams were dragging them down to their level. They drew with Leeds, won nervously against Aston Villa, then dropped two points against Liverpool, a result that infuriated Roy. They were 2–0 up. The match was all but won. Then they stopped concentrating. It was just cumulative exhaustion. Oyvind Leonhardsen won a penalty for an artless dive in the box. Denis Irwin – Mister Dependable, remember – got himself sent off for kicking the ball away. Then Paul Ince equalised and Anfield celebrated as if denying United the league was a greater cause of joy than winning it themselves. Which, to Liverpool's fans, of course, it was – a mark of how low standards had slipped at the club, Roy would cuttingly observe.

'Yeah, good man,' I remember him saying to the television as he watched Ince's fist-pumping celebration again on Sky News the next morning. 'I wonder will you ever win another medal in your life?'

And, of course, he never did.

Arsenal should rightly have won the league. They'd been out of Europe since the beginning of December and had no excuse for tiredness. But then they lost to Leeds and the entire league season came down to the final day, when United – I'd noticed weeks earlier; that's how on top of things I was – were down to play Ginola's Tottenham. The job was simple. If United won, the league was theirs.

Yes, I gave Roy one or two notes, but I never really doubted the outcome. They came from behind to win and that was that. I *could* point out that Ginola played like a man who had his Worthington Cup medal, his two Player of the Year awards and a goal against Barnsley for his career highlights reel and that was more than enough for him for one year. But, like Roy, I've learned to take the high road.

The players went out to celebrate the following night. Initially, Roy wasn't going to go. 'Season's not over,' he said. 'What's there to celebrate?'

I blame myself for what happened next because I talked him into it. All I can say in my defence is that I saw the tense line of his features when he walked through the door the night they won the league and I thought, 'Now there's a man who needs a drink.'

'You've been uptight for months now,' I said. This was the following morning. We were in the back garden and I was watching a bee, swollen with pollen, careen from flower to flower. Roy, I remember, was finding it difficult to sit still. 'Might do you good to let off some steam.'

Gary Neville was organising the night out. Naturally, I thought, how bad could it be? I hate to sound like a bitch, but Gary's idea of excitement was letting the petrol in his car run down until the fuel light came on.

Roy must have made his mind up and changed it a dozen times that morning and afternoon. He was going. Then he wasn't. Then he was again. Finally, at about seven o'clock that night, he said no, he was staying in and that was that. The others could do whatever they wanted, he was going to wait until the season was over. End of discussion.

An hour later, I heard the front door click shut and he was gone, the jasmine and black pepper notes of *Moves* by Adidas following him up the road like the contrails of an F15.

I went to bed that night a happy dog – it was still only twenty-four hours since Roy had lifted his first trophy as captain of Manchester United – and I slept soundly, apart from one nightmare in which Ole Gunnar Solskjær's disembodied head hung before me, saying, 'Football ish not jusht about eleven men againsht eleven anymore. Itsh alsho about the shtrength of the bench, which I think I have proven with the contribushions I have made when I have come on ash a shubshtitute.'

Oh, the horror of it.

I slept until ten the following morning, which was almost unheard of for me. The season had taken a lot more out of me than I realised. When I woke, it was as if my mind had been rebooted. I bounded up the stairs to Roy's room, my thoughts already fixed on the FA Cup final against Newcastle the following weekend.

You can imagine, I'm sure, the fear that quickly gathered in me when I discovered that he wasn't there. Instinctively, I ran for the bedroom window and threw my front paws up on the sill. There was a small clot of photograhers outside the gate, a sight I'd grow accustomed to in time.

It wasn't until the early afternoon that I heard the electronic gates spring open. Through the living-room window this time, I watched him walk to the door, his shape told in silhouette against the halogen flashes going off behind him.

There was a small cut under his eye.

He didn't tell me anything for at least an hour. He sat in the living room, staring at nothing, muttering little admonishments to himself. 'How could you have been so fucking stupid' and 'Why the fuck did you get sucked in?'

I jumped up on the sofa beside him. The leather sighed wearily. He hung his arm around my shoulder and pulled me close to him. I melted into his side and we stayed like that for an hour or more, ignoring the phone, which trilled away in the hall, neither of us saying anything. We didn't need to say anything. When a man and a dog are as close as we were, you wouldn't believe what can be communicated by simple silence.

The time passed.

'Spent the night in a police station,' he said eventually.

'Oh,' I replied.

I didn't know if I should ask him what he'd done. From the sad pall that hung over him, I could have believed almost anything. After another short silence, he volunteered the details. A row in a bar. Words exchanged. Insults thrown. A champagne glass hurled. Roy got cut. He reacted. There was a fracas. And between one thing and another, the police ended up being called.

Yes, I was disappointed. I admit it. The whole thing was . . . well, it was such a cliché.

'Fucking stupid,' he said.

And it was. I think he really hated hearing himself use that same old formula of words that he'd heard a hundred other players use to excuse their behaviour.

I didn't think it was necessary for me to say anything. He

was mad enough at himself. Besides, I was feeling a good measure of guilt for talking him into going out in the first place. I was probably relieved that he wasn't blaming me.

We sat there for a little while longer, then he stood up and took a look through the blinds at the crowd that was still swelling beyond the gate. From the defiant set of his chin, I knew what was coming next.

'Let's go and stretch our legs,' he said.

Looking back, this was the start of it really – the performance aspect of our walking together.

'You, er, wouldn't prefer to wait until all those photographers are gone?' I said.

'No,' he said. A look of outrage spread across his face. 'What, stay in here like a couple of trapped animals?'

He went to the hook under the stairs and got the lead. Sixty seconds later, we were walking down Bankhall Lane with dozens of journalists and photographers shoaling like hungry pilot fish around us. Amid the percussion of camera shutters going off, the questions came from every direction.

'What happened?'

'Are there going to be any charges?'

'Is it true that Alex Ferguson had to come and bail you out?'

Roy answered only one. A thick-set, unhealthy-looking man with a strong Manchester accent, who was having to run alongside us to compensate for the length of our stride, asked, 'What's the dog's name, Roy?'

Roy fixed him with a look and said, 'Triggs.'

And I realised in that moment that I would always love this man, no matter what.


It was a strange feature of that season that, while, for United, it built to a glorious crescendo in the city of Barcelona, for

Roy, it withered away to a disappointing end on that booze-sodden night he spent as a guest of the Greater Manchester Police. It would have taken the hardest of hearts not to feel sorry for him. While the others were preparing for the week of their lives, his season was as good as over.

He was carrying an ankle injury the week of the FA Cup final. We both knew that he didn't have ninety minutes in him. I doubted he had forty-five.

He didn't bother shaving for two or three days before the match, I remember. He needed a haircut, but he let that go, too. I tried to interest him in my assessment of Didi Hamann and Gary Speed as a midfield pairing, but he shrugged indifferently and said, 'Doesn't take much to beat Newcastle, Triggs. Jesus, it's like having a birthday. You turn up, it happens.'

He was right. The last time Newcastle won anything worth winning, of course, Winston Churchill had just left office – and weren't there still coal mines in that part of the country?

As it turned out, it was almost disappointing how routinely it all passed off. Roy hobbled off after six minutes, after Speed tackled him from behind. It should have been the fillip that Newcastle needed – instead, they played as if stricken by palsy. Sheringham scored in the first half, Scholes scored in the second and absolutely nothing else happened.

People who talk about Roy missing the Champions League final due to a silly trip on Zidane always leave out the important part of the story – he was injured. He wouldn't have been fit to play anyway. It's not that I expected him to find solace in that. But he could have stopped beating himself up at least.

Had Roy had his way, I don't think he'd have gone to Barcelona. If he wasn't the captain of the team, I think everyone would have understood had he stayed at home and watched the final with me.

I'm going to tell you something that I've never openly expressed before. I didn't think United had a chance against

Bayern Munich. With Roy and Scholes missing, I thought Stefan Effenberg and Jens Jeremies would win the battle with Beckham and Butt for the centre of midfield.

Was I wrong? Well, happily, only about the result.

United were bested everywhere on the field. I spent the half-hour after Mario Basler's first half goal stretched out on Idina's sofa in Cheadle, with my head in her lap, wondering what Roy was making of it all. Then the camera caught a brief flash of him in the crowd, with a funereal expression to match his sober grey suit. I looked at him through the choking fug of Idina's cigarette smoke and I knew what he was thinking: 'Jesus, I could be at home now, watching this with Triggs.'

Bayern bore out all the clichés about Germans and their logical minds. Everything functioned well in relation to everything else. I just couldn't see United getting back into the game.

Then Ottmar Hitzfeld did something I didn't expect. He took off Lothar Matthäus and Basler. Yes, they were tired, but I would have left Matthäus on for his organisational abilities alone. There was suddenly a discernible shift in the weight and momentum of the game. Without Matthäus, the Bayern defence looked like they believed in themselves less.

As the game entered its final minutes, I remember thinking United could score a goal from a set piece here. This time, I *was* wrong. They scored two. First Sheringham, then Solskjær.

Naturally, I ran yelping from the room when Solskjær's laughing face filled the screen. Idina chased after me, saying, 'What is it, Lover? What's frightened you? Was it that funny-looking fella on the telly?'

She had a real gift.

Anyway, she managed to coax me back into the living room in time to watch the lap of honour. I kept trying to pick Roy out from among the celebrating players, but I couldn't. Then I thought, of course, he'll have slipped back to the dressing room the moment the presentation was made. I could almost picture him, sat back there, checking his watch, wondering what time the bus was going to leave, to get him away from this scene.

Clive Tyldesley said the crowd were chanting his name. Then I could hear it: 'Keano . . . Keano . . . Keano . . .'

Someone was dispatched to the dressing room to get him. Out he came. Secretly dying, I could tell, behind that painted-on smile. The crowd cheered him. The players put their sweaty arms around him and told him that none of this would have happened if it wasn't for him. He stood there in his sharply cut suit looking about as comfortable as a sow in wellies.

I decided to go to bed. The treble was won, but I knew I still had a job ahead of me persuading Roy that he'd been a member of a European Cup-winning team. I could guess the kind of thoughts that were going through his mind as he sat, no doubt alone, at the back of the plane. Won nothing. Proved nothing.

The following day, he returned home. He wasn't downhearted like I expected him to be – in fact, he was positively prickling with energy. If you'd told him that the new season was starting the following day, he'd have said it wasn't soon enough.

'Why don't you just take time out to enjoy what you achieved this year?' I asked. This was during the drive from Cheadle to Hale.

'I know what you're going to say next,' he said, smiling at me slyly.

'What?' I wondered.

'That they would never have reached the final if it wasn't for me. Maybe wouldn't have got out of the group stage. That I played my part in winning the Champions League – doesn't matter if I didn't play in the final.'

'Well, exactly. It's not about one match.'

'The thing is – end of the day – I don't *feel* like I'm a European Cup winner. So, for me, I'm not.'

We had many conversations like this over the years. I remember once losing it with him and saying, 'If David May can celebrate it, why can't you?'

(Like tens of millions of United fans, I remember watching May on television, leading the party, and wondering – again, pardon the bad language here – who the fuck is that?)

I never could get Roy to change his perspective. My fear was that it might lead to a career of frustration. United might never enjoy a year so perfect again. And Roy might never get to play in a European Champions League final. Of course, he wouldn't have thought that conceivable at the time.

I never gave up trying to convince him that he was as much a European Cup winner as Giggs and Beckham and Cole and Stam. He has a medal that says as much. I've never seen it and I'm not sure he even knows where it is anymore. But maybe one day, hopefully before I'm gone, he'll find it in a drawer somewhere and he'll look at it, still shining proud in its presentation box. And if it's one of those days when he's not being hard on himself, he'll think, 'You know what? Triggs was right. I earned it.'

That would make me one happy dog.

# 7.

# *Allo Conclusione del Giorno*

I COULDN'T PLACE THE TONELESS, DISEMBODIED voice coming from the kitchen. I was lolling about in the laundry room, tending to a rawhide bone, when I heard it.

'*Ovviamente, come ho detto prima . . .*'

It was one of those voices that insisted upon itself, melodramatic and a touch self-regarding. It couldn't be Andy Cole, I thought. He was in Ireland with the rest of the squad for the Beckham wedding. I cocked my head at various angles, to try to improve the frequency. And that's when Roy's voice emerged, small and faltering, and repeated the line.

'*Ovviamentay, come haaaw detaaaw preema . . .*'

Naturally, I had to investigate. Across the hall I padded. I reared up on my back legs – I was now almost a fully grown adult – pressed down on the handle of the kitchen door, then let my full weight fall on it to throw it open. It was a simple enough trick, which I'd mastered in about fifteen minutes – the same length of time it would take Alex Ferguson to work out that Massimo Taibi was not a £4.5m goalkeeper, shortly after he paid £4.5m for him.

The door gave way to the sight of Roy, sitting at the freestanding island, his eyes closed in an attitude of concentration. It turned out that the voice was coming from the CD speakers on the kitchen countertop opposite.

'Tooo be fayer tooo the lad,' it said, all didactic and latin-sounding. '*Per per essere giusto al ragazzo.*'

Roy repeated the final line like he was saying his catechism. '*Per per essere giusto al ragazzo.*'

'What's going on?' I said.

Roy opened his eyes – fainlty embarrassed, I thought – and said we needed to talk. And that was when he told me that he might be leaving Manchester United.

It turned out that his existing contract was coming to an end and the club was understandably anxious for him to sign a new one, preferably for a fraction of his real market value. Roy chose not to involve me in the matter at the beginning. While he'd come to respect my views on players and systems, I don't think he'd imagined yet how my tactical expertise might be applied in the area of salary negotiations. Maybe it was because he didn't want to worry me. But then it came to the point where he was phoning around, asking questions about the quarantine requirements involved in bringing pets to mainland Europe, and he decided that I had a right to know.

This thing was going to affect both of our lives.

He got up and pressed the stop button on the CD player, lifted the lead from its hook under the stairs and indicated the door with his eyes.

Of course, I was never known to say no to a walk.

Five minutes later, we were cutting through the grounds of The Priory Clinic and along the little path that bisects Hale Golf Course and Roy was explaining the ins and outs of Manchester United's wage structure to me. It seemed that the club had placed an upper limit on what it was prepared to pay its key employees and that this limit was determined by, oh, just what some stuffed suit in the boardroom thought it should be.

Napoleon was right about the English being a nation of shopkeepers, by the way. This was supposed to be the biggest football club in the world, yet the people in charge wanted to run it like they were flogging beds and divans from a warehouse on the side of a motorway.

Being a dog, I should point out that I had no real concept of money, other than as a means of necessary consumption. But I understood relativity. And when Roy told me that he was earning £8,000 a week less than Michael Owen was at Liverpool, I was too shocked to even form a complete sentence.

'But he's . . .'

'Won fuck-all,' Roy said, helping me out. 'Obviously, no disrespect to the lad.'

'And he's earning . . .'

'I know, it's a joke. It'd be the same for the lad Desailly at Chelsea. And the lad Lebouef.'

Two men in bright jumpers and trousers with razor creases came from behind us, dragging their grumbling golf trolleys behind them. We stopped to let them pass us out.

'Morning,' one of them said.

They didn't seem to recognise him.

'Morning,' Roy said.

'Wonder will the rain hold off?'

'Well, it's been a tremendous summer so far. Obviously, can't have too many complaints.'

'That's true.'

We watched them shrink towards the clubhouse.

'Anyway,' Roy said, 'the reason I'm explaining all of this to you, Triggs, is, well, because it might be necessary for me to move.'

'Move?' I said. 'Move where?'

'Maybe Italy. That's why I'm trying to learn the language — one or two phrases I'll maybe need. But it could just as easily be Germany or, obviously, Spain.'

'Oh,' I said.

Well, I didn't know what else to say. It was a lot to get my head around.

'Obviously,' he said, 'my first choice is to play for Manchester United Football Club. But as I think I've said in the past, it's a short career. There's maybe only two or three times in your life when you're in a strong enough bargaining position to maybe make demands . . .'

'Of course.'

He could tell that I was struggling with it. We understood each other like that.

'Listen,' he said, 'I'm not looking to bankrupt the football club here. All I'm looking for, at the end of the day, is what *I* believe I'm worth. They've offered me what *they* believe I'm worth. To be honest with you, I've no interest in splitting the difference and neither do they. So that's where we are.'

I tried not to ask the question, but I'm ashamed to say that I did. 'What will happen to me?'

Inside, I cursed myself for being so weak. Roy was quiet for a moment, then with a nod he indicated the little bench that overlooked the first tee box. We wandered over to it and sat down.

He took a breath. 'As I said before, Triggs, I spent a day, maybe two, ringing around, making inquiries about obviously quarantine arrangements. There's no rabies in this country, they stamped it out – take a bow, son – but there's still obviously rules about bringing dogs into other countries. Red tape and all the rest of it. But the thing is, Triggs . . .'

I heard a tinge of regret in his voice.

'. . . it might be necessary to maybe leave you here.'

'Here?' I said.

'In obviously England.'

'Oh.'

He looked away, in the direction of the car park. 'It's just, you know, wherever I do end up, I'm probably not going to have a house like the one we have here. Definitely not for the first while anyway. Be maybe living in hotels, like I did when I came to Manchester first. Possibly an apartment . . .'

'Okay.'

'And obviously, at the end of the day, there's rules about dogs living in hotel rooms and apartments.'

'Of course.'

He looked at me again, searching my face for a reaction. I assembled my features into a look of patient forbearance, not unlike the face that stares out at you from the cover of this book. He leaned down and pinched the back of my neck lovingly. 'Are you okay about it?' he asked.

'I understand,' I said. 'If you have to go . . .'

'It's obviously important for my career.'

'There you are then. You know, I'm not really sure I would have liked Italy anyway.'

'Well, like I said, it might even be Germany or Spain.'

'Well, I just feel that England is my home.'

It was a lie, of course. My home was with him. It always would be. But I was trying to sound selfless to make it easier for him. The fracture in his voice told me this was hurting him as much as it was hurting me. He took my face in his gentle hands, then he offered me the bone of a vague promise. 'Maybe when I'm settled,' he said, 'possibly in a year or two . . .'

'Don't,' I said.

'. . . I might send for you then.'

'Please,' I said, 'I'm fine with it. Or I *will* be fine with it. You've got do what's best for you. I understand that. And if that means having to find a new home for me . . .'

'I wouldn't leave you with just anyone, Triggs.'

'Dogs are adaptable,' I said. 'Especially Labradors.'

I know I tended to propagandise the breed, but there was a reason why we were America's most popular pet, notwithstanding Marley's efforts at assassinating our character.

'It'd obviously have to be someone I know who would definitely look after you, okay?'

'Okay.'

We walked back to the house. My heart was sundered. I returned to the laundry room and a moment later I heard that voice again.

'*Allo conclusione del giorno.*'

And I cried. I cried until I had no more tears left in me.

It hit the papers a day or two later. Roy had turned down Manchester United's offer of a new contract and was considering his future abroad.

Of course, I was devastated, but I sublimated my hurt feelings into a kind steely acceptance and a resolve to be a pillar for him during what was going to be a difficult time. Valiant, steadfast – you know the script.

I followed the story on Sky Sports News. I remember there was a lot of talk about loyalty and I must admit, it rather confused me. I thought I understood the concept. I was loyal to Roy Keane because I loved him, and because one hundred and forty centuries of breeding told me that he was my master and because – well, as any dog who ever found true happiness with their owner will tell you – in him I felt I had found my true complement.

But Roy was loyal to a public limited company whose reason for existing was to make cash profits for its shareholders. And the loyalty ran in only one direction. Players were being forever reminded what an honour it was to be employed by a particular club, with its history and its traditions and its famous shirt and its fans and, frankly, lots of other sentimental rubbish that wasn't going to buy you groceries. But as soon as your club found a player who could do a better job for a thousand pounds a week less, they were reminding you that football was a business, a brutal business, but a business nonetheless – and hey, don't be a stranger.

I pointed out this moral dichotomy to Roy many times, but it would be another six years before the penny truly dropped.

I didn't want Roy to go away. Of course I didn't. My heart ached at the very thought of him being somewhere where I was not. But deep down I knew that he had to go abroad and that conviction hardened as the summer weeks slipped by.

I kept watching the news, expecting to hear an announcement that United had finally signed one of the marquee players who, Roy assured me, Alex Ferguson was pursuing aggressively. Well, it turned out to be as forlorn a dream as Rio Ferdinand's hope that sucking on a 2p piece would help him beat a breathalyser test. There was talk of Rivaldo, Ronaldo and Gabriel Batistuta. They ended up with Quinton Fortune, Mikaël Silvestre and Mark Bosnich. Yes, it was disappointing. They were the champions of Europe. They were entitled to go out and buy the best players in the world. Instead, it seemed that, having seen for how little money the Champions League could be won, they wanted to see could they do it even more cheaply next year.

More and more I was convinced that the right thing for Roy was to go. I nursed this quiet fear that missing the final the previous season would be a permanent scar on his life unless he got to play in another one. But this season, it was going to be even more difficult. In their thirst for TV revenue, UEFA had conjured up the idea of a second group phase before the knockout dimension of the competition began. United needed to strengthen their squad. They didn't.

Roy tried to put a positive construal on it, I remember. He didn't want to be the one always whinging.

'The lad Silvestre's a player,' he told me. It was a muggy Friday night at the end of his first week back at pre-season training. We were sitting in the swing chair on the deck at the back of the house, me in the hinge of Roy's elbow, my head resting on his right shoulder, a faint air of sorrow about us – I suppose we were both aware of our ever-shortening time together. 'The lad Fortune did well at Atletico Madrid. Peter Schmeichel's obviously moved on to – as everyone knows – Sporting Lisbon. But Mark Bosnich will bring something to the club.'

Of course, the only thing that Mark Bosnich brought to the club was about five kilos more Mark Bosnich than Alex Ferguson had paid for. I'm sorry, I just couldn't believe the cut of him when they introduced him to the press as a Manchester United player. Look, I'd had my own issues with weight – but this was a joke. Then he showed up an hour late for his first day of training. Ferguson wasn't around so Roy took it upon himself to have a chat. 'Why are you fucking late?' he asked him in that signature way of his.

Bosnich, obviously badly misjudging the mood, told him he got lost on his way from the hotel.

'Your first fucking day at Manchester United,' Roy said, 'and you turn up fucking late for obviously training?'

I knew why Roy was upset. He'd been defending him to me for days. 'A good lad,' he insisted. 'That's according to Yorkie. And a top, top shot-stopper, at the end of the day.'

But he changed his tune after that. 'When I joined Manchester United,' he told me later, 'they put me in the exact same hotel. The morning of my first training session, I phoned a taxi and told the driver to lead the way to The Cliff – full credit to him – with me following behind. Jesus, I was an hour early!'

I didn't say a word.

I just hoped he would see what I could see – that Manchester United weren't worthy of his loyalty. And also that the team was a busted flush. In truth, the Bosnich business was just one part of a more serious malaise. Yes, the club was cheap, but worse than that, it was also fundamentally and fatally pleased with itself. And so were far too many of the players. Roy was sharp enough to spot that within an hour of the final whistle in Barcelona.

'Jesus, Triggs,' he told me later, 'they were all in the fucking bath together, passing obviously the champagne around – on about they didn't care if they never won another thing in their lives. They didn't care if they never won another thing!'

All too easily, I could picture Roy sitting there, still in his sober grey suit, giving them the cold eye and filing away who said what in his hard drive of grievances.

'Maybe they were just intoxicated by the moment,' I suggested. 'They have a few weeks now to come down from that high.'

'For me,' he said, 'the high is gone nearly straight away. Whenever I win something, I'm immediately thinking, okay, what's next?'

As the first few weeks of the season slid by, I saw what Roy meant when he talked about a big warm blanket of complacency enfolding the entire club. The general smugness was abetted by the ease with which they were racking up points. With my help, naturally. Rightly, it should have been an in-between year for United, but no one else had improved, except Leeds, who were a young team and, I was certain, wouldn't have the legs to stay the pace beyond Christmas.

United won six and drew three of their first nine Premiership games.

Now, I don't want to give the impression here that everything good that happened during that time was down to me. That *would* be conceited. My observations and suggestions didn't always yield results. And I was occasionally wrong in my judgments, although I was wrong far fewer times than I was right.

Not that I was counting or anything, but I reckoned I was responsible for ten – or arguably thirteen – of the points that United accumulated that August and September. They beat Arsenal at Highbury and Liverpool at Anfield. In my mind, the league was as good as over and it was still bright at seven o'clock in the evenings.

I remember Roy and I were walking through Hale a couple of days before the Arsenal match, under the firehose of a heavy rain. We were skirting around the bigger puddles and shooting the breeze about how old and frail Arsenal's back four suddenly looked and how it might be a couple more seasons before they were in a position to challenge for the league. He was distracted, though. His future at Old Trafford had been back-page news again that morning.

Depending on what newspaper you read, the club was lining up Rivaldo, Edgar Davids or Marcel Desailly to replace him. I know those stories hurt him. The same newspapers said that Juventus, Inter Milan, Real Madrid, Roma and Bayern Munich all wanted him. One or two had even mocked up photographs of him wearing various other teams' colours. I'd caught him staring hard at those Photoshopped images over his breakfast cereal and wondered for the first time whether Roy was capable of making the leap of imagination required to leave Manchester United.

'Italy would be a whole new challenge,' I reminded him. We'd had to double-back to the Co-op because he'd forgotten to buy milk. Like I said, his head was elsewhere. 'A chance to measure yourself against Zidane and, well, the best players in the world. Instead of arguing with Bosnich about his timekeeping. And the size of his arse!'

Roy offered a sour haint of a laugh. Bosnich had lasted less than three hundred minutes of the new season and was now on the injured list. And the club that liked to mind its pennies was back in the market for another goalkeeper.

We'd reached the bottom of Bankhall Lane and were preparing to cross when a black Porsche Boxter pulled up alongside us. David Beckham stuck his head out of the driver's window. 'Alright, Roy?' he said.

'Alright, Becks.'

'You out walking your dog then?'

Roy answered him, even though it probably wasn't strictly necessary. 'Er, I am, Becks, yeah.'

Beckham was wearing what looked, to my admittedly untrained eye, like a leather catsuit. Smell is the dominant sense in dogs. In humans, it's vision, although from the way Beckham dressed, I often wondered if that was true.

'Obviously,' he said, 'the papers have gone and had a field day this morning, haven't they? All the speculation about obviously your future.'

'That's what papers do,' Roy said. 'You should know that better than anyone.'

'That's true. I can safely say that. At the same time, I think it'd obviously be a massive, massive blow for Manchester United Football Club were you to leave. You've been – I think I've used the word before – immense for us. Phenomenal is another word. On a different footballing planet. And obviously a tremendous servant to the club going way, way back . . .'

Good God, I thought.

'You're one of the main reasons we've had the success we've had, including obviously the elusive treble. Looking back, I feel total respect for what you've done for me as a player. I think all of us would be obviously devastated if you left, even if you did end up at another massive, massive club.'

'Well, we're still talking, Becks. We'll see.'

By that point, I was sniffing the car's rear kerbside tyre, only vaguely following the drift of the conversation.

'Have you thought about what you're going to do with him yet, Roy?'

'Who?'

'The dog.'

I looked up.

'It's a girl, Becks.'

'What?'

'Triggs is a her – not a him.'

'Oh, sorry, Roy – I just presumed . . .'

Everyone just presumes.

'But have you decided what you're going to do with her – if you do go away to obviously Inter Milan or Bayern Munich, or possibly even Juventus?'

'Not yet.'

'Because Victoria, I think, is on the record as saying that she'd love a dog. And she saw you walking yours a few months back, obviously on the television.'

I looked at Roy and shook my head in a tight little movement, at the same time trying to communicate my feelings to him with my eyes. Roy thought this was hilarious, of course.

'Go on, Becks,' he said.

Our friendship was always the richer, I think we'd both agree, for a bit of good-natured mockery.

'Well, she said, "I'd love a dog like what Roy Keane's got." I think anyone who knows us would tell you that we'd obviously really look after her well.'

Roy looked at me. 'I don't know – what do you think, Girl?'

'She'd have a tremendous life with us,' Beckham said, 'and that's not being disrespectful to you, Roy. Them dogs are the ones what are on the Andrex ad, aren't they?'

'I think they are.'

'That's what Victoria thought. She loved those ads as a little girl. Did you know there's shops in Amerca where you can buy, like, designer gear for them? Dresses and – I can safely say – fur coats. Even jeans, to be fair.'

Roy could see the stomach-curdling terror in my face – I was about to lose my breakfast – so he decided to put me out of my misery.

'Er, like I said, Becks, nothing's been decided yet. Everything's still up in the air.'

'Oh, right. Think about it anyway. As I said before, we would love to have her, even though it would obviously come as a blessed relief if you did decide to stay at the football club. Anyway, I'll see you at training.'

And then he was gone in the wet slap of a tyre spin. Roy asked teasingly if I'd like to go and live at Beckingham Palace.

'I'd rather pass a slow-moving gallstone through my urinary tract,' I said.

He laughed.

'You might like it there,' he said. '*She* might even paint your fucking nails for you!'

On a more serious note, though, Beckham *had* become a worry to me. It was no secret that he and Ferguson had had a blow-up over the issue of his honeymoon. Between them, the Beckhams had decided that David's holidays weren't long enough to allow them to go somewhere 'right exotic', and they felt he deserved more time off. Except he didn't knock on Ferguson's door to ask him. He had his agent ask the club chairman if he could have the extra days instead. That was Beckham for you. Terrific guy. But what he lacked in intelligence, he more than made up for in stupidity.

You can imagine Ferguson's reaction to being treated with the same casual dispatch as, say, the person whose job it was to make sure that two thousand tealights were each fifteen centimetres apart at their wedding.

Roy played magnificently against Arsenal, by the way, and scored both of United's goals. Yes, there was some measure of personal satisfaction for me in seeing that he clearly remembered our conversation about Arsenal's increasingly decrepit defence – he passed his way through them for both goals. He commanded the field in a way that as good as placed a moral imperative on the United board to give him whatever he wanted to stay. Patrick Vieira seemed almost spooked by the level of his performance and could come up with no riposte other than to try to slap him and hit him with his forehead.

Roy was more than a little pleased with himself when he arrived home from London. 'Do you think Edgar fucking Davids could do that?' he asked, already knowing the answer.

Oh, I loved him.

Then, fifteen minutes later, I heard that voice again – '*Per me, el ragazzo ha dato centro dieci per centro*' – reminding me that one day, very soon, we were going to have to say goodbye.

*'Pop her up there so I can have a look at her,' the vet says.*

*Roy ships groans like the sound of air leaving a balloon as he heaves my seventy-four pounds of deadweight up onto the examining table.*

*'The vet in Manchester,' Roy says, 'did he send you through her obviously medical records?'*

*The vet looks at Roy wearily over the top of his glasses, then I notice his eyes rivet to a tower of pages piled up beside the fax machine. 'It's been spitting out paper all morning,' he says. 'I had to fill the tray twice.'*

*Roy favours me with an indulgent smile as I lie there on my side on the cold of the steel table. 'Yeah, no,' he says, 'she's had a lot of things wrong with her over the years.'*

*Dr Hutton pulls back my eyelids with his thumbs and studies the whites of my eyes. He pokes around inside my mouth. He feels my abdomen at various points, like he's frisking me for contraband.*

*Then Roy helps me to the ground. The vet washes and dries his hands, then indicates for Roy to follow him into the poky little office just off the consulting room.*

*Roy holds up a staying hand. 'Be out in a minute, Triggs.'*

*I strain to hear what's being said, but I catch only snatches of the conversation.*

*'Just what happens . . . Slowing down . . . It's nature . . . An old dog . . .'*

*A moment later, Roy emerges from the room with a tense smile strung across his face like a tightrope. He knuckles the back of my neck and I follow him outside to the car. He straps me into the back seat and points us in the direction of home.*

*Through the window, I watch the variegated fields flash past.*

*A voice on the radio says that Ipswich lost to Coventry last night, Clive Platt and Lukas Jutkiewicz scoring the goals to arrest the Sky Blues' woeful away form of late and record their first victory at Portman Road since 1994. But Ipswich will be wondering how they didn't come away with at least a point after Jason Scotland . . .*

*Roy reaches out and switches off the radio.*


That autumn, I developed an itch. And when I say an itch, I don't mean a restless desire for a new experience. I mean an itch. It was a Saturday night, I recall. Roy was on the road home from Coventry and I was settling in for an evening in front of the television. The Discovery Channel was showing an interesting programme about the lives of wombats and I worked out that I could watch twenty-five minutes of it before the start of *Match of the Day.*

That's when I noticed myself going at my neck – ten or fifteen seconds of sustained scratching with a hind paw. Which was nothing unusual in itself. You've seen dogs do it. Except there was no satisfying this itch. Because scarcely a minute later, I had to go at it again. And still I couldn't get any relief.

I tried to concentrate on the programme – they can run at a speed of up to forty kilometres an hour, did you know? – but the urge to scratch myself refused to be ignored.

It crossed my mind that it might be a nervous reaction

to the stress of Roy's continuing contract uncertainty. The negotiations had lengthened into the early autumn of 1999. Offer was followed by refusal. Demand was followed by revised offer, followed by new refusal. I stayed mostly out of it, but I could see what it was doing to Roy – and now, I thought, what it was doing to me.

It was just as *Match of the Day* was beginning that I noticed something. The itch had begun to migrate down my back and was worst in those areas of my body that were tauntingly beyond my reach. And that's when I realised that this was no anxiety rash. No, this was millions of years of evolutionary hardwiring to guarantee the survival of the cleverest and most insidious parasite known to man or beast. I had fleas.

My first thought was that Roy didn't need this on his plate right now. In less than three months' time he would be entitled to open negotiations with other clubs for his services. The club was still talking to him, but everyone seemed to have accepted the inevitability of him leaving. Fleas were the last thing he needed on top of everything else. I made a silent pledge to keep it to myself until his future was sorted out.

He was in good spirits when he came home that night. Coventry were one of those teams that United tended to beat as a matter of boring routine. I'm not sure I ever had to share a single insight about them with Roy. I'd turned in early. Not long after eleven o'clock, he pushed open the door of the laundry room and I heard him say, 'What about Scholesy?'

As my eyes adjusted to the light, I noticed that he was rubbing his hand up and down the jamb of the door as if smoothing it, an action calculated to hide his embarrassment.

'Scholesy?' I said.

'Yeah, would you live with Scholesy – obviously the Ginger Magician?'

'Em . . .'

'He said he'd take you. He's a smashing lad, Triggs. Obviously a tremendous player. Does his talking on the pitch. Although any of the lads will tell you that when it comes to obviously practical jokes, there's no worse offender.' He chuckled fondly. 'Don't leave your mobile phone or your car keys down when he's around, that's all I'm saying! And don't jump into a hotel bed until you check he hasn't put something in it first!'

Football was the best excuse in the world for a lifetime of adolescence.

'For me,' he added, suddenly serious, ' Scholesy maybe hasn't got the credit he deserves for obviously Manchester United's success. But world-class. No doubt about that. Some of the things he does – take your breath away.'

'Er, yeah,' I said. 'I mean, I like Paul.'

Which I did. Certainly on the basis of the two occasions on which I'd met him – once, briefly, when we were pulled up at a temporary traffic light near Birkinheath Covert and he and Roy exchanged some car-related banter ('Fifty-five grand a week and you're still driving that bucket of rust,' was Paul's contribution in that tiny, adenoidal voice of his), then another time in the short-stay carpark at Manchester Airport. Roy was collecting some friends who were coming from Ireland. I don't know why Paul was there, but he acknowledged me with a friendly, 'Hello there, Triggs.'

I don't remember who United had just beaten, but Paul must have scored twice because Roy said, 'You must be obviously happy with your brace.'

Paul was as inscrutable as they come – he had a range of precisely three facial expressions and I couldn't read any of them.

'Ever so pleased – stuff of fantasy,' he said. 'Still having to pinch myself to believe it.'

'You took the second one well.'

'Yeah, no, obviously swivelled on the proverbial sixpence.'

'Unlucky not to get the hat-trick, *I* thought.'

'The last minute. Sad to say, my goal-bound effort was scrambled off the line.'

Yes, he was a little dull, but I was sure I could adapt to a quieter life. Maybe I could teach him how to tackle.

Like a lot of dogs who are forced to part with their owners, my main concern was how Roy was going to cope when he no longer had me at his side. But I decided to stay positive for his sake. Things were difficult enough for him.

'Listen,' he said, 'as I've been saying quite a lot of late, Triggs, my first choice is to stay at Manchester United. But obviously time is running out and I've got to start maybe thinking about my future outside of England.'

'I think I'd quite enjoy living with Paul.'

'Really?'

'I think so.'

'Because Becks is the only other lad who said he'd take you.'

'Well, that's that then.'

He laughed. It was hurting him, though. I could see that.

While this exchange was taking place, by the way, my eyes were stinging with the effort of not scratching myself in front of him. It was torture.

I doubt I had more than fifteen minutes of unbroken sleep that night. I went at myself until I could feel twists of my own skin gather under my nails. I knew there were powders you could get, but I didn't want to encumber Roy with any more concerns. Instead, I suffered it with the dignified tolerance that distinguishes my breed and concentrated as best I could on the football.

Despite the diversions of their captain's uncertain future, the lack of a credible replacement for Schmeichel, the bad soap that Beckham's life was becoming and a whole heap of problems in defence, there was still no team in England to touch United. Arsenal seemed to be suffering from some form of collective post-traumatic shock as a legacy of what happened the previous season. Chelsea, under Gianluca Vialli, fielded English football's first ever all-foreign eleven that year. But, for all their big names, they hadn't improved and, watching them on television, playing in a stadium devoid of atmosphere, I got the sense that they were losing their audience. Leeds were a good young team, but their time was still a year or two away. Liverpool had a fine young midfielder called Steven Gerrard – 'He's definitely going to be a player,' Roy told me – but Gerard Houllier, an unfathomable man, seemed intent on surrounding him with fair-to-middling players from the French league.

Meanwhile, while the richest club in the world dithered on a new pay deal for – and you can say I'm biased here – the best player in the world, they saw fit to pay £4.5m for Massimo Taibi, an Italian goalkeeper, whom one or two cards in the United dressing-room – you can probably guess who they were – soon nicknamed, 'The Blind Venetian'.

Alex Ferguson's brother had apparently seen him and reckoned he was good. He wasn't good. He *really* wasn't good. The signs were there in his first game against Liverpool, when he misjudged the trajectory of a free-kick, running from his line, flapping his arms like a man trying to take flight. The ball cleared him and Sami Hyypia dipped his head to help it into the goal. He did make a couple of saves in the second half and someone had the bright idea of giving him the Man of the Match award. But I could read Ferguson's mind when I saw him interviewed afterwards – he had the look of a man who thought he might have left the gas on.

The man's instincts were seldom wrong. Taibi then let in three goals against Southampton, including a weak shot from Matt le Tissier that managed to percolate first through his arms, then through his legs, then over the line. Four years at clown school and you couldn't have made it look more convincing. A week later, he conceded five against Chelsea, and he was on the next flight home. The club that talked about sensible financial husbandry and ensuring that the fundamentals remained sound took a two million pound loss on the deal.

And Roy still had no contract.

The frustration occasionally got to him and resulted in yet more efforts to train me. I had a habit back then – I admit – of trying to get at my food before the bowl had been laid on the floor. Now, suddenly, Roy was insisting that I sit motionless, staring at the thing until he said a trigger word, which, as it happened, was 'Eat!'

The man was under a lot of pressure. So, for once, I went along with it, much as it reduced us both.

Looking back, it was a tough time for me too. I admit it, I struggled with it, like [*name removed on legal advice*] struggled with his marital vows – not to mention those of his brother. I was existing on never more than an hour's sleep per night. There were times when I thought the itching and the sleep deprivation would push me over the edge. I continued to do all of my scratching in private and even took the precaution of watching the television from the hallway, so as not to spread the infestation to the sofa.

There was one afternoon when I almost told him. I'd have done anything to end the agony of those little bloodsuckers slowly leeching the life from my body. It was October. Roy came home from training and told me that the club had decided to pull out of the FA Cup. I don't remember having an opinion about this either way, but Roy read – or rather, misread – something in my expression and, well, out shot the defensive quills.

'I don't know why people go on about the FA Cup,' he said, his voice surging then falling away. 'The mythology. The folklore. The red carpet. Obviously the royal box. The FA Cup is bollocks.'

It struck me that he had looked happy enough lifting it five months earlier. I was going to say that to him – just to give him a ribbing. But in the end, I didn't. 'So why have you pulled out?' I wondered.

'We're going to be playing in obviously the World Club Championship in January,' he said. 'It's in Brazil.'

This threw me for a moment. United were playing Palmeiras in the World Club final in Tokyo in four weeks' time. I knew that because Roy had arranged for me to stay for a few nights at a boarding kennels near Droylsden. Idina, it turned out, was in Rhyl, looking after her sister, Elsie, who'd broken her kneecap in a fall.

'I thought that was happening in November,' I said.

'No, no,' he said, 'that's the World Club final in Japan.'

'Okay.'

'I'm talking about the World Club Championship in Brazil.'

'Indulge me just for a moment, Roy – do they not sound like the same thing to you?'

He turned his bottom lip out. 'I suppose they do. Anyway, it's a new competition that FIFA are after starting up. And they're keen for us, as obviously European champions, to be a part of it. Triggs, are you okay?'

'I'm fine,' I said.

His forehead was corrugated with concern. 'It's just that your eyes are streaming.'

He was right. I hadn't noticed, but I was crying from the effort it took not to scratch myself in front of him.

'This place in Droylsden,' he said, 'it's a top, top kennels. Approved by obviously whoever checks these things out. Be a little holiday for you.'

'It's not that.'

'Is it the FA Cup then?'

'What?'

'Might have been a bit harsh. What I maybe meant was that it was only third on our list of priorities.'

'No, it's not the FA Cup.'

'What is it then?'

'I've got . . .' I almost blurted it out. But then I performed a neat save. 'I've got . . . Well, I've got a feeling that I'm going to really miss you when you go.'

Roy presumed I was referring to the trip to Tokyo, or Brazil, rather than to us saying goodbye to each other forever.

He leaned down to me, smoothed my coat and told me that the time would fly. And do you know what? From the very moment his fingers were in my coat, the itching stopped. I thought, my God, even the fleas defer to him. Within half an hour, though, they were back to work. Like Roy, all I could do was try to keep my mind on football.

Mark Bosnich was soon back in goal, but I knew the man was beyond redemption. Steffen Iversen beat him at the near post when Tottenham beat United at the end of October and I remember thinking, as Bosnich struggled to get to his feet, how much he resembled an upturned Beetle. And yes, that upper case B *is* deliberate.

The Premier League wasn't what it was about anymore. The whole point now was Europe. And it was in Europe that United's parsimoniousness truly revealed itself. They skipped through the first phase. Marseilles, Croatia Zagreb and Sturm Graz – it was no group of death.

I know Roy thinks his game suffered while the uncertainty over his future persisted. Take it from me, he was playing some of the best football of his life, and I'm not just saying that out of loyalty. He scored three goals in that opening group stage and – just as I suspected after the final in Barcelona – it was as if getting United to another Champions League final was a personal crusade.

I knew in my heart, though – as I think Roy probably did,

too – that there wasn't another European Cup win in this group of players.

The second group stage dealt them Fiorentina, Valencia and Bordeaux and you knew that the real business was only beginning. I watched a DVD of Fiorentina that Roy had brought home from work and I offered him one or two pointers.

I thought Stam might have it in him to stop Gabriel Batistuta from scoring, but only if someone marked Rui Costa out of the game. But then, no one could have done that on that particular night. I watched the match sitting under the lintel of the living-room door, mesmerised by his performance. As it happened, though, it wasn't Rui but Roy who put Batistuta in for the opening goal, with a slovenly back pass. Frankly, I knew the night was over from that moment.

He was furious with himself when he returned from Florence. I think this was the origin of the myth that the contract business was affecting his game.

'Obviously, my mind's not on the job,' was all he said to me about it.

Then off he went to Japan.

The kennels in Droylsden turned out to be – like Stam's defending that autumn – just about adequate. There were no television privileges, which I wasn't happy about. But it was warm and dry and the people who ran the operation followed Roy's instructions regarding my diet to the absolute letter. Soya protein. Scrambled eggs. Boiled rice. Tofu. White bread.

Yet I was miserable. By now, my coat was hopping with fleas and scratching had become a full-time, round-the-clock preoccupation. My Ole Gunnar Solskjær nightmares had returned, despite Roy's assurances that, 'Anyone who knows him will tell you that he's a good lad and obviously a tremendous goalscorer – doesn't miss many – which is why they call him The Baby-Faced Assassin.' But he was back haunting my dreams, telling me: 'No, I never feel bad about obvioushly being the thirteenth man. I think it's obvioushly a shign of our shtrength in depth. Like I shaid many timesh in the pasht, I accshept that it's a shquad game and I'm happy jusht to play whatever part the gaffor wantsh me to play.'

Terrifying.

And then there was something Roy said to me the day before he left. We were out walking – weren't we always? Halfway down Bankhall Lane, he stopped at the little wooden stile at the top of the muddy narrow pathway that led down to the river. Roy always went over it, I always went under it – you probably saw us do it a dozen times on television. Anyway, before he threw his leg over it that day, he looked down at me and said, 'I might have some news for you when I get back from obviously Tokyo.'

'News?' I said.

'About my move. Well, nothing's cast in stone yet, but by the time I get back, I'm probably going to be in a position to make an announcement about obviously my future.'

So that was that then.

I tried to be happy for him. What kind of dog wouldn't have? The Fiorentina match had borne out my belief that for Roy to fulfill his potential, he had to get away from Manchester United. No, I had to scarf down my own personal feelings and offer him my support. But that was easier said than done, sitting in my kennel in Droylsden, clawing at my coat until it was blood raw and contemplating the end of the beautiful urban pastoral we'd shared for two-and-half years.

Then he arrived home. He turned up, fresh and smiling, in the middle of the morning and I followed him out to the car. He ushered me into the front passenger side, which was unusual, because I generally sat in the back, so as not to distract him with my incessant chatter.

There was something different about him – barely discernible, but enough to change his whole aspect. He turned the key in the engine and soon we were on the M60.

'So how did that match go?' I asked.

'Beat Palmeiras 1–0.'

'That's good.'

'I got the goal.'

'Great.'

'Although, at the end of the day, the goal means absolutely nothing to me. It's obviously the result that counts.'

'Obviously.'

We were stuck in a tailback approaching the Audenshaw Reservoir when he told me. 'That bit of news I was talking about,' he said. I turned my head and looked at him eagerly. 'Triggs, I'm staying.'

'What?' I said.

'I'm staying at Manchester United.'

Never in my life would I experience the sense of pure, unadulterated happiness that I did in that moment. I've never been much of a barker – never saw the point of it, to be honest – but Lord, did I bark in that car!

Roy laughed. 'Are you pleased?' he asked.

'Pleased?' I said. 'This means we're going to be together, doesn't it?'

'Er, no,' he said. 'Listen, I did tell Scholesy he could have you, to be fair – and a promise is a promise at the end of the day.'

My mouth just fell open. But then he reached out and locked me in the crook of the arm that wasn't steering the car. 'I'm only joking, Triggs. Scholesy can obviously fuck off, to be fair to the lad. It's you and me.'

I was going to have to lighten up. I laughed along. 'So,' I said, 'what changed your mind?'

He shrugged. 'As I've said in the past,' he said casually, 'I like the football club. I like playing for the manager. I like the dressing-room – a good set of lads.'

The tailback began to dissolve and we got up a bit of speed. And that's when I decided to tell Roy *my* news.

'I've, er, got something to tell you,' I said. 'I've been meaning to say it for a while but you had a lot on your . . .'

He looked at me askance. 'What is it, Triggs?'

'Well, there *is* no easy way to say this, so I'll just come straight out with it. I've got fleas.'

I watched his face lengthen. 'Fleas?'

'It's nothing to be ashamed of,' I said defensively. 'They're mostly drawn to a clean host.'

'Fleas?' he said. I could hear the suspicion in his voice. 'Triggs, if you'd fleas, you'd be scratching yourself.'

'I have been scratching myself,' I said. 'But I've been doing it mostly in private. Like I said, you had a lot on your mind.'

He pulled into the hard shoulder just before the turn-off for the M67. He pulled me close to him. I felt his hands explore my coat, his fingers picking through my hairs with a surgeon's intensity. He did this for about a minute, then he said something that I didn't expect.

'Triggs, there's not a flea on you.'

'What are you talking about?' I said. 'I'm riddled with them.'

'Triggs,' he repeated, 'there's not a fucking flea on you.'

Extraordinary. Because now that he mentioned it, the

itching *had* stopped. But where did all the fleas go? Well, that remains a mystery to this day.


It was the first week in December when the news broke, the evening United played Valencia in the Champions League at Old Trafford. It was a match they couldn't afford to lose yet the atmosphere surrounding it – I could sense it from watching on television – was light and skittish. The word was already out before they announced it over the public address system. Roy was staying.

He scored the first goal. And can I just mention here that I'd been telling him repeatedly since the beginning of the season that he should shoot from the edge of the box more often?

'Keano!' the crowd crooned. 'Keano! Keano! Keano!'

The goal was the foundation stone for a three-nil win. Everyone went home happy.

The following day I heard on the news that the club's share price went from £1.87 to £1.91½ on the back of Roy's decision not to leave. I thought, of course! There was no way in the world that United were going to let him walk away. They couldn't. He was the heart that beat life into the team. His performance against Valencia bore out the fact that without him, there would be no success in Europe. And no success in Europe meant a drop in revenue. Once you could put what he meant to the club onto an Excel spreadsheet, they were always going to see the light.

But I did wonder, in the weeks and months that followed, whether he'd done the right thing. It was the right thing for me – like Manchester United, I was still going to have him in my life. But for him, I had to wonder. Would he one day regret never moving to Italy or Spain to take his measure against the best players in the world?

Who knows?

United finished 1999 as champions of England, champions of Europe and champions of the world. In a few weeks time they'd be setting off for Brazil, to try to become champions of the world. (No, no one could explain that one to me – and, remember, I was a smart dog.) For better or worse, we were staying where we were. And whatever my differences with the club, I was going to rededicate myself to Roy and his endeavours for Manchester United. That was my job, *allo conclusione del giorno.*

# 8.

# The Real Thing

HE LOOKED WELL. I TOLD HIM SO. HE GAVE ME A hard, unblinking stare. 'We weren't out there fucking sunning ourselves, Triggs.'

God, he was testy this morning. Of course, being a member of the most famously compassionate dog breed in the world, I just put it down to the long flight from Rio and the missed hours of sleep.

'I'm just saying, you look rested,' I told him, jumping onto the back seat. And he did. His face was the colour of hot buttered toast. He got into the front seat, pulled the seatbelt across himself and started the engine.

'You haven't asked me how we got on,' he said, his left arm around the front passenger seat and his body twisted around so he could see where he was reversing. 'In obviously the World Championships.'

The truth was, I didn't care. But then, nobody else in football cared either. I just wanted to get home. It had rained the eleven days I was in Droylsden. My coat was full of anxious tangles. My breath stank. I needed a bath. I needed my bed. But most of all, I needed television.

Roy insisted on filling me in on the details anyway. The only point I found even vaguely interesting was that Mrs David Beckham had apparently confided in some show business reporter or other that her husband liked to wear her smalls.

No real surprise there, I thought. But then Beckham, in an apparently indiscriminate rage, got himself sent off in United's first match against Necaxa for a challenge on Jose Milian, which Jamie Redknapp – with his wonderful capacity for understatement – would no doubt have described as 'late', but would have been construed by everyone else as an assault occasioning actual bodily harm had it happened outside the stadium rather than inside.

'The tournament was a bit of a joke,' Roy allowed. 'The heat was unbelievable. Stadium was half fucking empty. Less than half.'

I feigned interest. 'You didn't win it then?'

He laughed. 'Went out with a bit of a whimper. Drew the first match. Then we got beaten by obviously Vasco da Gama. Gary Neville had a bit of a torrid time of it. Then the manager threw the rerserves on against *South Melbourne.*'

South Melbourne? I'm sure you can imagine how I felt. I'd just spent two wet weeks in a boarding kennels in Droylsden – honest to God – watching my hair curl for the want of something to do. South Melbourne. Jesus Christ, I thought, there's two weeks of my life I'll never get back.

I said nothing, though. We Labradors – we live by enduring.

No, I just wanted to get on with the season and I was happy that Roy was of the same mind. After a long shower, I stretched out on a soft towel in front of the television with a couple of Pink Ladies and tried to catch up on what I'd missed.

It turned out that while Roy and the others were browning themselves in Rio de Janeiro – he definitely sunbathed out there, despite his protests – no one could establish any kind of lead over them in the league.

They had Arsenal at the weekend. While Roy went to bed that afternoon to try to acclimate himself to the time lag, I sat at the window of the kitchen, staring out at the branches of the elms gesturing in the chill January wind, and I thought about Freddie Ljungberg. He worried me.

The continuing disaster story of United's efforts to find a (preferably cheap) replacement for Peter Schmeichel had taken some of the heat off Jaap Stam. But he was still there, as slow and as prone to moments of gross stupidity as ever. The thought flashed into my mind that Ljungberg was going to score for Arsenal and that Stam would be somehow complicit in it. Ljungberg was just too fast, too clever, too everything for him.

I said it to Roy when he got up. He was mid yawn, rubbing his shaven skull, while absently sorting through the post that had accumulated during his time away.

'You're on about Ljungberg,' he said. 'And obviously he's a top, top player – always shows his quality in the big games. For me, he's one of the most difficult players in the game to mark. Obviously got a lot of pace. Very tricky. As I said before, there's no doubt he can hurt you.'

He said this, I couldn't help but notice, in a perfunctory sort of way. Maybe his mind was still somewhere over the Equator. One thing's for sure, he didn't take my warning seriously. He liked Jaap and still believed he'd come good.

Naturally, it gave me no pleasure at all to be proven right. A long ball from the Arsenal penalty area was headed on and Stam – caught at cross-purposelessness – let the ball bounce. Ljungberg purloined it from between his feet and put it into the net.

United were almost too bad to be believed that day, and Teddy Sheringham's late equaliser was an act of pure larceny.

Roy was in a right humour when he got home that night. I was still up, watching a biography of Cary Grant, when he walked in, shaking his head and huffing quite a bit. 'We've gone soft,' he mentioned more than once.

It hardly merited saying that *he* hadn't. Ljungberg's goal had stung him into a fury of effort. He threw himself into tackles. He screamed himself hoarse asking his team-mates to give more of themselves. He was outstanding.

'Just too fucking pleased with ourselves,' he said. 'All that stuff from obviously last year. "The elusive treble." Lads maybe happy if they never won another trophy in their lives. And there's the fucking proof of it tonight.'

The folly of the Brazil junket, I think, was also becoming clear to him. What the hell had they been doing five thousand miles from home, playing in a tournament that none of the United players seemed too exercised about winning?

'Our fucking heads are still over there as well,' he said.

I waited out the storm, then rolled my eyes in the direction of the front door and asked if he fancied a walk.

He laughed – I think, despite himself. 'Triggs, it's one o'clock in the morning.'

I just stared back at him. He laughed again, then shook his head. 'I'll get the lead,' he said.

The twinkle of ground frost lent Bankhall Lane a certain hauteur at that hour. Oh, how I miss that road today. I knew the pitch of every incline, the camber of every turn. Our breaths smoked in the gelid darkness and I dared to ask him the question.

'Do you regret staying?' I said. 'At United?'

'Regret it?' he repeated. He was processing. 'Do you mean do I regret not going to Italy? Or obviously Spain?'

They amounted to the same thing. 'Well, yes.'

'No,' he said, 'because I want to play for Manchester United Football Club. It's just, at the end of the day, you do have to wonder sometimes about our ambition. You're on about emulating the feat of the Busby Babes. Fucking blah, blah, blah. So two European Cups in, what, thirty years – you're happy with that, are you? You think that makes us a great side? I'll tell you something for nothing, Triggs – it doesn't. For me, the mark of a great team is one that wins something, then everyone gets up the next day and says, "Right, now we need to win it again." That's what made Liverpool great. AC Milan. Ajax. Obviously, as I've said in the past, Bayern Munich.'

'And you don't think everyone shares your ambition?' I asked.

He harrumphed at this. 'They *don't* share my ambition,' he said, his voice rising up through the scales. 'Except, obviously, the manager. He knows the kind of players we need. I've spoken to him about it. But the money's not there. So obviously we've got to get on with what we have. But listen, they're not bad players, Triggs. They're just not doing it. I mean, we stood off Arsenal. How we didn't lose that match I'll never fucking know.'

He fell silent then. For the next few minutes the only sound was the hungry munch of our footfall on the frozen road.

'I went hang-gliding,' he said – this, out of nowhere.

'Hang-gliding?'

He laughed. He continued staring straight ahead, his eyes fixed on some distant memory. 'When we were in Brazil. Myself and the lad Butty . . .'

Of all the Class of '92, as the younger players styled themselves, I think Roy was fondest of Nicky Butt.

'Hang-gliding?' I said again. It just seemed so out of character for him. What was going through my mind were the insurance implications. I thought like him sometimes.

'It was Giggsy's idea,' he said. 'Then Coley got in on it. But then Coley remembered it was Friday the thirteenth and obviously the two lads bottled it. But me and Butty went up.'

I laughed. The idea of it.

'Were you scared?' I wondered.

He snorted. Of course he wasn't. He was Roy Keane. 'The definition of happiness is not being afraid' is probably the most sensible line I ever heard him quote from calendar or book.

'The funny thing is,' he said, 'the rest of the lads were sitting around the pool, including the manager. Someone pointed up into the sky at these two obviously lunatics and said, "That's two of our players up there, Gaffer." And the manager said, "No way! None of my players would fucking dare do that!"'

I wondered what it meant, this small act of rebellion. Or maybe it meant nothing at all. Roy could be so serious at times, so determinedly detached from the fun that everyone else seemed to be having, that you could forget this silly-hearted side to his personality.

'I'll tell you something, Triggs – it's beautiful from up there.'

'Rio?'

'The world.'

I thought about saying something suitably philosophical, like, 'It's not too bad from down here either, Roy,' but then I thought, don't go spoiling the moment.

We reached the bottom of Bankhall Lane and in the cold blackness stared off in the direction of Hale village. 'Do you want to keep going?' he asked.

And I said, 'I'm good for a few miles yet.'

*It's a sharp, bright afternoon in October and I'm staring through the window of the car across miles and miles of unbroken heathland, the bedstraw seeming to beckon us in the wind. The air is thick with the smell of distant fires. And the only noise that sounds above the soothing silence in Knettishall Country Park is Roy talking to someone on the hands-free carphone.*

*'In the second half, obviously we got back into the game late on,' he says, 'but we gave ourselves another mountain to climb. We're obviously not scoring enough goals. Listen, we're creating chances – don't get me wrong – but it's maybe that final pass, that final bit of quality, that's missing.'*

*Who's he talking to, I wonder? A journalist? The chairman?*

*A man's voice emerges through the speaker, thin and reedy. 'You freshened things up in the second half,' he says. 'You must be pleased with the way the lads responded?'*

*'Yeah, as I said before, there wasn't a lot in the game. First goal, we should have maybe defended it better. Second goal — what was it, two minutes later? Obviously, that was the sucker punch. Made it hard. The lads came on — obviously Connor Wickham. Ronan Murray. The lad Edwards. And they gave us that extra edge. One or two of them will maybe feel a little bit aggrieved that they didn't score. They certainly caused Watford a few problems, but obviously, as I said before, they've won the game and we've not.'*

*The conversation continues this way, a catechism of upbeat question followed by stilted answer.*

*'Two defeats on the bounce,' the voice says. It must to be a journalist. 'I presume no one's hitting any panic buttons just yet?'*

*'Yeah, obviously — as I said — it's disappointing. If you want to make progress at any football club, I think I've said from day one, you have to keep clean sheets. And we've not done that. But I can't fault the effort of the lads out there. Damien's done well for us today — obviously, first start for a number of months. Tamas did well, even though I took him off when I thought we needed to maybe freshen up our approach a bit. And obviously Murph, who never lets us down. Yeah, no, obviously it's difficult to lose — as you said — two on the bounce, especially with another tough game against Forest at the weekend. But we'll keep at it, keep plugging away and hopefully the results will come.'*

*'Thanks, Roy.'*

*He hangs up and sits motionless for a short time, then he gets out of the car and opens the rear passenger door for me. 'Come on, Triggs,' he says — the words almost a sigh — 'let's walk — even just to the picnic tables and back.'*

*I jump out of the car, then I stop for a moment. A sneeze gathers in my nose. Then it passes.*

*I think about the conversation I've just heard. Mostly I think about the names. Murph. Damien. Connor Wickham. The lad Edwards. All Ipswich players. But I don't know anymore who they are or what they do.*

*Up ahead, Roy gives me a summoning whistle. I put my nose down and follow his scent along a carpet of decaying leaves.*

After what happened against Arsenal, Roy decided that the match against Middlesbrough the following weekend was the most important game in United's season. Which it wasn't, of course. But it goes a long way towards explaining why what should have been just another workaday Saturday ended with me barking madly at the television and the behaviour of Roy and his teammates being discussed in parliament.

For what it's worth, I thought Middlesbrough might get something from the match. Their little Brazilian, Juninho, had brilliantly fast feet and I could already picture Stam struggling with him like a Chow Chow looking at long division. I didn't mention it to Roy. I was blue in the face telling him about Stam, and it was beginning to sound like I had some kind of vendetta against him. Besides, I didn't think it mattered a whole lot. I could see that United were so much better than everyone else that all they had to do was go through the boring exigencies of gathering the required number of points.

A draw wouldn't be a bad result for United, I figured. Middlesbrough were one of those teams who were too good to be involved in a relegation battle, but not good enough to be involved in the competition for places. Only the occasional cup run or a victory over one of the big sides prevented them all from dying of tedium.

Nonetheless Roy had decided that this was the day when they'd reassert their right to be considered the best team in

England after their feeble performance against Arsenal and, well, there was no talking to him.

I got my first insight into the way he was thinking when we ran into Dwight Yorke a couple of days before the match. He was coming out of the Carphone Warehouse on Market Street in Manchester City Centre.

'Alright, Skip?' he said. He always called Roy 'Skip' or 'Skipper'.

'Alright, Yorkie.'

A great guy, Dwight — one of the nicest human beings it's been my pleasure to know. Always that smile on his face, like a man who couldn't believe his luck. And, well, that's how he lived his life as well. And sadly, that was the problem.

He told Roy a story about something he'd gotten up to once — an escapade I read about again in *Born to Score*, his autobiography. It might have been the one where he had sex with four women in a twenty-four-hour period. Or his romantic entanglement with a woman in a Glasgow taxi. Or the one where he filmed himself cavorting around in a female acquaintance's clothes, only for the video tape to fall into the hands of a tabloid newspaper, who naturally went and had a field day.

Well, I'm sure it was one of those.

Now, I don't want to come across all judgmental about human sexual mores here. I'm a dog, for God's sake. But I do remember thinking, 'Jesus, Dwight, why would you think that Roy was a suitable audience for a story like that?'

I remember Roy deflected the conversation back to football, mentioning that Middlesbrough on Saturday was a chance to arrest a recent slip in standards. 'At the end of the day,' he said, 'I think we've all become maybe a bit slack. Maybe one or two of us are finding life a bit too easy. Maybe we're all a bit too satisfied with our Ferraris and our big watches and whatever else. *Is it not strange that desire should so many years outlive performance?*'

That was Shakespeare.

Dwight had a good idea that this little speech was directed mostly at him, but he took it with his usual happy even-headedness. You had to say it, life just brimmed in the guy.

'I think one thing I can safely say, Skip, is that my lifestyle has never affected my performance on the pitch, where it matters. Anyone who knows me will tell you that I play hard, yeah, but I also work harder than any other player. Once I cross that line, I always give a hundred and ten percent.'

Poor Dwight was one of those people who careened through life, from incident to accident, somehow always managing to miss the point. At the start of his book he tells a dramatic story about kicking and punching a man who tried to rob him of his £45,000 watch at knifepoint in a nightclub toilet. It's a pretty standard plot device to draw the reader into the narrative – didn't feel the need to use it myself – but it concludes with the payoff: 'I realised that my life was in freefall.'

When I read that, I just wanted to scream, 'That wasn't the moment, Dwight! That was *not* the moment!'

Beautiful person though he was, he just couldn't see it. He didn't understand what Roy was trying to tell him – to tell them all. To be successful, in Roy's and Alex Ferguson's terms, you had to want to win like you wanted your next breath. Dwight continued to score goals for United, but the clock was ticking for him. And, poor sap, he didn't even know it.

I can only imagine the talking-to the rest of the players got before the match, because they went out to play Middlesbrough fired up like a pack of squaddies on furlough. And what should have been just another ho-hum afternoon in the life of a team going about the metronomic business of winning championships turned into something else.

The match wasn't televised live, and the first I knew of what had happened was when I caught the news headlines. I was flicking between a hugely enjoyable biography of Walt Disney and a documentary on the history of Basque separatism when I inadvertently hit the button for Sky News and discovered that the match at Old Trafford had, for some reason, made it to the top of the news cycle.

There, filling the screen, was a photograph of four United players surrounding referee Andy D'Urso with pure, naked violence in their faces. Roy was the worst of them, right in the middle, his eyes popping, his neck muscles cinched tight and, yes, that vein in his forehead, pulsing like the Niagara River.

I thought, Oh, no, Roy, what have you done now?

It turned out that the photograph didn't even begin to do it justice. You had to see it in real time to appreciate the ugliness of that aggression display. I did when I watched *Match of the Day* later that night.

I should have mentioned that the entire game was played in a spiteful atmosphere. Paul Ince was now playing for Middlesbrough and the fans who once loved him now booed his every touch. Christian Ziege got sent off for two fouls that Beckham managed to turn into minor theatrical productions. It was all irredeemably ugly stuff until Juninho spirited past Stam – again I've never been one to say I told you so – who swung his leg blindly at him and brought him to the floor.

I have to say, I thought it was a penalty myself. The United players didn't agree. Roy, Giggs, Beckham, Butt, as well as Stam himself – the nerve of him! – disagreed so strongly that poor Andy D'Urso started backpedaling like a man who'd somehow found himself in the bear enclosure in the zoo – or, worse, a burglar who'd just run into Duncan Ferguson on the landing of his home.

I watched Roy's right arm semaphore wildly, then he went after him with rage in his eyes. I was filled with something that felt like fear. I realised that I couldn't bring myself to watch it and I backed out of the room, barking madly, and stayed in the laundry room until I was sure it had passed. A few minutes later, I laboured slowly back to the living room to see that Middlesbrough had missed the penalty anyway, but, far more shockingly, that Roy was still on the field.

United went on to score a winner and went top of the league. But that couldn't have seemed more beside the point that night.

He at least had the humility to look embarrassed when he arrived home, although at first he tried to play it for laughs, probably trying to gauge my feelings.

'Jesus, Triggs, I'd say you thought I was back listening to Dylan again, did you?'

I won't lie, the thought did cross my mind. I was in no mood to joke about it, though. 'I didn't recognise you,' I said.

I was in my basket in the laundry room with the lights off. Roy sat on the floor, with his back against the washing machine and gently stroked my coat. 'Didn't recognise myself,' he said.

How *could* I stay mad with him?

'What happened?' I asked.

'I lost it. Obviously we all did. The manager had a right go at us afterwards.'

'Well, he was right to.'

'Said it'd only turn referees against us at the end of the day. They'll maybe be waiting for one of us to step out of line now. Did I scare you, Triggs?'

'No,' I said.

That was a lie. He did scare me. But that wasn't the reason I was upset. Look, I didn't live under a rock. I watched the television and read the papers like everyone else. I knew what people said about him. That he was a hothead. A bully. A raving madman. But he was none of those things. Take it from me. I knew him better than anyone.

'It's just . . .'

'Go on, Triggs.'

'Well, those people who talk about you like you're some kind of monster. People who don't know the real you . . .'

'Listen, I'm beating myself up over it, Triggs. I mean, obviously the lad D'Urso, he didn't deserve that. Don't get me wrong, I stand by what I said. I still think he made a mistake, obviously with the penalty decision. But, at the end of the day, he's only human. And no human deserves to be treated like that. Disproportionate. That's the word the manager used – hats off, he was right. He said there's very little in life that matters that much.'

Smart man, Alex Ferguson. He was right about a backlash too. The newspapers said that United had grown arrogant and needed to learn humility. A couple of weeks later, Roy collected two yellow cards in a 3–0 defeat to Newcastle – the first for suggesting to a linesman that prescription lenses might improve his decision-making skills, the second for a foul on Robert Lee that was singularly lacking in malice. There was no point in Roy complaining that referees were being overly sensitive towards him. He knew he just had to take his medicine.

By then, United had racked up a couple more wins and I noticed that the William Hill in Hale was already paying out on bets on them becoming champions. Arsenal didn't have the heart for the race. Leeds didn't have the legs – and United had the chance to burn them off once and for all at the end of February.

Leeds were a team full of youthful promise. Lee Bowyer was a spiky central midfielder broken from the same mould as Roy. Harry Kewell, with the ball at his feet, was the most exciting young player in England. But their squad was thin and tiring fast. They'd lost their last two matches – to Arsenal and Aston Villa – and in both games I noticed their tendency to overcommit personnel to the attack, leaving themselves vulnerable to a fast counter-attack. All four defenders liked to cross the halfway line and Ian Harte especially had this tendency, I noticed, to take his time returning to his post.

The match was overshadowed by other events that week. It was a Friday lunchtime, I remember. I was in the kitchen, playing with a length of insulating tape that had worked itself loose from the underside of the window sill, while thinking about how Andy Cole might fare in a one-on-one situation with Lucas Radebe. That was when Roy arrived home. He seemed a bit distracted.

'The manager's had a right go at Becks on the training ground,' he said. 'Tore him a new one. Then told him to go and train with the reserves.'

By now I should have been inured to Beckham's occasionally boneheaded behaviour, but this was a new high in stupidity even for him. It seems that Beckham's boy had gastroenteritis. (Both ends. We've all been there. And it's no one's idea of a fun time.) So David skipped training. Fair enough. I'm not a parent myself, but you know enough about Labradors at this point to know what a generally empathic lot we are.

The problem was that Mrs Beckham was photographed that very night, *rocking* – I believe is the phrase – a pair of green satin Maria Grachvogel hotpants on the London catwalk. Well, you can understand how it looked – to everyone except Beckham, that is, who thought optics were devices that barmen use to measure spirits. I mean, what he did think Alex Ferguson was going to say?

*'Would a lime green, one-shoulder number with silver sequins and trim go with those pants? Wouldn't mind asking your wife for me, would you, David?'*

No. What he said was: 'You were at home babysitting while your wife was out fucking gallivanting.'

Right or wrong, you just knew that's how Ferguson was going to see it. He was as furious as poor Ashley Cole when

Arsenal offered him a contract for a measly £55,000 a week.

Roy filled me in on the full exchange, which happened within earshot of the rest of the players. He waited for my response. I had long ago realised before that it wasn't a question of who wore the knickers in the Beckham house but who wore the trousers. But I decided to keep my comments measured. In the end, I didn't get to say anything, because there was a neat report of sharp knocks on the door. Roy went out to answer it and the next thing I heard was Beckham's voice rattling in the emptiness of the hallway.

'Obviously, I'm sorry to disturb you, Roy. As I've said in the past, you're someone who I definitely respect and look up to, not just as a captain but as a player who's obviously world class and who's been colossally influential . . .'

'Yeah, yeah, yeah,' I heard Roy say, 'what do you want, Becks?'

'Well,' he said, 'I don't know if you've heard, but the manager's gone and dropped me from the team for obviously Leeds. He's told me not to even report.'

I heard Roy sigh heavily. He might have been trying to give him the impression that he'd been doing something. 'You'd better come in.'

Beckham caught sight of me with a length of insulating tape hanging from my face like a set of Chinese whiskers and said, 'You've still got the dog then, have you, Roy?'

Roy didn't answer. It would have been a waste of everyone's time. Instead, he said, 'What the fuck are you at, Becks?'

This clearly threw him.

'As I've said before, my little boy was running a fever. At the end of the day, it just felt wrong to leave him and Victoria, so I've stayed down in London. Anyone who knows me will tell you that my first priority is always my family. Then in the afternoon, he was feeling better and Victoria's decided to honour obviously a long-standing commitment . . .'

'Becks,' Roy cut him off. 'I don't give a shit about that. *He's* the manager.'

'Obviously, yeah. But it was the way he's gone and spoken about my wife. It was disrespectful and at the end of the day, that's not something I think I'd ever take lightly.'

'Disrespectful?'

'Well, it was the sneering way he said that word. Obviously, *gallivanting*.'

Four syllables? Someone was clearly home-schooling him, I thought.

'Becks,' Roy said, his eyes closed in an attitude of forced patience, '*he's* the manager. He told you to go and train with the reserves. And what did you do?'

'When someone attacks my wife, as I said before, I consider that an attack on me . . .'

'You got dressed and you got in your fucking car. Whether you're in the right or in the wrong, you didn't do yourself any favours there, Becks. He's the manager. He tells you to go train with the reserves – whether you agree with him or not – you go and fucking train with the reserves.'

'Don't get me wrong, I can see the other side of the argument . . .'

I watched Roy bristle, the way he does. 'Becks, what are you doing here anyway?'

'Well, as I said before, you're the captain and obviously a huge part of the reason that the team has done so fantastically well over the years . . .'

'For fuck's sake.'

'You've been obviously a talisman for us and hopefully that can continue into the future.'

'Go and talk to the manager.'

'I was hoping you could give me some obviously advice . . .'

'I've given you my advice. Talk to the fucking manager.'

Beckham had one eyebrow raised in that expression of utter cluelessness that was a default look for him at that time and became his stock in trade when he went into modelling.

Ten seconds after that, Roy was showing him out the door. I said nothing. There was nothing *to* say.

Beckham went off to find Alex Ferguson. But I think Roy and I both understood that he was probably going to make matters worse by – and this was my guess from the drift of his conversation with Roy – telling him that he was sorry he felt the way he did, even though he respected his right to an opinion having achieved everything he's achieved as a manager. Vanity had become the mainspring of Beckham's character. Nothing was going to change. He wasn't going to play against Leeds, that was for sure.

As it turned out, they didn't need him. They won 1–0 at Elland Road. With Leeds heavily committed forward, Paul Scholes hit a beautiful pass from the back to send Andy Cole racing clear with only Lucas Radebe for company. It happened just like I saw it. The television showed the goal from six different angles and Ian Harte didn't make it into a single shot.

The league was over and everyone knew it. Now we could all concentrate on what really mattered.

Europe.


United beat Fiorentina at Old Trafford. Roy scored with a perfectly executed volley – he was spectacular that night. Then they drew with Valencia away to win the second qualifying group.

The quarter-final draw threw them Real Madrid.

'Oh, fuck,' seemed to sum up the general attitude of the team, although Roy, like me, was positively straining at the halter to get at them. 'How can you claim to be the champions of Europe,' I remember him saying to me, 'if you don't beat the best teams in Europe?'

This was on a blustery Sunday in early spring. We were in the back garden. I was chasing an Asda carrier bag that had assumed a jellyfish-like life of its own in the wind, while Roy was sitting at the little patio table, laughing at the spectacle. Exhausted, I eventually joined him, stretching myself out at his feet. And that's when we got talking about Real.

I'd been watching quite a lot of Spanish football that season. I don't think I was telling Roy anything especially new when I mentioned that he had to win his personal battle with Fernando Redondo for primacy of the midfield, and that Stam – unlikely as it sounded – had to do the same with Raul.

'Raul's obviously a top, top goalscorer,' he said. 'The best in the world when he's on form.'

'But don't forget about Fernando Morientes,' I said. 'The thing about Raul is that he drags defenders out of position and creates space for Morientes. That's why Morientes scores so many goals.'

He nodded his agreement. 'But I think we've got players who can obviously hurt them,' he said.

'I agree.'

'I mean, Andy Cole's in top, top form at the moment and his confidence is obviously sky high.'

It was interesting that neither of us mentioned Dwight.

I was worried about Roberto Carlos and the damage he could do with his pace down United's right flank. Neither Beckham nor Gary Neville were quick and Neville's confidence was on the floor at that point. It didn't require any special skill at reading human bodies to see it.

'Although defensively,' I added, 'Roberto Carlos does tend to make two or three serious errors per game.'

I watched him slowly process this and I think he realised that I had a point.

The first match, in Madrid, finished scoreless and no one seemed to know whether it represented a good night's work or not. I tended towards Alex Ferguson's view, which was that they'd needed an away goal. Roy was inclined to focus on the narrative of the match more than the outcome.

'They gave us a serious chasing,' I remember he said. 'I don't know why people go on about us being a great team. We've a lot to learn from the likes of obviously Real Madrid.'

He was right and he was wrong. Real *were* a better team, but I didn't believe the gap was anything like Roy thought it was that night. United might have even won had Cole not managed to somehow sky a simple header over the bar.

But Roy was terribly uptight around that time. Fearing a repeat of the Andy D'Urso incident, I was trying to keep things light – thus my little comic routine earlier with the plastic bag. I was doing other little turns, too. Wrestling with the garden hose like it was an anaconda that had come to attack the house and barking at racehorses when they came on the television. Another time I pretended I thought the fibreglass Labrador outside Boots in Altringham, into which people dropped coins for the Blind Society, was a real dog. I started growling at it – gave it the full aggression display, in fact – just to draw a laugh from Roy. Yes, I was out of my comfort zone but I think he appreciated my efforts, especially in the days immediately before the second leg, when I think the final he missed in Barcelona might have been on his mind.

As it turned out, the match was another of those that reminded me I didn't know everything about football after all.

'What kind of way is that to line out?' I remember thinking, as the Real players resolved themselves on the screen into a shape that I'd never seen before on a football field. I was as baffled as Jonathan Woodgate having algorithms explained to him.

They played with three central defenders and two wingbacks

– okay, there was nothing new in that – but Redondo was on his own in midfield. They had three players up front, while Steve McManaman – who I'd always dismissed as a dilettante when he was at Liverpool – was given *carte blanche* to play wherever he wanted.

I wondered how it was going to work. The answer, it turned out, was very, very well. It was the perfect system for counter-attacking football. They could cover the length of the field in three passes.

While I was still trying to discern the shape of the game, Roy put the ball into his own net. I thought something like that might happen. There is such a thing as wanting it too much. He tried to intercept a low cross from Michel Salgado and suddenly he was lying on the ground with his eyes shut tight, wishing – I could read him like a book – he was at home with me. And I could see what he thought of the supportive chorus of 'Keano!' that rang around the stadium as well.

Redondo was having the better of him – anyone could see that. But then he had Raul dropping back to help. Or when it wasn't Raul, it was Salgado, or McManaman, or Morientes.

I was convinced that Ferguson was going to change things around at half-time. But he didn't. He was convinced that if his players kept doing the right things, then they'd score. Didn't they always? But what they were doing was as pointless as, well, explaining algorithms to Jonathan Woodgate, and I was disappointed to see them returning to it after half-time. What they should have done, I thought, was switch to a 4–3–3 system that would force Real to withdraw their forward players and also make their three central defenders work.

But that was me.

I had to answer a call of nature. In normal circumstances, I would have tried to hold it, but I'd had a bad bout of diarrhoea recently and I wasn't one hundred percent sure I could trust myself.

I was unburdening myself on a patch of grass behind the oil tank, wondering how long Ferguson was going to wait before he tried something else. Sixty-eight minutes seemed to be the average point when managers made tactical substitutions in a match. I had no idea why, I thought, as I assumed the sitting position and wiped my bottom on the grass.

I was outside no more than five minutes. When I returned to the living room, the score in the top left-hand corner of the screen said 0–3. I wondered was it a mistake. But then Clive Tyldesley mentioned that two goals in two minutes from Raul had left Manchester United with, well, really a mountain to climb and that their reign as European champions looked like coming to rather a sad end.

'We keep giving ourselves too much work to do,' was Roy's rather neat précis on events when he returned home in the infomercial hours of the morning.

I was still sitting in front of the television, watching a man with a cockney accent pitching 'the only knife that you will ever need', which, as it happens, came with a free set of ten other knives – not to mention a pen that could write underwater. Stone Age man might have domesticated the dog, but much human behaviour remains a mystery to me.

'We've been getting away with things in obviously the Premiership that you just can't get away with against the top, top sides in Europe,' he went on. 'Concede three goals against the likes of Real at home, you don't deserve to be in the competition. Listen, to do what they did to us tonight, Triggs – take a bow – that's the standard that we should be setting ourselves. But I'm blue in the face saying it.'

Personally, I thought Ferguson erred in not changing the shape of the team at half-time. But I also agreed with Roy. In fact, it would become a regular plaint of mine over the coming years that United's failings in Europe were down to their failure to add to their squad in a way that improved it.

So they were trapped in that stasis between being too good for England but not good enough for Europe.

In the four Premier League matches that bookended the two games against Real, they scored eighteen goals. They won the league with four matches to spare. A record. They won it by a margin of eighteen points. A record. They scored ninety-seven goals. A record, too. But the point was, they weren't learning anything. They weren't improving. I'd gotten into the habit of zoning out whenever Roy threw lines from his desk calendar at me. But his thought for the day when United made the league safe in Southampton had a logic to it that was irresistible – *if you're not going forwards, you're going backwards*. I think he feared that that would be his fate, too.

If I have a favourite memory of Roy, it was the morning late that spring when I tipped upstairs to his bedroom and found him standing in front of the mirror in his dress suit, his neck straining against the imagined tightness of his shirt collar. Some men could wear a tuxedo like it was a secon layer of skin. Not Roy. He always looked strangely out of sync dressed up like that.

'A big night tonight,' I said.

He was off to London for the PFA Awards. He turned and noticed me for the first time, then pulled what I'd come to know as his difficult-to-impress face.

'Obviously, as I've said in the past, individual honours don't concern me,' he said. 'Listen, don't get me wrong, it's obviously an honour being recognised by your peers. But as I keep saying, the important thing is obviously that the team is doing well.'

Then I watched his hairpin features twist into a smile. 'Anyway,' he said, 'who says I'm going to win?'

Of course he was going to win. He'd been the best player in England by a distance that was incalculable, just as he'd been the best player in England the year before as well.

While Roy took his measure in the long mirror, I told him about a documentary I'd seen recently about Orson Welles, who was the victim of arguably the greatest injustice in the history of the Oscars when John Ford's *How Green Is My Valley* took the 1941 Best Picture award ahead of *Citizen Kane*. I was never much into movies, so I'm no kind of judge. But thirty years later, the embarrassment of having got it so wrong prompted the Academy of Motion Picture Arts and Sciences to offer Welles an honorary Oscar. The legend has it that on the night of the presentation, Welles got drunk in a bar somewhere and sent John Huston along to collect it.

Roy loved that story. 'Maybe I should go to The Bleeding Wolf,' he said, 'and get Ginola to pick it up for me.'

I did my impersonation of him from the L'Oréal ad – 'Because I am worth eet!' – which Roy always got a kick out of.

He took off his tux then and slipped it into its cover for the journey to London.

When he'd gone, I was struck by a sudden fear that he might in fact be right. The Player of the Year award was decided by other footballers and they'd gotten it so wrong the year before. God knows they weren't the brightest stars in the sky. Couldn't they get it wrong again?

I couldn't relax. All day and all night. Of course, later on, I could have put myself out of my misery at any moment by switching on Sky News and discovering the result for myself. But I couldn't bring myself to do it. I kept thinking about what it would do to him to have to sit through that again. Another Ginola-style travesty.

I lay there in my basket in the laundry room, silently torturing myself with that thought until, some time around seven o'clock the following morning, I must have drifted off.

When I woke up I had the impression that it was some time late in the afternoon. My eyes were gummy with sleep and even before I managed to pry them open, I was aware that I wasn't alone in my little room.

It was there, right in my line of vision, the size of a small child. The PFA Player of the Year award. He'd quietly left it there for when I woke up. I suppose it was the nearest thing Roy and I ever had to a *Marley & Me* moment.

When you own a dog – I think Roy would back me up on this – a little bit of that animal's light enters you. And, I can tell you from happy experience, the transaction works two ways.

# 9.

# Mick McCarthy Comes for Tea

MICK McCARTHY CAME TO THE HOUSE ONE DAY in the summer of 2000. Like Tony Blair and Gordon Brown splitting an aromatic duck with Chinese pancakes in Granita in Islington in 1994, the meeting between Roy and Mick assumed a kind of mythic significance in the light of, for now, let's just call them, later events.

No doubt there'll be a movie one day. More work for Peter Morgan.

Unlike Peter, though, I wouldn't be required to dream up the conversation. Because I was there. I heard every word that passed between them, even though I still find it difficult, looking back through the prism of – again – those later events, to believe that it really happened.

I remember asking Roy to repeat himself. He was plumping cushions, sweeping my chew toys into a corner and generally making sure that everything was just so.

'I don't see what the big fucking deal is,' he said.

Oh, he saw what the big deal was alright. We both did. In the three years we'd known each other, I'd heard him refer to Mick in the most imaginatively disparaging ways. So when he said to me that morning, 'Mick McCarthy is going to be calling in,' I couldn't be certain that this wasn't another of my more outré dreams.

'But why?' I wondered.

Roy laughed at me like I was the one being ridiculous. 'Because I'm the captain of my country,' he said, warbling the words in a defensive way. 'And obviously there's a World Cup qualifying campaign about to start.'

In three sharp movements, he pulled the retractable flex out of the body of the Hoover, then he stopped, his face configured to say something significant. 'For the want of a nail,' he said, 'the shoe was lost. For the want of a shoe, the horse was lost. For the want of a horse, the rider was lost . . . All for the want of care about a horseshoe nail.'

I took this as a parable about the importance of preparation, which was becoming a kind of obbligato in Roy's conversation. Later, when I checked his *Encarta Dictionary of Quotations*, which someone had given him as a Christmas gift, I discovered it.

I decided to get out from underneath his feet. I had to – suddenly he was pushing the Hoover head in my direction in big, purposeful sweeps. So I padded back to my basket in the laundry room and did some quick arithmetic. Roy was about to turn twenty-nine. By the time the World Cup came around, he would be almost thirty-one. Given the attritional way he played football, it was likely to be his last opportunity to appear in a World Cup finals.

There is an age, in my experience, when humans begin ticking things off a mental checklist.

We watched Euro 2000 together. Every single match – even as Roy went through the expedient of telling me that he wasn't a great watcher of the game. The football, if you want my opinion, was some of the best I ever saw, although Roy reckoned that Ireland were better than about half of the teams in the tournament. That got him wondering and as he said himself – one morning while I was reading another dog's pheromone scent from the base of a bin outside the Britannia

Ashley Hotel in the centre of Hale – 'Why the fuck aren't *we* at the European Championships?'

The impression I had was that the meeting with Mick happened at Roy's instigation. I could be wrong – look, I had my views, which Roy knew about, so I decided to stay the hell out of it – but that was certainly the sense I got when I heard him greet Mick at the door.

If he didn't say, 'Thanks very much for agreeing to come,' then he certainly conveyed it.

I sat listening from my basket as they moved into the hall, the air strung tightly with the forced politeness of a first meeting, the conversation peregrinating awkwardly from subject to subject – congestion on the M1, holidays they'd both enjoyed in Albufeira and the way that Hale had retained its country feel despite its close proximity to Manchester's urban sprawl. I suppose in human terms they were circling, sniffing each other out.

I'm an especially sensitive dog – you'll have picked that up by now – and I could feel the atmosphere in the house tighten, like soon there wouldn't be enough oxygen in the place for the three of us.

I didn't move from my basket. I decided to just leave them to it. I knew the effort it must have caused them just to be in the same room. Take it from me, Roy disliked Mick very, very intensely and I can't imagine the feeling was anything other than mutual.

Roy had filled me in on the whole history of antagonism between them. Mick seemed to have enjoyed some kind of headboy position under Jack Charlton, the last Ireland manager, who Roy also disliked very, very intensely. Roy was still in the rambunctious flush of his hellraising youth back then. There was a trip to America. The way he tells it was that he staggered out of a pub and onto the team bus, stinking of beer and wearing a 'Kiss Me Quick' hat. So the head prefect decided to deliver him a lecture about professionalism – as a riposte to which Roy pointed out that Mick had a first touch like an elephant (which he did – I've seen clips), then told him to sit the fuck down.

Unsurprisingly, Mick didn't take this with the smiling equanimity of a man trading little nuggets of repartee with a fellow professional footballer.

Fast forward four years. Mick became the manager of Ireland. I got the impression that he attempted to reach out to Roy in some way. The cynical view, of course, was that he had to. Roy was the best player in his position in England. And at a time when there was a dearth of leaders in the Ireland squad, Roy was the only young player he had who was clearly officer class.

Look, it's a difficult one for me to talk about. Along with Bob Dylan and, well, the way Roy sometimes dressed, Mick McCarthy was one of the few sources of serious disagreement between us in my thirteen years at his side.

Because I liked Mick McCarthy. There. I've said it. I didn't love him like I loved Roy. But I could see there was a streak of decency in him and an instinct to try to make the best peace, which was a product of his working-class, north of England, post-War upbringing.

Back in 1996, the year before I was born, he'd made Roy captain for the second half of a best-forgotten friendly against Russia in Dublin. Roy responded by kicking some player who'd been pissing him off all night. He didn't have me in his ear in those days, of course. Off he went.

A couple of months later, there was another trip to America. Roy didn't fancy it. But he didn't phone Mick to tell him he wasn't going. Had I been around, I'd have made sure he did. Instead, he phoned the FAI and told some flunky. Mick said he didn't hear from any flunky, then he found himself, a couple of days before they were due to fly out, having to answer questions about where his captain even was. And Mick said it straight out. He didn't have a clue. One of the newspapers eventually caught up with Roy – and I still struggle with this – at a cricket match, drinking Pimm's No. 1 Cup. Or maybe I added that final detail myself.

The next time Roy played in Dublin, the Irish fans booed him every time he touched the ball. His own fans. I know Roy held Mick personally responsible for hanging him out to dry and over the four years that followed, his feelings for him calcified into pure, hard loathing.

And I told you about *They Think It's All Over* and the hairy kebab business.

So there's your backstory. It was a mess. And to be truthful, I wasn't sure either had it in him to completely let go of the past. It was the alpha thing again. Let me get this straight, I was never against the idea of Roy playing for Ireland. I just didn't think it was a good idea while Mick was the manager.

So now you can understand why, as they moved into the kitchen, discussing how Roy had really fancied Italy to win the European Championships and the discrepancy in house prices between Hale and Alderley Edge, I had one car primed for the sound of furniture breaking. I don't know whose welfare I was most concerned about. Mick was a big man. But as Roy said to me a few weeks later – it was a couple of days before he was sent off for leaving his mark on Gus Poyet in the Charity Shield – it's not the size of the teeth that matters, but the anger of the mouth.

I listened closely, then I heard a sudden machine gun blast of laughter – Mick first, *then* Roy – and the air cooled somewhat.

That's when I thought, okay, I need to be a witness to this. I had a sense, even then, that this was going to end up being a significant episode in all of our lives.

So I ambled into the kitchen, all innocent-like. Mick was a dog-owner. I could just tell from the kindliness of hands as he smoothed my coat. And he said, 'Hello, Girl!'

He noticed!

'What's her name?' he wanted to know.

I should perhaps mention that my fame then wasn't a fraction of what it would become.

'It's Triggs,' Roy said.

Mick laughed, then stood to his full height again. 'Here, you've not gone and named her after Jason, have you?'

Did I mention that Jason McAteer's nickname was Trigger?

'No,' Roy said in a long aspiration, at the same time handing Mick a mug of tea with the bag still in it. 'Not after Jason, no.'

'I've got two meself,' Mick said, fishing out the teabag without the use of spoon, squeezing it dry between his forefinger and thumb, then dropping it into the sink. 'Yeah, they're Staffys.'

Staffordshire bull terriers. Hard dogs. Hard man.

'They're great company,' Roy said. 'I think I'm on the record as saying that, obviously being around footballers all day, talking to Triggs is the only intelligent conversation I get!'

I watched the laughter lines spoke from Mick's eyes. 'I do the same,' he said. 'I do the very same. You know, there were a woman lived up the road from us in Barnsley when we were kids. And she used to say that dogs knew how to speak – they just never bothered.'

Roy tilted his head. 'She was probably bananas, in fairness to her.'

'Oh, she were mad as a fucking hatter. Mad as a hatter. But I like to think sometimes that there were something in it. I chat to my two all the time. And sometimes, yeah, I like to imagine what they're saying back to me. Like you said, Roy – sometimes it's for the want of intelligent conversation.'

I moved over to the mat by the back door and lay down, watching as much as listening. I know that Roy thinks I'm a bit too hung up on the whole alpha thing. But what I was looking for, I suppose, were submission signals – the human form of the play bow, the tail between the legs, the head held low, the eyes turned away.

'I think it's time, Mick, we started maybe giving ourselves a bit more credit,' Roy said, apropos of nothing. They were facing each other across the free-standing island. 'Like I said before, I watched Euro 2000 and I thought, 'We *should* be there. We should be there – and we're not.'

Mick drew a slow breath. 'Well, obviously, Roy, we've had to rebuild . . .'

Roy cut him off. 'The rebuilding's done. It's fucking done, Mick. That's what I'm saying to you. We have to maybe start raising the bar for ourselves.'

Mick put his mug down on the island. I watched his outline stiffen. Then he did something that was typical of a human alpha. He tried to restart the conversation on his own terms. 'I'm glad I've come here today, Roy, because it's given us a chance to – *I* think – clear the air.'

Even with words, one was constantly trying to blot out the urine scent of the other.

'What do you mean, clear the air?'

'Look, I know *you'd* rather be stood in the kitchen here having a cup of tea with Ratko Mladic. And I think it's fair to say that you're never going to be on *my* Christmas card list either. We've both done a lot of things. Both said a lot of things. Maybe some of us wish we'd handled things a bit better. The point is, Roy, that it's the past. If I'm hearing what I think I'm hearing from you . . .'

I watched Roy bristle. 'What do you mean, what you *think* you're hearing?'

'Well, that you want to play for me.'

'It's not a question of playing for *you*, Mick. It's a question of playing for my country . . .'

'Of which *I* am the manager.'

'I've *always* wanted to play for my country.'

'Well, that's good. That's what I want to hear from *all* my players . . .'

All my players? Roy let that one go. I could only imagine the effort it took.

'The point is, Roy, that you and I have got to start with a clean slate. Look, no one's saying we've got to be bosom buddies. I'm not your kind of person and, well, I think it's fair to say that you're not mine. But if you're going to play for Ireland – *under* me – we've got to at least appear to be singing off the same hymn sheet.'

'Why is that important?'

'Because I can't have you undermining me, Roy. I can't have it and I won't have it. If you have a problem with the set-up . . .'

'I've plenty of problems with the set-up, Mick. You know that.'

'Then you, as my captain, should be able to come and talk to me about it.'

*My* captain. Was he doing it on purpose?

Roy started rhyming off a long corpus of grievances, most of which I'd heard before. 'We travel to away matches – we're sitting at the back of the plane. Like fucking livestock. The training facilities are terrible – obviously the pitches, the surfaces. Just not good enough, Mick. We don't get proper meals before matches . . .'

'Obviously, Roy, you're comparing us to the way things are done at Manchester United . . .'

'That's not the point, Mick. It's nothing to do with the way things are done at Manchester United. There's a right way and there's a wrong way. People maybe saying that we don't have the resources – blah, blah, blah. Listen. How much would eleven plates of pasta cost?'

'I've no idea, Roy.'

'Jesus, I'll give the FAI the fucking money myself? Take my fucking match fee and give the lads a feed before they go out to play. Chicken. Pasta . . .'

'I'm hearing you.'

'Obviously cereals . . .'

'I'm hearing you, Roy.'

'I hope so, Mick. Because I've been saying it for years. I'm blue in the face saying it. I'm not asking for anything out of the ordinary. Special treatment – blah, blah, blah. We're talking about obviously basics here.'

'Look, *you* want to improve things. *I* want to improve things.'

'I'm glad to hear it, Mick. I'm glad to hear it.'

There was an instant of silence then. 'Because I'm going to tell you something,' Mick said. 'I think we have a very good chance of qualifying.'

From the way he said it, he clearly expected this to come as some kind of revelation. But Roy just frowned at him across the island and said, 'Of course we have,' as if it was self-evident.

'I'm just saying, the papers – as soon as they saw Holland and Portugal in our group – they said, that's it, Mick McCarthy's for the high jump.'

'Listen. Don't be worrying about the fucking papers.'

'I'm just saying. Especially when they both got to the quarter-finals of Euro 2000. They're already writing us off, you know? Before we've even kicked a ball.'

'As I said before, it's just the fucking papers, Mick.'

'The thing is, I've always said that the time to get these teams is right after a major finals. Because they're knackered, see. Sometimes they have to rebuild. They've maybe got a new manager. They've not yet got their heads around starting the whole qualifying process again. That's why I arranged for us to play our two toughest away games first.'

He seemed to be inviting praise from Roy. Even the subtlest

submission display would do. Roy just spat out his bottom lip. Wasn't impressed.

'For me,' he said, 'it doesn't matter when we play them. If your mental state is right, obviously your preparation – if that's right – if you've a gameplan, you can beat any team in the world. Doesn't matter if you play them at six o'clock on Christmas morning. That's what I'm saying to you, Mick, about maybe giving ourselves a bit more credit. Other people saying we maybe don't have the players. We *do* have the players.'

'We've got good players. I always give them credit.'

'We've got *very* good players. Shay Given in goal. Obviously, Kells and Hartey – everyone's saying Leeds are going to be the team to beat over the next five years. We'll see about that – they've obviously achieved nothing in the game – but we've got their two fullbacks. We've got Richard Dunne in there. Obviously myself in midfield. The lad Kinsella. Duffer on the left. Duffer's a player. Listen. *Jason's* a player. Things have maybe not worked out for the lad at Liverpool, but he's another one who could do with maybe taking himself a bit more seriously. Robbie up front. A top, top goalscorer. Proven. Obviously Niall, who'll do a job for you. Vastly, vastly experienced. Other lads coming through . . .'

'I'm agreeing with you, Roy.'

'Well, let's stop all the talk about rebuilding then. We *have* the players now.'

I watched Mick shift his weight forward onto the balls of his feet. 'And what about you and me?'

Roy shrugged softly. 'As you said, at the end of the day, we're never going to be friends. For me, that's not important.'

'Me neither. But you've got to respect me, Roy.'

Respect. That word again. It might have been around that time that Andy Cole started referring to himself as Andrew and we were all supposed to do the same. I went on calling him Andy. Roy will tell you that. I thought the whole thing was stupid.

'Listen,' Roy said, 'the question is, can we work with each other? I think we both agree that things maybe need improving – obviously within the set-up. But at the end of the day, we both want Ireland to qualify for the World Cup finals.'

Mick nodded evenly. 'And then we can say our goodbyes.'

Roy smiled. 'Never have to look at each other again,' he said.

Mick suddenly had the attitude of being ready to go. He hadn't drunk a drop of tea, I noticed. Neither had Roy.

'It's hard,' Mick said. 'Management, I mean. You'll discover that yourself one day, no doubt.'

And Roy stared hard at him and said, 'Who says I'm mad enough to ever want to be a fucking manager?'

Mick let himself out. Roy didn't walk him to the door. He stood at the window of the kitchen and watched him leave. With his back to me, he said he thought that went okay. I kept my mouth shut. I, in fact, thought the opposite was the case. The meeting went horribly. But he couldn't have known that. He wasn't a dog.

Humans, you see, are often too preoccupied with their higher motives to recognise their base ones. Herd packs are ruled by a strict social hierarchy that recognises one pack leader. Only another dog could know the sense of uneasiness that hardened like a lead ball inside me as Mick McCarthy pointed his Renault Mégane in the direction of London, with the issue of dominance and submission left unresolved.

It wasn't over. That much I knew for certain.


*'You know whose car that is?'*

*Two passersby stop and goggle through the window at the walnut dash.*

'Whose?'

'Roy Keane's.'

'Fuck off!'

'It's Roy Keane's.'

'How do you know?'

'Because I've fucking seen him in it. Loads of times.'

Two men. In their forties, maybe. Wearing dark overalls with white spatters. Painters would be my guess. Possibly plasterers. One of them shields his eyes with his hand and presses his face closer to the glass.

'Here, look, it's . . .'

'Who?'

'His fucking dog – what's he called.'

'I don't know.'

'You do. He's always on the news. He's fucking famous. Any time Roy's out walking . . .'

'Oh, yeah – look at him there!'

'You do know it. It's always, 'Roy Keane pictured yesterday walking his dog . . .' Awww, it's on the tip of me fucking tongue, man.'

'Beautiful dogs, them . . . Marley.'

'It's not fucking Marley.'

'I'm saying he's like fucking Marley.'

I'm fucking not, I think.

We're parked on Tavern Street, in the centre of Ipswich. Roy is in River Island, picking up one or two things. I'm listening to this conversation through the two-inch crack he left in the rear passenger window.

'It'll come to me, man. The name – it'll come to me. I'll tell you something for nothing, though. He's not long for this world.'

'The dog?'

'Fucking Roy Keane. Did you see the match on Saturday? Forest?'

'Told you, I don't really follow the football anymore.'

'Well, you've got more fucking sense than me then. Fucking shite.'

'Who won?'

'Forest, of course. And I mean shite, by the way. Should have been more than two-nil as well.'

'So where are they now? In the table, like?'

'Bottom half is all I know. I said it to one of the fellas who's on this job with us, I said, you can forget fucking promotion. At this rate, we'll be lucky to stay up. I said that to him.'

# 10.

# Prawn and Bred

BOB DYLAN RE-ENTERED OUR LIVES THAT SAME summer. He was back like the peripatetic boy from the Bible story. And he didn't even have the good decency to sound remorseful about it either. Through the study door, one Monday lunchtime, I heard the clumsy acoustic chord changes from 'It's All Over Now, Baby Blue', then his voice dully vocalising some tiresome dispatch from his random imagination and I thought, 'Oh, no, Roy, not again.'

The Charity Shield was still a week away. He was bored and he wanted the new season to start as desperately as David O'Leary enjoyed the sound of his own voice.

I'm painfully aware, incidentally, that Dylan still enjoys a certain popularity and that some of you will be reading this and thinking, what the hell does she know about popular music? She should stick to football. Well, believe it or not, dogs are rather astute music critics. In fact, the great English composer, Sir Edward Elgar, was convinced of it. The man who wrote the Pomp and Circumstance Marches was terrific friends with a bulldog called Dan, who belonged to George Robertson Sinclair, the organist of Hereford Cathedral. Kind of became his sidekick, in fact. Elgar was convinced that the dog could pick out the chorister in a group who was singing out of tune, just as I could pick out a centre-half who was a yard behind the pace of a game. If you ever take the time to

listen to Elgar's wonderful *Enigma Variations*, the eleventh —
the most beautiful, in my view — was inspired by Dan.

Knowing what constituted bad singing, you can be
reasonably certain that Dan would have hated Dylan and, had
he been in my position, would have communicated this to
Roy, who'd had the bare-faced gall, remember, to carry out a
home deafness test on me! Maybe *I* should have stood behind
*him* with a wok and metal spoon. Wondered what he was
hearing.

Yet still, once or twice a year, Dylan would insinuate his
way back into our lives. I could never reason out what it was
about the man and his music that Roy found so inspiring. I
mean to say, he wouldn't have been Roy's kind of man. I knew
that much. I'd made it my business to do as much background
work as I could on him, watching a couple of documentaries,
reading two or three biographies that Roy bought and left
lying around the house, unopened, then listening to his entire
back catalogue in an effort to better understand why it was
that Roy felt such an affinity with him. It sounds extreme, I
know. But the attitude that seemed to come over Roy when
he had Dylan in his ear, well, it was affecting my life, too.

I even compared their histories, to see if I could draw
some parallels between their backgrounds. They were both,
reputedly, perfectionists, although Dylan, I would argue, set
the bar far lower for himself than Roy ever did. They could
both be a bit perverse in their judgments and, dare I say it,
a tad crabby at times. They both left home at the age of
nineteen: Roy to play football for Nottingham Forest; Dylan
to follow in the footsteps of Woody Guthrie, the legendary
folksinger from whom — if you want my opinion — he ripped
off his entire early act.

But what else?

Well, Dylan famously found God in the late 1970s, after
which he took to making hostile sermons to his concert

audiences about how they were choosing to live their lives. At a stretch, you could say that Roy was conveying a similar message to his teammates, especially the bit about rampant consumerism leading them to forget their true heart's desire – the Champions League in Roy's case; salvation through Jesus Christ in Bob's. But like I said, that's a stretch.

Apart from that, there really wasn't anything they had in common. In fact, as far as I could see, Dylan was a checklist of all the things that Roy despised in people. He was a fraud. A middle-class boy from Minnesota who was deliberately vague about his comfortable upbringing because he had no narrative context for the music he played. Roy believed in being true to oneself; Dylan was determinedly never himself – his songwriting style, his way of dressing, his manner of speech were all filched from Guthrie, even as the old man lay dying of Huntington's disease in a New York hospital bed.

Roy was a consistently brilliant performer. He felt he owed it to himself and to his audience to give his best every time, with no exceptions. Anyone who ever saw Dylan live on stage will tell you that he turned it on when he felt like it, which, as it happened, wasn't very often. He was the David Ginola of music.

Roy loved being the man of the moment, especially when the moment mattered. He lived for it. Dylan shrank from it. The voice of America's disaffected youth turned his back on the protest movement just as the 1960s were warming up, to become a commercial artist. By the time psychedelia came along and threatened to make him at least artistically interesting again – drug-fuelled gibberish was his stock in trade after all – he'd gone country.

And talk about people who'd become smug and sated by success. Dylan was the ultimate exemplar of it. The man who once urged his audience to question authority and to revolt against everything their parents believed in was, within the course of a couple of decades, advocating a slavish devotion to Christ and selling his songs through Starbucks.

Oh, Roy would have hated him had they ever met. I was sure of it. 'A fucking bluffer and a spoofer.' I can hear him saying the words.

I did try to communicate all of this to him. Naturally, I didn't say it straight out. Roy could be quite willful. If you knew anything about him, you knew that much. It would have only driven him deeper into Dylan's embrace. So I used more subtle methods. I tried to steer him towards *Self Portrait* or *Planet Waves*, albums that even devotees accept represented a career slump for Dylan. I also made occasional observations – digs, Roy might have called them – based on my research, my intention being to slowly loosen the bonds of the attachment.

So that lunchtime, when I heard him playing 'Baby Blue', I waited two or three hours, until he was in the garden, hanging out the laundry, then I drifted outside, with a look of studied nonchalance on my face. 'Yonder stands the orphan with his gun,' I said, with a subtly mocking inflection in my voice, 'crying like a fire in the sun. Tch.'

'I think I'm on the record as saying it's definitely one of his best,' he said. He had a clothes peg in his mouth, clamped between his teeth like one of Ché Guevara's cigars.

'Of course,' I said, 'he played that one at the famous Newport Folk Festival. Don't know if I ever told you about the Newport Folk Festival.'

'Go on.'

'Well, it was the day that Dylan plugged in, as they say. Turned his back on his folk roots and embraced rock and roll. Anyway, the crowd booed his electric set . . .'

'Being popular's not the most important thing in the world, Triggs. You're on about booing? Listen, it's part and parcel when you're playing at that level.'

'But then afterwards, being essentially a people-pleaser, he was persuaded to go back out on the stage and give the people exactly what they expected of him – an acoustic set. So he played that song.'

He didn't look at me. 'I know what you're trying to do, Triggs.'

'*Do?*' I said, all wounded innocence.

'You don't like him?'

'If vomit could sing,' I said, 'it would sound like Bob Dylan.'

He laughed. 'And you don't like when *I* listen to him, because you think I start acting a bit . . .'

'Extreme,' I said.

He laughed at that, too, then pegged the final piece of washing to the line – a round-necked Diadora sweatshirt that, I often tried to persuade him, made him resemble an ASBO teenager.

'Listen,' he said, 'I like the lad's music. The other thing about Dylan is, he was right about a lot of things.'

'Okay,' I said, 'is there a specific line, Roy, that you're finding particularly resonant?'

'Jesus, Triggs, calm down, will you? I'm just saying he'd a good attitude, that's all.'

'Did he?'

'It's in the lyrics. Obviously, 'Baby Blue'. It's all about, as I've said in the past, not settling for what you've got. Don't allow yourself to go soft. And don't be afraid to maybe rip it up and start over.'

'You might as well take your cues from a child,' I said, 'gibbering drunk on his mother's sherry.'

He laughed. He picked up the empty laundry basket and walked back to the house.

I watched an interview once in which Pete Seeger said that if he'd had an axe at the Newport festival, he would have chopped Dylan's power. Well, I knew exactly how he felt when Roy went back inside and put on *Subterranean Homesick Blues* at a volume loud enough to disturb the foundations.

I had a sick sense of foreboding for what was to come.

I never saw his PFA Player of the Year Award again, after the happy afternoon when I woke up to find it staring me down in the laundry room. I have honestly no idea what he did with it. I could say the same about any of the medals he won. He was never one to turn our home into a shrine to himself – that kind of vanity always smacked of weakness to him. Like white boots. Or hair gel.

The most cringeworthy mistake that Roy ever confessed to was the personalised licence plate –'Roy 1' – that he bought for his first very Mercedes. Like Diego Forlan at United, it didn't get many outings and he got rid of it when it became the subject of embarrassing questions.

The award was in the attic. That was my guess. Because to put it in the middle of the dining-room table would have been a sign that he'd gone soft. And going soft, or rather fear of it happening, had been a recurring motif of his conversation all that summer.

'Definitely took a backwards step last season,' he said to me one evening. We were walking along the little towpath that skirts the River Bollin at the back the golf course. 'Obviously not just in terms of what we won, but I think mentally as well. Mentioned before players being maybe happy with their lot. Turning up late to training. That's been well documented. Maybe not training as hard as they could. Then still winning the league by – what was it in the end?'

'Eighteen points.'

'Eighteen points. Jesus! Do you get what I'm saying, Triggs?'

'I do,' I said. Because anyone could see that, as I said before, they were stuck in a limbo between being too good for England

and not good enough for Europe. 'Winning the European Cup should have been the beginning of something,' I said. 'It seems to me that, for too many people around the club, it was an end in itself.'

He stopped abruptly, as if this was some eureka moment for him. I wasn't telling him anything he didn't already know. It might have been my rather neat phrasing that made it sound more profound than it actually was.

'That's *exactly* it,' he said. 'Everyone's way too happy with themselves. *Still!* Still talking about that night in obviously Barcelona. Fergie's Fledglings emulating the achievement of the Busby Babes. The history. The glory. The elusive treble. Blah blah fucking blah. Listen, if it had been up to me, I'd have let the lads have their celebration – then I'd have said, "Now I never want to hear it mentioned again." That's what happened – we spoke about it in the past – at Liverpool. Soon as they won it, all they cared about was going out and obviously winning it again the next year.'

For the second summer in a row, United had resisted the temptation to part with any serious money. They'd made an offer for the striker Ruud van Nistelrooy, but he got injured before they'd even put a down-payment on him. The only new arrival, in fact, was Fabien Barthez, who'd won the World Cup and European Championships with France and who was, as Roy was quick to point out, 'a phenomenal shot-stopper and a huge personality obviously in the dressing room'. But sorting out the team's goalkeeping issues struck me as the stuff of house maintenance. It wasn't a declaration that, after a year of preening its coat, the team was serious about winning the European Cup again. I thought I'd find common ground with Roy on this point. I was surprised when he cut me off.

'I know what you're about to say, Triggs.'

'What?'

'You're on about, maybe the manager hasn't been given the money to spend. I don't agree with you. Well, I do up to a point. But we *have* players. Becks is a player. Giggsy's a player – you're on about real quality there. Obviously Scholesy. World class. Proved it. Obviously, we've got Andy Cole, who'll score goals no matter where he plays. Yorkie, in fairness, if he sorts himself out. Obviously, Teddy – who's typical of our strength in depth. Okay, maybe we haven't added any – we spoke about – big summer signings. But listen. We can't keep using that as an excuse. The players we have, who've already won the Champions League – *they* need to think about maybe stepping up now. *Opportunities usually come disguised as hard work – that's why we don't recognise them.*'

This was still the talk in the days leading up to the first match of the season – the Charity Shield against Chelsea.

'I think I said it before, we have to maybe prove to people we haven't gone soft,' he told me two days before the game. I was lying in the kitchen, watching dust motes move in a shaft of sunlight like bubbles in carbonated water, thinking about nothing much. I must confess, I found it very difficult to get excited about the Charity Shield. Suddenly, Roy was standing above me, just home from training, with a water bottle in his hand.

'I think it's fair to say there's a perception out there,' he said, 'that, obviously, after the way we won the league last year, we might have maybe lost a bit of our hunger. It's up to us to prove that we haven't. There's teams will try to maybe intimidate us. Especially the likes of obviously Chelsea. Physical teams who try to beat you up. End of the day, we've got to prove to them that we're still in fucking business.'

Well, between that kind of talk and then Bob Dylan in his ear, I had a fair idea how the day was going to go. The only surprise was that he took as long as he did to get himself sent off. Oh, and that it was Gus Poyet, not Jimmy Floyd

Hasselbaink, who was left writhing around on the deck like a landed marlin. It was an especially robust tackle on him by Hasselbaink, I recall, that set Roy off on a quest for justice. In my imagination, at least, he was listening to Dylan curling that supercilious top lip of his around the words of *Maggie's Farm* and telling himself that he wasn't going to take shit no more. Poyet just happened to be the player with the ball at the time. I watched it, stupefied, not knowing how to react – like the barman, I imagine, who caught [*name removed on legal advice*] whipping out his sexual organ in a crowded pub and urinating into a pint glass to save himself the walk to the toilets.

I have to say, though, I was surprised by Roy's mood when he arrived home that night. There was none of the usual whaling on himself. His attitude was that it had been necessary, that he was happy to sacrifice himself to make a point that needed to be made. And though I never usually enjoyed these Hydesian changes that came over his personality from time to time, I decided that for once Roy might have been right. The summer was over. They all needed to be told.

Happily, it was nine months before I heard Dylan's voice again.

It worked. Certainly in the first few weeks of the season. Beckham, Scholes and Giggs were playing some of the best football of their lives and Teddy Sheringham, who had flirted with the idea of moving on that summer, was scoring goals – as Gary Neville pointed out when we ran into him one night, coming out of a chip shop in Salford, still wiping away the gravy splashes that had adhered to his face with the back of his hand – 'for fun'.

The other good news was that Jaap Stam got injured in August and wouldn't be back until after Christmas.

'Doctors make mistakes,' I told Roy, who often had trouble

seeing the silver lining for the clouds. 'He might be out for the whole season.'

This earned me one of his famous beady stares. Roy thought I was fixated with the man and, well, he might have had a point.

United scored seventeen goals in four games that September – yes, I was still contributing advice and observations – and I knew that once again there was no one in England strong enough to stop them winning a third league in succession.

Arsenal had opted for another gap year by selling Emanuelle Petit and Marc Overmars. Chelsea dumped Gianluca Vialli after a poor start and were already too far adrift. Gerard Houllier seemed hellbent on delivering Liverpool back to a time before football tactics were invented, with his hoof-it-long-and-live-in-hope style. And Leeds United were about to start a slow process of unravelling. A teenager had been found beaten up in Leeds city centre and two of their players were about to stand trial. Whatever the outcome, I sensed, with my nose for these things, that it was the beginning of the end for O'Leary's 'babies', as he cloyingly referred to them. (The average age of a Leeds first team player, by the way, was twenty-three.)

It was the beginning of the end for someone else, too. I remember I was in the front garden one morning that September, nosing through some rubbish bags that Roy had carried down to the gate in anticipation of the bin lorry arriving. There were some carrot peelings in one of them that interested me. I was tugging at the plastic when I spotted, through the bars of the gate, an anxious-looking figure loitering outside on Bankhall Lane, wearing a sheepskin coat, a beanie hat and so much gold around his neck that he could have been the mayor of any Russian town. He seemed agitated and a full minute must have passed before I recognised that it was Dwight Yorke.

I caught his eye and he flashed a smile at me. Jesus, he had a set of teeth on him that would give a Tibetan mastiff pause for thought.

'Alright . . .' he said by way of a greeting, then he paused, as if searching his memory for something. I wouldn't imagine it was the first time he'd forgotten a female's name. I didn't take offence. I turned and trotted back to the house.

'Dwight Yorke's outside,' I said.

Roy was sitting at the desk in his study, thumbing through his dictionary of quotations, as he was wont to do with an hour or two to kill, filling the margins with his own scribbled thoughts.

He looked up. 'Yorkie?'

'Yeah.'

'You're saying the lad's here?'

'He's outside the gate.'

'Did he say what he wants?'

'Er, no. He didn't talk to me at all.'

For the sake of context, I should mention that Roy tended to treat home visits from his teammates like some of the Liverpool team of the nineties regarded training. It was an unwelcome intrusion into his life. He got up from his desk and I followed him outside. He didn't open the gates, I remember, just talked to him through the vertical bars.

'Alright, Yorkie?'

'Alright, Skip?'

I might have mentioned it already, but Roy had a soft spot for Dwight that he found difficult to conceal.

'What the fuck are you doing here?' he asked. 'And obviously that's not meant to sound disrespectful.'

If Dwight had a little stump speech prepared, the words deserted him in that moment. The poor guy struggled to get beyond the first syllable. 'I . . . I . . .'

'What is it, Yorkie?'

Then he blurted it out. 'I want to play for Man United, Skip!

And that was when the tears started coming. Now, Roy was as comfortable around crying men as Dwight was with the idea of a quiet night in.

'Jesus Christ,' he said, 'what the fuck are you crying for?'

'Like I said before . . .'

'You want to play for Manchester United. I heard you. What are you doing at *my* house?'

'At the end of the day,' he said, wiping his cheeks with his open palm, 'you're a massive player, who's obviously one of *the* main reasons, if not the main reason, why we've done so tremendously well over the years . . .'

'Jesus, Yorkie.'

'Immense is the word you always hear used. I was hoping you might have a word with obviously the gaffer.'

Dwight had recently been dropped from the team. All of my fears about the way he'd been living his life had been realised in a bevy of tabloid newspaper headlines. Dwight enjoyed having sex with beautiful women, a considerable number of whom just happened to enjoy talking to reporters.

Actually, can I make a point here – not about Dwight, but about footballers in general? What is this thing they have for Page Three models? (Debbie, with daddy issues, from Halifax.) They never seem to wise-up to the fact that Page Three models like to get their photos in the newspapers – preferably on Page Three. You could say their lives depend on it. Yet these footballers still march on in there – '*Wanna see what I was 'angin' out the back of last night – she was only a fackin model!*' – as dumbly as a mouse who can't spot the trap for the smell of the bacon rind. Then a day or two later, they were reading a deconstruction of their performance and, very often, a disappointing rating out of ten in a national newspaper. '*Ere, she's only gone and sold me dahn the fackin rivah. They've gone and had a field day ere!*'

Sorry. Roy always loved that little routine when I did it for him.

But back to Dwight. He'd been pushing his luck for a while. The previous season, even as he kept up his high goals-per-game average, I heard that Alex Ferguson had told him, 'You're failing.'

But he didn't listen. He didn't get it. He never got it. So Ferguson dropped him. And Dwight, the poor, lovable lug, was heartbroken. I mean, genuinely heartbroken. He could have sat around, collecting his wages and sulking like other players I could mention but won't. Ah, what the hell – William Gallas, Nicholas Anelka, Dimitar Berbatov. But that wasn't Dwight. No, this was more his style. Turning up on Roy's doorstep, with his heart exposed, like a wayward husband desperate for just one more chance.

'Yorkie,' Roy said, 'you're talking to the wrong man. Speak to the manager.'

'I've spoken to him, Skip. But you know what he's like. At the end of the day, if you cross him – it's well documented – there's no way back.'

Roy's voice was calm and measured. 'Yorkie,' he said, 'you're still a top, top goalscorer. I think I've said from day one that you were an exceptional acquisition and you've gone on to prove your quality since then. The treble year – obviously phenomenal. But for me, you haven't exactly covered yourself in glory with maybe your attitude, which obviously isn't good enough at this level . . .'

'I've always given a hundred and ten percent where it matters.'

'And obviously your lifestyle.'

'End of the day, though, to be fair, it's never affected my ability to score goals for the football club.'

'It's affecting it now – because you're not in the fucking team! The manager's talked to you about it. Turning up late to training – all the rest of it. You didn't listen. Not interested. In one ear, out the other. And now you turn up at *my* door, crying your fucking eyes out . . . You're on about, you want to play for Manchester United. Blah, blah, blah.'

I watched Yorke's fingers curl around the upright bars of the gate. There was desperation in his voice. 'Is there a way back, Skip? End of the day, that's all I want to know. Is there a way back for me?'

I could see that Roy's heart was breaking.

'Of course there's a way back. Too fucking right there's a way back. You put your fucking head down and you work. You don't go storming out of fucking training – you didn't do yourself too many favours there doing that.'

'I was upset.'

'That's neither here nor there. Whether you're upset or not means absolutely nothing. Get a fucking hug off someone. At the end of the day, the only thing that's important is what's best for the football club.'

'I know that,' he said morosely.

'As I said before, put your head down. It's a long season, Yorkie. There'll be injuries. There'll be chances.'

Dwight nodded tightly, dabbed at his wet cheeks and his streaming nose with the back of his hand, then turned and shuffled – a broken man – back to his white Lamborghini Diablo.

While Dwight was frozen out, Teddy Sheringham and Andy Cole – I'm still not calling him Andrew – formed the most peculiar front partnership in football – peculiar because, as I've already mentioned, they didn't talk to each other. Even more bizarrely, it worked. I mean, it was compelling to watch.

I asked Roy about it. I confess, I was fascinated by it. We were walking back from The Park Dry Cleaners, I remember, lengthening our stride halfway up Arthog Road, as we often did, for the final hill before home. It was the first day that Roy let me walk without the aid of the lead and halter.

'Goes back to the time Coley made his debut for obviously

England,' Roy said. 'Came on for Teddy. Second-half substitute. Coley says Teddy didn't wish him well . . . Triggs, don't even think about picking that up . . . Anyway, they just never got along from that moment on.'

It was a chip bag, if you must know, and I was only sniffing it.

'But why has Alex Ferguson never banged their heads together?' I asked, catching him up.

It seemed a reasonable enough question. Roy popped his bottom lip out and shook his head. 'It's not important that they get along, at the end of the day – as long as they're both professional enough not to let it affect them out on the pitch where it obviously matters.'

And in that moment, I thought – like he was no doubt thinking – that if Teddy and Andy could work together, then maybe Roy and Mick could, too.

I was surprised at Alex Ferguson for not getting on top of it, though. He never usually left these things to chance. But then I was still only learning the oceanic depths of his cleverness. What would be achieved by trying to force a détente between them? No one told Teddy what to do. And Andy, it seemed to me, could hold a grudge like no man since Sinatra. But if enjoying Teddy's respect meant that much to Andy, then the partnership might, in a perverse way, work.

That was how I read it anyway.

Ferguson was the most masterful manipulator of people and situations I've ever known. I mean, you didn't think he and his good friend Alastair Campbell bonded over a shared love of vintage Fords and Thai fusion cooking, do you? No, it was because one looked at the other and saw himself reflected back in his eyes. And one thing they certainly had in common was that they both knew how to get people to do their bidding. In Ferguson's case, I saw an example of it that winter that was so masterful that even now, as I think about it, I find myself having to sit down.

I could sense the frustration gathering again in Roy as my assessment of United going into the season began to look more and more accurate. They lost to Arsenal, although that didn't matter so much – they'd be gone from the race by the time the evenings lengthened again, I was sure of that.

No, it was the defeat to PSV Eindhoven in the Champions League at the end of September that really shocked Roy. My warnings about Mark van Bommel's brilliant awareness of space – which I'd picked up watching a DVD that Roy brought home from the club – as well as Mateja Kezman's quickness of thought, were borne out.

'A bad night at the office,' was Roy's effort to put a positive twist on it as we were crossing the railway tracks on the way into Hale a day or two later. But PSV were by some considerable distance the better team that night – and they weren't even that good themselves. I hated repeating myself. But when Anderlecht did the same thing to them a month later, Roy had no choice but to accept the veracity of what I'd been telling him – United were falling behind the rest of Europe.

It wasn't long after that that Alex Ferguson called to the house. It was a Sunday morning in early November. I was still in bed. I hadn't had a good night. Ole Gunnar Solskjær was back, tormenting my nights.

'Of coursh I shtill feel that I have a role to play at the football club. I'm shure the manacher wouldn't have me here if he didn't think I could shtill contribute. Even if thatsh coming on ash a shubshtitute, thatsh shomeshing I will gladly do.'

It was no surprise that I needed a lie-in.

The hallway seemed to swell with voices, as it always did when Ferguson called around. There was a lot of loud and garrulous chat about the weather and the case for a second ring-road for Manchester and the improvements that Roy had made to the place since the last time he was here. They stepped into the kitchen. I heard Alex ask after me.

'No Triggs?' he said. Which was nice.

'Still asleep,' Roy said. 'She's a bit quiet today. Doesn't seem like herself.'

'That'll be the time of year.'

'Probably is.'

'No, I won't have coffee, Roy.'

'What about tea?'

'I won't have anything, thanks. Is that cobblelock you've got out the front there, Roy?'

'Er, it is, yeah. As I've said in the past, it's much easier to maintain than obviously the grass.'

'Aye, you don't have to cut it for one thing.'

'Yeah, no, you just need to maybe power-hose it down once a year. You'd have to say – take a bow.'

'Might look into it myself. Don't want to be still pushing a lawnmower around in my old age, do I?'

There was a long moment of silence, as if Alex was building up to say something but wanted to make sure the phrasing was right.

'I'm finishing up, Roy.'

There was no response. I could only presume that Roy was in as much shock as I was.

'Aye, finishing up,' he repeated. 'Retirement – know?'

'I didn't think you'd *ever* retire,' Roy said. He had his brave face on – I could tell that even from the laundry room. 'I thought you were planning to go on forever.'

'Already feels like I'm doing it forever. Aye, fourteen years is a long time. Missed out on a lot of things, Roy. Time with my wife. Missed my kids growing up. I just think maybe it's time now to get my life back. Do the things that I've always wanted to do. Travel. Learn to play the piano.'

'The piano?'

I could tell from the upward cant of the final note what Roy thought of that.

'Well, who knows?'

'Will you obviously miss it?'

'Oh, I'll miss it alright. I just want to go out on my own terms – know? Don't want to be carried out of the dugout with a heart attack, like poor Jock Stein.'

'When are you going then?'

'Well, my contract runs out the end of *next* season. I'll see it out out. But I'll not sign another one.'

The end of next season? That was still eighteen months away. I wondered was Roy thinking what I was thinking – about the wisdom of making an issue of it now. Could he exercise the same control over players if they knew he'd be out the door in a year and a half?

'Well, just to remind you,' Ferguson said, as if reading my thoughts, 'I'm not gone yet. And I'm going to be very disappointed if I have to retire without winning the Champions League again. I dare say you feel the same way – eh, Roy?'

'Well, obviously – I've been saying it a lot of late – the Champions League is the ultimate prize. It's what a football club like Manchester United has got to set its sights on winning – obviously year in, year out.'

But United were in trouble. And Ferguson was worried. I could hear it in his tone. The defeats to PSV and Anderlecht had left United requiring a win against Dynamo Kiev to be sure of getting out of the first group phase.

'Things have fallen a bit flat,' Ferguson said. 'Do you not think so, Roy?'

'With the players?'

'No, just the air around the club. What – nearly ten years of success now, the supporters are maybe taking us a wee bit for granted.'

Roy and I had already talked about this. Twice after watching United that season, I had to ask him to check whether the volume on the television required adjusting, so tranquil was the atmosphere at Old Trafford.

'No,' Roy told me when he'd finished fiddling with the remote, 'the fans are always like that until they see maybe two or three goals go in.'

'You'd have wonder sometimes,' Ferguson said, 'have we got the balance right between the real fans and what you'd call the corporate supporters?'

'What do you mean by obviously the corporate supporters?' Roy said.

'It's just, you know, they're up there in the boxes. They're eating their miniature prawn varuvals and their Stilton and chutney rarebit bites. Drinking the Bollinger – you know? And then they go out to their seats. And because they don't know the first thing about football, they think it's all about how many goals they see scored . . . Er, maybe I will have that coffee after all, Roy.'

How naïve did I turn out to be? Because I had no idea what Ferguson had been up to until the night of the Dynamo Kiev match.

If you want my opinion, by the way, the vapid atmosphere around Old Trafford had nothing to do with United's corporate fans. They were only a tiny percentage of the gate.

No, the problem, I realised, was the so-called ordinary fans. You only had to look at the number of camera flashes going off in the crowd to realise how much of the ground was taken up by day-trippers, who went to one or two matches a year and expected to see a decent return in goals.

Well, they didn't get it against Kiev. United were a stuttering mess. They managed to bundle one goal over the line before it almost ended in calamity, when Georgi Demetradze stole in – 'Tell Wes Brown to watch Demetradze's late runs,' I told Roy at least three times – but somehow turned the ball wide from five yards out.

Despite my unflinching loyalty to Roy – all I ever wanted in life was to see him happy – I did wonder whether it might have been better in the long run if Demetradze had put the ball the other side of the post. The loss in Champions League revenue would have forced the board to do something. Instead, they were content to just plod on with the players they had.

I saw a spark of something in Roy's eyes when he was interviewed after the match. I realised he had something that he wanted to get off his chest.

'Sometimes you wonder, do they understand the game of football?' he said, referring to the fans. 'We're one-nil up, then there are one or two stray passes and they're getting on players' backs. It's just not on. At the end of the day, they need to get behind the team. Away from home, our fans are fantastic. I'd call them the hardcore fans. But at home, they have a few drinks and probably the prawn sandwiches and they don't realise what's going on out on the pitch.'

I laughed out loud, I must confess. He couldn't think of the word varuvals, so he said sandwiches instead. That was very much a footballer thing – if in doubt, put it between two pieces of bread. And Roy wasn't the most adventurous eater in the world, chicken and pasta being the usual standby. Once, I persuaded him to try farfale instead of penne and I'll never forget the look on his face as he cooked it – he looked like he was enriching uranium.

Prawn sandwiches indeed! Yes, we had a good laugh about it when it made the papers for days afterwards. Roy's scathing attack on football's corporate culture. It took me a good twenty-four hours before I realised what a masterstroke it had been from Ferguson. You see, he understood class politics and he knew what the outcome was going to be. Being a corporate fan was suddenly akin being a holocaust denier. No one wanted to be identified as one. So everyone started making noise again, even if the football didn't always demand it.

And the genius of the trick was that no one even saw Ferguson's lips move.


*Today is a good day. One of our better ones. I have a kind of giddy awareness of myself.*

*We're out worrying the roads again in the lurid sunlight of a November afternoon. It's two nights since Guy Fawkes and there's still a faint wraith of charred wood in the air. We've always loved this time of year. The first week of November was when the league table resolved itself into something that made sense. You knew what kind of a contest you were going to be facing come the spring, if there was going to be a contest at all.*

*It'll be dark in an hour, but there's no suggestion of us turning for home yet.*

*Ipswich beat Sheffield United yesterday, their second win in seven days after the 2–0 victory over Millwall last weekend. From bottom half of the table to sixth in the measure of a week.*

*That's something I remember from his first season managing Sunderland – how two or three good results in this division can change the entire complexion of a season. A lot of fair to middling teams, you see. He took Sunderland from a relegation placing to promotion as champions in much less than a full season. All it takes is a good run.*

*A good run and a good walk. We give each other a sideways look. He smiles. Yes, a look was all we ever needed to say everything we ever wanted to say.*

## 11.

# Hup Haaland Hup!

SANDWICHES WERE FAST BECOMING A THEME OF that 2000/1 season. There were the prawn ones that Roy imagined the corporate crowd were noshing on in the sterile little greenhouses where they gathered to ignore the football. And then there were the cheese ones that he was served an hour before Ireland played Holland that September. He wasn't happy about that one. In fact, he till hadn't calmed down by the time he came home from Amsterdam.

'At the end of the day, Triggs, you heard me,' he said, his voice reaching up into the sonic range, 'in that kitchen out there, tell Mick McCarthy the kind of the things that players should be eating before we got out and play a football match. You're on about chicken, pasta, obviously cereal . . .'

I was enjoying a documentary about the sixty-five-day search for James Earl Ray, the man who assassinated Martin Luther King, but now Roy was standing between me and the television.

'I said it to him, Triggs. I said, "Mick, do you think Jimmy Floyd Hasselbaink is eating cheese fucking sandwiches?" One or two of the lads rang room service in the hotel. They were fucking starving! Ordered pizza. Two hours before a World Cup qualifying match and they're eating fucking pizza!'

Yes, I pulled all the right faces, but Roy understood my position. It wasn't even like I'd made a secret of it. I was against the idea of him playing for Mick McCarthy while the issues of submission and dominance remained unresolved. Because much as I was devoted to Roy, cheese sandwiches were not the real issue here, even if he couldn't see it himself.

The match had finished 2–2. I didn't watch it. It wasn't that I wasn't interested. Idina, who was back from nursing her sister in Wales – smoking more and weighing less than before she went away – switched the television on for me. The problem was that Holland were wearing orange and dogs see orange and green as the same colour. It was like regarding the world through six inches of glass – the action on the screen as unfathomable to me as Gerard Houllier's decision a couple of years later to spend £20m on El Hadji Diouf, Salif Diao and Bruno 'The New Zidane' Cheyrou. The more I tried to concentrate on the figures on the screen, the more my head hurt, so I retired to my basket in the kitchen and slept.

'Shame, Lover, you not wanting to see the match,' Idina told me later. 'Ireland (*Island*, she pronounced it) did very well.'

That was at sharp variance to Roy's own view, which was that they'd squandered two points. They were two goals ahead halfway through the second half, then allowed Holland to come back and equalise.

Mick was happy with a point. 'If you'd offered me that at six o'clock this evening, I'd have had your hand off,' is what he, well, almost certainly said.

Roy was seething. It was always difficult to convince him that the glass was half-full when he could plainly see that it was half-empty. I gave up on ever finding out how they caught James Earl Ray.

'Should have been three points in the bag,' he said. 'Except now you've got the likes of Mick saying it's a positive result. Blah, blah, blah. People saying you don't come to Amsterdam expecting to beat the Dutch in their own backyard. You're never going to fucking win if that's your attitude! They said the same about Manchester United going off to play Juventus in obviously the Stadio delle Alpi. Never won in Italy before. I said, what the fuck does that matter? It's just two football teams playing against each other.'

He sat down on the sofa beside me. I edged closer to him, sought the awning of his armpit. He draped his arm around my shoulder, his agitated fingers teasing my coat.

'*The art of losing isn't hard to master,*' he said.

'Yes,' I said.

'And the Dutch were gone, Triggs. When Jason McAteer scored the second, you could see it in their eyes. Weren't up for it. Then we give them a goal – a silly goal to give away, especially at this level – and they suddenly fancy their chances. Then obviously Giovanni von Bronckhorst has a go, beats Shay all ends up and we're suddenly celebrating a draw. Celebrating? It's fucking typical of the Irish. Nearly prefer the moral victory. And we all go off and get pissed – people slapping each other's backs – celebrating a draw that should have been a win, except we don't have the belief and obviously the moral courage to finish the job.'

This, by the way, was a full twenty-four hours after the event. I remember thinking, if this is the way he was talking in Amsterdam, I know what the other players will have been thinking. They'll have been thinking: which of these two men is in charge?

It wouldn't be overstating the case to say that I came to dread his trips away with the Ireland team, which seemed to serve no purpose other than to increase his sense of frustration with the world.

A month later, Ireland drew 1–1 with Portugal in Lisbon. I saw the highlights later on and considered it a good result, especially given the clear shortfall in class between the teams. But when he got home, Roy was like a bear just out of hibernation. Uttered not a word to me during the drive from

Cheadle to Hale, then, once he'd pulled into the driveway, insisted on going for a walk before we'd even entered the house. I wasn't going to argue, having always believed in the restitutive value of stretching one's legs.

So off we set. Half-eight on a wet October morning. Down Bankhall Lane. Roy laid his left hand on the top bar of the stile and jumped clean over it. I went under and soon we were descending the narrow trail to the Bollin. It had rained heavily overnight and two or three times he almost lost his footing in the glutinous mud. We reached the river and he sat on a fallen bough, with me at his feet, listening to the urgent murmur of the water for a long time before a single word was spoken.

'Obviously a bit wound up,' he said, squeezing the folds of skin at my withers. He knew I liked that.

I came straight to the point. 'You don't like him,' I said, 'and he doesn't like you . . .'

'Obviously, as I've said in the past, that shouldn't matter.'

'But it does matter. Look at you. I just don't see how this thing can work.'

'Well, it's not Mick I've a problem with, at the end of the day. It's the set-up.'

'What do you mean, the set-up?'

'The officials – obviously the FAI – sitting in first class, while the players are sitting back in economy with the press and the fans. Listen, I'm not asking for special treatment. These are things that obviously at club level you take for granted. Then you travel with the Ireland set-up and there's big Niall – Jesus! – folding himself in fucking half to try to fit into a seat. And up in first class you've got some lad in a suit who doesn't know the first thing about the game.'

I didn't say anything, just sat and watched the current froth on the rocks of the riverbed.

'Then obviously the training ground. I've said that to you

in the past. It's a fucking disgrace. You know, you're on about players running the risk of maybe getting injured.'

After ten or fifteen minutes of this kind of talk, he admitted that Mick *had* in fact annoyed him in Lisbon by suggesting that he act a bit chummy with him in front of the cameras. Okay, maybe Mick did care too much about what the press thought of him. But wasn't it part of the deal they struck that day in our kitchen, that they'd present at least the outward impression of being on the same side?

'You're not saying anything,' he said.

'You know how I feel.'

'Jesus, not the two pack leaders thing again. That might be the case with dogs, Triggs. But we're not dogs. And at the end of the day, me and Mick both want the same thing, which is for Ireland to qualify for the World Cup finals.'

And that's where we left it.

The year turned. In the spring, Ireland went to Cyprus. I watched the match from Idina's sofa. Her sister, Elsie – an older woman, stout, with pendulous jowls and grey hair set in a sort of dandelion puffball style – had come from Rhyl to stay and was more than a little put out to be told that she couldn't have the television.

'Triggs is watching the football, aren't you, Lover?'

The skin folds on Elsie's neck shook incredulously. 'But I've got all my programmes.'

Idina blew a trumpet of cigarette smoke out of the side of her mouth. 'Don't touch that remote control, Elsie. I mean it.'

'But it's *Family Fortunes*!'

'She likes watching *him*. Oh, she'll sit like that for the whole match. And when *he* comes on the screen, she gives a tiny little bark. Well, it's not so much a bark as a huff . . .'

'You know what your problem is, Dina – you never had kids.'

'I don't see what my not having kids has to do with anything . . . There! Did you hear that? *Huff!* I think it's sweet!'

'There's always been a want in you. So will you meet him then?'

'Who?'

'Hugh.'

'Who the bloody hell is Hugh?'

'I've told you three times. He's an uncle of Janis, my daughter-in-law. I told you – his wife died a few months ago. He lives in Stalybridge.'

'Good for him.'

'There's no harm in meeting him, is there?'

'Jesus, Elsie! I'm too old to be set up.'

'You're not *being* set up.'

'Why am I meeting him then?'

'For, well, for friendship.'

'I'm too old to be making new friends.'

'If you're not careful, Idina, you're going to die a lonely old woman. And you won't be found for weeks. Bloody dogs will have eaten your face. Don't laugh. You read about it all the time.'

'That's cats.'

Idina was right, by the way. It is cats. But then Elsie was right about it never being too late in life to make new friends. I couldn't get into it, though. There was a match on.

It seems odd to talk about a team labouring to a 4–0 victory, but that was what happened that night. The only memorable thing about the match were the two sets of backing vocals that echoed around the largely silent stadium, urging the Ireland players to wake up. One was loud and industrial and very north of England, the other mellifluous and permanently outraged and unmistakably Cork.

It might have sounded like Roy and Mick were on the same side, but by then their relationship was all subtext. Roy had done a newspaper interview with a journalist called Paul Kimmage and gone public with most of the things he'd told me about the set-up. Even the cheese sandwich episode enjoyed a reprise. Well, the FAI boys were so in awe of Roy that they immediately offered up their premium seats to the players. A small victory, but then you had to wonder, at what cost?

If you want my opinion – and, God knows, Roy heard it enough times over the years – that was the real end of the affair. Forget what happened in Saipan a year later. The faultlines were drawn from the moment that Mick was so publicly undermined.

I did say it to Roy when he arrived home from Cyprus. He was vacuuming dog hairs from the back seat of the car with a little hand-held device he'd picked up in Dixons Travel at Manchester Airport.

'Isn't it, em, Mick's job to demand better treatment for his players?' I wondered casually. Don't get me wrong. I was on Roy's side. He was never in any doubt about that. The little motor died.

'I know what you're getting at, Triggs,' he said. 'Obviously, by saying what I said, you think I made Mick look maybe small.'

'Well, I know you didn't do it deliberately.'

'We spoke about training on shit pitches. We spoke about travelling in steerage. Jesus Christ, Triggs. You heard me say it to Mick, at the end of the day – inside in the kitchen there. Nothing changed. I'm the captain of my country. I'm entitled to bring it up. I don't have to just go along with it. Only dead fish go with the flow, Triggs.'

This was a piece of fridge-magnet philosophy he'd picked up from somewhere and no doubt you remember him quoting it in various interviews over the year that followed. The big joke – shared by those of us who watch a lot of Discovery – was that it wasn't even true. Atlantic salmon, for example, allow the current to do almost all of the work for them when they're travelling to the ocean from the freshwater streams of their birth. Sometimes, just going with the flow is the sensible thing to do. I was always surprised that Mick, who was a keen angler, never pulled Roy up on that point.

'It's just, I'm thinking about the *realpolitik* of the situation,' I said.

'The what?' he said.

'People are going to be asking, who's really leading this team?'

'What people?'

'Well, Mick McCarthy for one. You don't think he's asking himself the question?'

He dismissed me with a shake of his head. 'We're on the same side, Triggs!'

Naturally, everyone wanted to believe that. A few weeks later, Ireland drew with Portugal again, this time in Dublin. I decided to park my reservations and get on with my job, which after all was serving Roy. I had watched the highlights of a number of Portugal's recent games and noticed that they were slow to pick up players at set pieces.

It is with all due modesty, naturally, that I point out that Roy scored Ireland's goal directly from a quick throw-in while the minds of the Portuguese defence were elsewhere. You'll never see a dog do *that* on *Britain's Got Talent*.

Roy was outstanding that day. I regard it as one of the five greatest performances of his career. And to top it all off, he even managed to pick up a booking, which meant he was suspended for the next match and didn't have to travel with the team – in business class – to Estonia the following day. That meant I got home from Cheadle three days earlier than expected. Everyone was a winner. And everyone seemed to believe that Ireland could continue with two men believing themselves to be in charge. I knew better. But for now, I had to just bite my tongue.

*It's amazing how attuned you can become to the noises of an empty house. I listen to the purring of the fridge, the muffled sound of the television playing some old classic match from the 1990s, the noise of the automatic central heating like some distant applause, while I await the sound of his key in the door.*

*Ipswich lost to Derby County this afternoon. A bad defeat. Two-nil at home. I saw Roy interviewed this evening, his face failing to filter his frustration.*

*'I keep saying it that it's consistency that wins you promotion,' he said, 'and that's what we've been maybe lacking of late. Winning one or two, then obviously losing one or two. It's not good enough, even though Derby are on a bit of a run, and their tails are obviously up. But I think I said it last week after we beat Sheffield United, it's important that we don't get carried away on the basis of obviously one or two results. We weren't all patting ourselves on the back a week ago and – as I said – we're not going to start panicking now.'*

*I hear the front door open, then his footsteps gather in the hallway outside. I don't even get the chance to stand up. He's suddenly hunkered over me, petting me rigorously, looking at me with the same joyful expression that he's always kept for me, saying, 'Are you going to tell me what to do, Triggs? Huh? Are you going to maybe tell me what to do?'*


Reflecting maturely on those times, as I'm apt to do now, I realise that it was a good thing that Roy had Ireland to distract him from the monotony of life at Manchester United. I have to admit it was hard for either of us to get excited about the Premier League. 'Piss-poor,' was Roy's view of the opposition United went through the motions of beating every week. Sunderland. Aston Villa. Ipswich. Middlesbrough. Charlton. Leicester. There was a workmanlike dullness to it all. When you're not being challenged, every job begins to feel like punching rivets into sheet metal.

Fabien Barthez was so bored, he started introducing little comic turns into every performance. He was like that. Barthez hated having nothing to do because he couldn't bear not being the centre of attention. He'd take throw-ins. Dribble the ball around centre-forwards. Try out the left-back position for size. He was – in the popular parlance – taking the piss. Everyone was taking the piss. Sixteen points clear with twelve weeks of the season to go, they could well afford to.

I must admit, I began to feel a bit redundant around that time. I remember offering Roy one or two observations about Oleg Luzhny before United played Arsenal that February and seeing his eyes glaze over, like David James when he was receiving a back pass. Difficult as it was for me to admit, United didn't need my help to beat the next-best side in England anymore.

I don't think I've ever seen a good team so effortlessly eviscerated as Arsenal were that day. It finished 6–1, but as everyone seemed to point out, it could have been twice that. Dwight Yorke was back, briefly, in Ferguson's good books – fulfilling the promise that Roy had made him through the gates that day – and he scored a brilliant first-half hat-trick. He even delivered a thank-you pass for Roy to score the fourth. I was pleased for him. I remember Roy, his face illuminated by a hundred watt smile, screaming, 'You're back! You're back!' at him after Dwight scored, I think, his third goal.

There was a kindness in Roy that was too seldom acknowledged. What he didn't know yet was that Dwight had invited the glamour model Jordan to the match and, with her, all the media fascination that attended these celebrity couplings. Every time he did something good on the field, the television cameras sought her out in the stand, with her honey-coloured hair and her bee-stung lips and her breasts that weighed the equivalent of a couple of Nicky Butts.

That's what I meant when I said Dwight just didn't get it.

Arsène Wenger was asked afterwards if he thought the league was now over. He gave one of those peculiarly French shrugs that required no further elaboration. 'It was over long before today,' he said.

Smart man, Wenger, even if, for all the players and money at his disposal, he failed to provide United with a consistent rivalry year-on-year.

Roy, I think, felt bad about the blithe way he'd dismissed my observations about Luzhny, who *did* lack pace, by the way – I stand by that. He said as much while we were stretching our legs the following day.

'Arsenal – I think I've said it once or twice of late – their defence was allowed to grow old together without players being maybe replaced.'

'It's true,' I said. 'And it's cost them.'

'*Sanctification is not regeneration.*'

'Er, yes,' I said. 'I suppose that's true.'

I was urinating against the gatepost of the Altringham United Reformed Church on Cecil Road.

'Obviously I was delighted for Yorkie,' he said. 'I think getting the first one obviously early doors helped his confidence. Although when you've got Jordan sitting in the fucking stand looking at you, you shouldn't have any problems in that regard!'

If there was disapproval in his tone, I couldn't pick it out.

'Dwight just keeps missing the point,' I said. 'He knows what Ferguson thinks of his lifestyle. He gives him another chance and then . . .'

'He scored a hat-trick, Triggs – full credit.'

'But if you take your job seriously, you don't go bringing your new girlfriend to work with you. It didn't work for John Lennon and he was a genius.'

Roy loved that one. Like I said, we laughed at the same things.

He had a switch in his hand, which he swung by his side as we walked towards Hale in a blaze of late winter sunshine and the conversation turned to Europe. Yesterday's result was already forgotten. That was always the way with Roy.

'People,' he said, 'getting carried away with obviously the Arsenal result. Best team the manager's ever had – blah, blah, blah . . .'

That had been Alex Ferguson's judgment the previous day. I tended more towards Roy's view that this team enjoyed its best days in 1999 and had been getting worse ever since.

'I'll tell you something, Triggs, I think it's time the manager broke this team up and maybe started again.'

'Do you mean that?'

'I do. We spoke about that quote before – *man cannot discover new oceans unless he has the courage to lose sight of the shore.*'

I said nothing.

'You know the point I'm trying to make, Triggs? It's easy to turn it on against the likes of Ipswich and obviously Leicester. I mean, Leicester! Jesus. Scoring maybe a hatful of goals. But no one's learning anything. It's no kind of preparation for the teams we're facing in Europe.'

He was right. There was a very pronounced difference between their performances on the two fronts. That winter and spring, they drew three successive Champions League group games – away to Panathinaikos, and home and away to Valencia. Three matches that they were never in danger of losing and never in danger of winning. Two hundred and seventy minutes of anodyne nothingness. What it meant was that they qualified from their group as runners-up. Their penance was a harder quarter-final draw. It was Bayern Munich.

According to Roy, they were all rolling their eyes at the club when they heard the news. Roy wanted it, though. They hadn't played a decent team since Real Madrid put them out a year ago. This would shake them from their torpor. 'How can you win the European Cup,' he said – and by that time it had become a kind of battle cry for him – 'without beating obviously the best teams in the competition? Jesus Christ, we haven't played anyone up until now.'

I threw myself into my work, immersing myself in Channel 4's Bundesliga highlights programme, then later DVDs of three or four of Bayern's Champions League group games. I didn't think they'd improved that much in the two years since United last beat them. It was largely the same team, functioning around the brilliant midfield pairing of Steffen Effenberg and Jens Jeremies.

Three days before the first leg, United lost 2–0 to Liverpool. I have to confess I didn't watch it. It was a beautiful day so I slept late, then took a rawhide bone outside and went to work on it, with the fresh smells of spring in my nostrils.

Looking back now, perhaps, without even realising it, I'd fallen into the same complacent trap as everyone else. I didn't think the match at all important. I knew that Alex Ferguson would rest players and that Liverpool would probably win, playing the joyless, Neanderthal Age football that led them that season to a treble of trophies that, frankly, no one else seemed to care very much about winning.

It was a mistake. It was almost criminally negligent of me not to watch it. Not because I missed Liverpool closing the deficit to twenty points or whatever it happened to be, but because I didn't see how flat and insipid and utterly unprepared for the Bayern game United were.

Roy knew it.

'You've lost to Liverpool before,' I said. I thought I was talking sense. 'Like you've said in the past, beating United *is* Liverpool's season.'

'Triggs, they took us apart. Played us off the park. First to every ball. We spoke about hunger the other day – well, they had it. And the lad Steven Gerrard, who's obviously come through, he looks like he's going to be a player.'

I was unconvinced by Gerrard at that point in his career. Too often preferred the spectacular option to the sensible one, which was why, in my admittedly jaundiced view, he was no Roy Keane.

Roy was right about United's lack of hunger, though. I presumed too much in thinking that it would come right on the night. That the players would arrive at Old Trafford and feel that extra frisson that comes from big European nights. That they'd hear the urgency in the manager's final instructions, the Babel of different accents in the tunnel, the Champions League anthem, and suddenly be ready.

There were only five minutes played when I realised the truth of what Roy had been trying to tell me. There was no energy to United's play. No tempo. No ideas. Their heads didn't even look in it. Effenberg and Jeremies subjugated Roy and Paul Scholes without any apparent difficulty, while Mehmet Scholl caused mayhem playing just behind the Bayern front two of Elber and Carsten Jancker. Containment proved too big a job for United for them to even think about committing bodies to attack.

A couple of minutes from the end, Effenberg lifted a free-kick into the box, Linke was allowed to head it across the face of the goal and Paulo Sergio smashed it over the line. You could almost see the belief leave the United players in that moment. Late goals. Didn't that used to be *their* shtick?

'Told you,' Roy said the following day. He was cleaning out my ears in the kitchen, forcing the cotton wool deep inside with his index finger to clear out a build-up of a wax that I was sure was responsible for the dizzy spells I'd recently been suffering. 'Flat. No hunger. As I said before – gone.'

The temptation was to remind him that it wasn't over. To reach for the cliché to chivvy him along. It was only half-time. They beat Juventus in Turin, didn't they? They could beat Bayern in Munich. It would have been a lie, though. I knew it. And I knew he knew it. They weren't that team anymore.

'I'm including myself in that,' he said, examining the cotton wool on the point of his finger. 'I played shit. Jesus, these ears are filthy.'

He'd had his finger in there for about ten minutes.

'There's an operation that Labradors can have,' I said. 'To shorten the ear canals. Rolf Harris was talking about it on *Animal Hospital.* They do it in Salford.'

'What'd be the point of an operation?' he wanted to know.

'Well, I wouldn't get so many ear infections,' I said.

'Triggs, you've never *had* an ear infection, that's because I fucking clean them out obviously twice a week.'

I know he thought that this was a little attention grab on my part. But it was Roy I was thinking about. Money wasn't an issue for us like it was for other people. But he was still spending a small fortune on lotions, drops and cleaning fluids. *And* medical bills. There'd been one or two occasions – five or six, if I'm being strictly honest – when I'd insisted on him running me to the vets, convinced I had a bacterial or fungal infection. I never did, as it happens, which explains his touchiness whenever the subject of my ears came up.

He navigated the conversation back to what happened against Bayern Munich. 'We've been sucked down by the Premiership,' he said. 'Playing rubbish teams week after week, it drags your own game down. We're too predictable. But we keep kidding ourselves that we're in competition with the likes of Real Madrid, Juventus. Obviously Bayern. It's just talk. Fooling ourselves. *If you do what you've always done, you'll get what you've always gotten.* We're going out there hoping these teams are going to have maybe a bad day.'

They won the league in the oddly flat fortnight between the two legs. Made the inevitable mathematically certain with a 4–2 win over Coventry.

'Yorkie bagged a brace,' Roy told me later, seeming more positive than he had been. This was often the way with him. All hope was lost, then he slowly came around. He was thinking about the Stadio delle Alpi in 1999. I knew it. 'It's one match,' he told me the night before he left for Munich. We were in the car on the way to Idina's place in Cheadle. 'All we need is an early goal and it's obviously honours-even.'

Now, I didn't want to sound a discordant note, but my feeling was that Ottmar Hitzfeld was too shrewd to lose to a team as predictable as United had become. And Yorke and Cole were no longer the irresistible force they had been in United's treble year.

'Tell Gary Neville to watch Michael Tarnat's runs down his flank,' I said. Beckham was suspended for the match. Ferguson, I understood from Roy, was toying with the idea of switching Scholes to the right and I knew he wouldn't offer much by way of defensive cover. 'Tell him to try to avoid getting sucked into the centre. Especially when Willy Sagnol is hitting those crossfield balls.' Then, just to be supportive, I added, 'An early goal, of course, would change the entire chemistry of the tie.'

An early goal did. Elber scored it for Bayern after only five minutes. And not for the first time it happened just as I saw it. Ryan Giggs stood off Willy Sagnol. Gary Neville got sucked inside and Sagnol hit a magnificent diagonal pass over his head to Tarnat, who crossed the ball for Elber to score.

Scholl scored a second before half-time. I couldn't believe the ease with which Jeremies beat Mikaël Silvestre down United's left. Or the jelly-hearted tentativeness of Wes Brown, who, I'd noticed, just from way he carried himself, had lost his confidence since the own goal he scored against Valencia in February. But that was it. Over for another year.

'Shush now! Shush!' I remember Idina saying to me. 'I don't know what's come over you tonight, Lover. Shush now!'

I'd apparently barked the entire way through Roy's post-match interview. I saw the stiff set of his mouth and the deliberate manner of his blinking and I knew that he was about say in public all of the things that we'd both been saying in private.

'We're not good enough,' he said. 'Obviously, it's hard to accept. But once again we haven't performed in Europe. Maybe it's time to break the team up. Maybe it's the end of the road for this group of players. And obviously I'm including myself in that.'

Looking back, I think the reason I was barking was pride.

By the time he arrived home from Munich, Roy was able to laugh about it – at least in his own grim way. You might remember that this was the night when a fan – dressed in the full United strip – ran onto the pitch and inveighed his way into the team photo. You might also remember that he chose to stand at the point furthest away from Roy. It was publicity he was after, not a summer in traction. Anyway, Roy was laughing about him.

'I should have asked him if he'd a pair of boots with him,' he said. 'He could have given me a fucking dig-out in midfield.'

'The club would have said he was out of their price range,' I said.

He laughed. 'That'd be right. That'd be right.'

I was worried about him, though. I was thinking, How much more frustration can this man take? There was nothing left to play for, but for the final weeks of the season the players had to go on punching the clock. Humans have a very good saying about the devil and idle hands.

It was out of nowhere one morning that he conjured up the name of Alfie Haaland. He emerged through the beaded curtain of the vegetable shop on Arthog Road – I was checking out some pheromone chemicals on the Plexiglas of the bus stop opposite – and said, 'See Haaland mouthing off again?'

I'd been encouraging him to book himself a holiday, to leave me with Idina for a week or two, or even in the kennels in Droylsden. It had been a stressful year for him. I'd been telling him about a seven-star hotel in Dubai that I saw advertised on the CNN Business channel. Every room had its own private bar and a piano.

'I think Giggsy's stayed there once or twice,' he said. 'Obviously Yorkie. Maybe Teddy. One or two others.'

He seemed quite enthused by the idea. Then suddenly he was muttering blackly about Alfie. I suddenly remembered that United were playing Manchester City that weekend. He must have seen a newspaper in the vegetable shop, I thought.

'What do you mean by mouthing off?' I said.

'*If Roy Keane is worried about the genuine fans, then he should think about maybe taking a paycut.*'

I laughed. 'You know what the papers are like. They'll have put those words in his mouth.'

Besides, it was months since he'd said it. In fact, it was before the last match between United and City. The newspaper had just reheated it for the week that was in it.

'He's got it fucking coming to him,' Roy said.

'Come on,' I said. 'What's that line you sometimes like to quote? A man only has so much energy – you must always ask yourself how much of it do you want to waste on this?'

'The guy's a fucking clown, Triggs.'

He turned for home. I had to run to keep up.

'He *is* a clown,' I said, 'but we already knew that. Come on, he's beneath you, Roy.'

I could discern the shape of the trouble to come that afternoon when I heard a harsh grating sound coming from the kitchen and I thought, either he's filled the food blender with gravel and switched it to the full speed setting or Bob

Dylan has found his way into our lives again. I wandered out to the kitchen and my worst fears were realised.

'A bit of Bob?' I said.

I thought I picked up a measure of guilt in his smile. 'Can't beat it, Triggs.'

*Curfew gulls and four-legged forest clouds and wicked birds of prey picking at his breadcrumb sins.* Jesus Christ. And they called him the heir to Rimbaud.

'Just forget about Alfie,' I said. 'Just, you know, take the high road, Roy.'

Of course, I might as well have been talking to the brickwork.

I still find it difficult to watch – hard as it was to avoid it at the time. Television is such an unforgiving medium. As the ball bobbled towards poor, unsuspecting Alfie, Roy's face betrayed his thoughts, which he later articulated in words: 'Take that, you cunt!'

The imagined debts of four years repaid in full with a stamp that could have snapped Alfie's leg like a burnt twig.

If you watch it back, you'll notice there was none of the usual pushing and shoving you expect to break out in these instances. Some kind of collective trauma seemed to fall on everyone. They all looked like they've been pulled from a burning building.

I expect I looked the same way.

On his way off the field, Roy made a quick detour to where Alfie was lying in a sorry bundle to get the last word in – as if he hadn't had it already.

Ryan Giggs, in his book, called it an 'over the top tackle' in that annoyingly effete way that footballers have of describing these things. His idea of over the top I wouldn't like to meet down a dark laneway in Moston at throwing-out time.

Roy didn't try any such nonsense with me when he got home. He came through the door, already apologising.

'I know,' he said, his palms spread in a submission display. 'I know, I know, I know,' and then he disappeared into his study, too ashamed of himself, I think, to even let me see his face.

But who was I to make him feel bad? Aggression is as much a part of the biochemistry of dogs as it is the biochemistry of professional footballers. And Roy had consistently stood by me after my various – let's just say – altercations with Ole Gunnar Solskjær, not all of which I've detailed in these pages. So I had to forgive him. It's what friends do.

A moment later, I poked my head around the study door. *The Encarta Book of Quotations* was on the desk in front of him and he was sliding the pages, looking for something that might make sense of what he'd done that afternoon.

'Walk?' I said.

I never saw a man get out of a chair so quickly.

Anyway, there was a postscript to this story. About a week later, I was in the garden at the back of the house, sniffing around the bins. As it happened, I'd developed a craving for turnip peelings – something about the taste or the texture – which I thought at first might have been a symptom of some underlying medical condition, such as anaemia, or lymphosarcoma, or inflammatory bowel disease, or even just a common-or-garden gastrointestinal maldigestive or malabsorptive disorder. I managed to knock the lid off the bin with my nose and there, covered in the remnants of last night's Chinese – sweet and sour pork with egg-fried rice – was his entire Bob Dylan CD collection.

I heard Roy's voice. I turned around to see him set in the centre of the doorframe.

'This hotel in Dubai,' he said, a holiday brochure folded between his two hands, 'it's got five swimming pools.'

# 12.

# A Halfwit Road Sweeper

ONE MORNING TOWARDS THE END OF AUGUST 2001, Roy woke me at an hour that was unnatural even for an animal hardwired by evolution to hunt in the predawn. Still groggy from sleep, I have no recollection of getting into the car. My first memory is of Roy slipping off the A538 onto the Airport Road, his knuckles tight in the ten and two position on the wheel.

The airport? I thought. It's not a Champions League week, is it? And has he forgotten to take me to Cheadle first?

But it wasn't a flight we were trying to catch. We pulled into the car park of the Radisson Manchester Airport Hotel and Roy stilled the engine. It was a dark and brooding morning and nothing sounded above the low, distant whisper of motorway traffic and the querulous grumbling of the occasional suitcase being pulled across the tarmacadam on its trolley wheels.

I was about to ask what on earth we were doing here when suddenly, through the front windscreen, I was looking at the hairless head and beaky features of the apparently once great — although I've never seen the evidence for this — Jaap Stam.

Roy pushed the button to open the electric window.

'Hello, Roy,' he said.

'Alright, Jaap,' came the reply.

Stam saw me in the back but we blanked each other.

'Who are you flying with?' Roy wondered.

'British Airways,' he said. 'Eight o'clock to London, then at 11.30am, a – how to say? – ur, *connection* to obviously Rome.'

Roy nodded profoundly, like this meant something to him. 'They're a top airline.'

'Yesh, I have flown with them many, many times in the pasht. You would have to shay quality. You would have to shay it.'

'Oh, no question. I think they've proved that over the years. Obviously, documented.'

There was a strange stiltedness about their manner. Roy's fingers fidgeted about the dash, while Stam just nodded at nothing.

'So anyway,' Roy said, 'I just wanted to wish you the best at obviously Lazio and say – speaking for myself – that, you know, obviously I'm sorry to see you go. For me, you're a top, top player, obviously a smashing lad . . .'

*Go*? Was I dreaming this?

'Thank you, Roy. Well, can I shay, for me, it hash been a privilege and an honour to play with you on the football pitch. You are obvioushly a tremendoush player and a tremendoush leader on the field. And I want to shay thank you to you for everything you did for me at the football club. For helping me to – how to shay? – shettle in, yes? You were great for me, at the end of the day.'

He thrust his hand through the window. Roy took it and pumped it thoroughly.

'We'll maybe have a drink,' Roy said, 'when Ireland play Holland in obviously Dublin.'

'Yesh, that would be very good.'

And with that, Jaap Stam was gone from our lives.

Well, almost.

A Prius dry-coughed to a halt a few yards away and Gary Neville was suddenly stalking towards us with his face all hagridden. 'Is it true?' he wanted to know. 'Is it true you've been sold to obviously Lazio?'

Stam gave him a curt nod. 'Yesh, it'sh true.'

'I'm gobsmacked! Gobsmacked! Because Phil's told me and I've not believed him. He'll tell you that himself. I've just straight out not believed him.'

'Well, it'sh true.'

'Is it because of your book? Because you've not exactly covered yourself in glory with it, Jaap'

'What?'

'Your controversial autobiography.'

He formed little quotation marks with his fingers when he said this, but ruined the intended effect by placing them around the third word rather than the second.

Stam shrugged, one-shouldered. 'I don't know. Maybe a little.'

'Is it because you've called me and Phil busy cunts?'

Stam shook his head. 'You *are* busy cunts. Many timesh I have shaid thish to your face.'

'See, I've said it to Phil. With Jaap Stam, that's like a term of endearment. I've said, when *he* calls you a busy cunt, well, it's like a hug, isn't it? The problem was obviously the serialisation. It don't look too clever when it's spread across two pages of a newspaper. I mean, it certainly wasn't something I relished reading.'

'Oh, well.'

'Hang about, I've still not properly taken this in. I'm mystified! If you'd told me a week ago that Jaap Stam – who's obviously done tremendously well for us since he's come in – would be transferred to obviously Lazio, I'd have flat-out not believed you. I'd have said you were mad. For me, this is a bigger bombshell than Sparky leaving.'

He looked at Roy for the first time. 'Have you told him he's been a tremendous servant to the football club?' he said, busily.

'Yeah,' Roy said.

'And part of the reason why we've done so fantastically well over the years?'

'Yes!' Roy said, his eyes lightly closed now.

'Three Premier Leagues in a row. Obviously, the elusive treble. I'd even use the word phenomenal . . .'

'I fucking told him, Gary.'

'Tremendous awareness as a defender. That's well-documented. Two good feet. Obviously a great touch for a big man . . .'

Roy turned the key in the engine, told Stam he'd catch up with him in Dublin and reversed out of the space. For the final time, I stared at Jaap Stam in the pale wash of Roy's headlights, looking shocked and disorientated, like a released hostage – Gary shaking his head at him, still saying, 'Mystified! Literally!' – and then we were back on the road to Hale.

Roy likes to say that nothing in football surprises him, but the quick and unsentimental way that Stam was dispatched shook him up quite badly, I think. He liked Jaap. Contrary to what some people say, Roy likes most people. I wondered if his view of Alex Ferguson shifted that day. All those years of service and then he's packed off without even a proper goodbye. I wonder now did Roy get a flash of his own future that morning.

We went home and sat in the garden for a while, watching two swallows frolic in mid-air, their hearts as giddy and light as those of the four Chelsea players who would soon be shouting abuse, stripping naked and vomiting in a Heathrow Hotel in front of weeping Americans on the day after the 9/11 terror attacks.

We watched television for a bit – a documentary about the Six Day War, then a biography of Benetton – and Roy groomed me with his open hand, an air of melancholy about him.

'At the end of the day,' I remember him saying, 'footballers are just pieces of meat. Like prime cuts of beef.'

Stam was far from that, I wanted to say. But I didn't. It wasn't the time.

'For me, Jaap is still a top, top defender. Obviously we wouldn't be in a hundred percent agreement on that point, Triggs. But he'll do well for Lazio. He'll win things with them.'

He won one Italian Cup with them. And it was nearly four years before Lazio settled the bill for him. I'm just making the point here.

I wasn't gong to weep any tears for Stam. Even if I felt the inclination, there wasn't time. The new season was already underway. It was one that promised so much but would yield only disappointment and bitterness and would end with the world's media encamped outside on Bankhall Lane and my name known across five continents.

But there I go, rushing the story again.


Roy and I were both excited about the 2001/2 season, not least because the club was at last spending some of the money that we'd made for them. Juan Sebastian Veron arrived with a reputation as one of the most creative midfielders in football – 'I think I've been saying it from day one that we maybe need a playmaker,' Roy said, 'and the manager thinks he has one or two of those tricks that we've been maybe missing in Europe' – while Ruud van Nistelrooy had recovered from his injury, completed his transfer and, again according to Roy, was showing in training why the manager was so keen to wait for him.

Teddy Sheringham was gone. Andy Cole saw the signs and was soon on his way too. Dwight Yorke – back on the naughty step – decided to hang on, figuring that Ferguson only had one season left and wagering that the next man wouldn't have quite so trenchant a take on his lifestyle.

Accommodating Veron in the team was the reason for United's unconvincing start to the season. So the popular wisdom had it. It meant that Paul Scholes was pressed into service either on the left or as a support striker to van Nistlerooy, where he wasn't happy, and it upset the delicate equanimity of the team. Take it from a dog who knows what he's talking about – that was all rubbish. Scholes could play football underwater and he'd still be great. Roy was too nice to say it, but the problem wasn't accommodating Veron. The problem *was* Veron. He thought work was something that footballers' wives had done to them in Harley Street in London. While Roy grafted like a kulak, he was happy to just ride the clutch. Brilliant, no question – he was just of the view that his genius was better demonstrated in little cameos.

I'm sure his career highlights make for far more entertaining viewing than Roy's if you watch them on YouTube. He just wasn't what Manchester United needed. Look, I knew Roy better than anyone and I thought I could sense a frustration growing in him during those first few weeks of the season, even as he was telling me, 'I've never seen a player who can play a pass like him' and 'You should see some of the things he's doing in training – one or two of the players used the word sublime.'

Training? When was that ever a mark of anything? How about doing it when there are a few more witnesses around and when there was an actual point?

He didn't speak English either, which made it difficult for him and Roy to establish any real understanding of each other. We'd meet him out occasionally – once coming out of Homebase in Worsley, once running in Heaton Park, once sitting in his yellow Ferrari in the lane behind us in the drive-through McDonald's on the Stockport Road – and Veron would smile and offer a thumbs-up – two, if the mood really took him – and say, 'Rykeen! Beeg, beeg player! *El ciento y diez por ciento! End of the day! Grande futbolista!*'

I know Roy feels he might have done more to help him settle in Manchester, but you just knew they weren't going to click. And that United weren't going to win anything that season. A month was all I needed to be certain of that. I mean, what the hell was going on at the back? Every team they played against suddenly fancied their chances of scoring two or three goals. They conceded four in their first two games. But then Stam was suddenly off to Rome and I was giddy with the thought that Ferguson already had his replacement lined – I almost said *tapped*! – up. Someone who, as I heard him say on television, could command the defence like Bruce and Pallister once had.

He got Laurent Blanc.

You have no idea how little effort it required to make that sound like a punchline just there.

*Blanc* was right. A substantial portion of my white hairs, I'm certain, were put there by his performances for United that autumn and winter. If Roy and Alex Ferguson were being honest, they'd tell you the same thing.

Ferguson had long been an admirer of his and had apparently tried to sign him twice before. But that was a long time ago. Now, he was thirty-six years of age. I was no fan of Stam, but where was the sense in selling a twenty-nine-year-old defender because you thought he'd lost a yard of pace, only to replace him with a man who was seven years slower than him? I hated to be the one forever cavilling, but all of the work I was doing on United's opposition was being undone by his errors at the back.

The upshot was that by the beginning of December, United had already lost five times in the league – to Bolton, Liverpool, Arsenal, Newcastle and Chelsea. Did you spot it? Of course you did. Their initials spelled out BLANC. I'm not a superstitious animal, but even I had to lie down for an hour in the laundry room with the lights off when I read that, on a page from *The Sun* that blew through the garden one early evening straight into my face.

'Are you absolutely sure,' I asked Roy one night while we

were passing The Hale Grill on Ashley Road, 'that it's the same Laurent Blanc who won the European Championships with France last summer?'

'Triggs,' he said, 'it's the same lad, I'm telling you.'

There was something else that no one liked to talk about. The unsayable. Ferguson's looming departure had changed the whole working environment at the club. As soon as he named a date, the players – and not just Dwight – began to imagine life beyond him. The newspapers were full of speculation about his successor. Ottmar Hitzfeld. Martin O'Neill. Sven Goran Eriksson. Fabio Capello.

One thing was for sure, it wasn't going to be Steve McClaren, the first team coach, who I quite liked. He saw the writing on the wall and left for Middlesbrough. And Ferguson couldn't find a replacement. Who was going to come to the club on a twelve-month contract? It all contributed to an atmosphere of between-times at Old Trafford.

So the frustration mounted in Roy. Oh, I could feel it, like a dog who senses electrostatic changes in the atmosphere and heads for higher ground. And, yes, there were further efforts to break me in, as it were, using click-and-treat, behavioural capture and physical prompting training techniques. I occasionally submitted to them. Much as I hated to reinforce, it was simpler all round.

I remember he finished his dinner one Tuesday evening and started talking about Eric Cantona – reminiscing about him in a fond way, as he was sometimes wont to do. It was something mercurial the man had said.

'Football is like a woman – when there is nothing left to say, you must walk away.'

Or something like that.

I think Roy always envied Cantona for the way he walked away from football on his own terms. With the audience wondering why. Without a backward glance. No sparks. No accusations of treachery or ill feeling. Didn't wind up like Peter Schmeichel – the idiot – keeping goal for Manchester City. Didn't end up playing for Sydney FC like Dwight. Just decided he didn't want it anymore and it was time for whatever life had for him next. I mean, who doesn't want to write their own ending?

That's the context for what happened at St James's Park in September.

The football I won't bother describing, mainly because I couldn't do justice to the performances of Blanc and Veron that day without libelling them. The news that I've decided to commit my memories to paper has already provoked interest from the lawyers of enough current and former footballers.

Newcastle won 4–3. Alan Shearer scored the winner, another of those ephemeral glories that were little consolations for Al in a career that had not seen a trophy since 1995 and never would again. I'm sorry. There was always something about Shearer that brought out the purebred bitch in me.

Anyway, this was the day when he and Roy had their little spat on the far touchline. Were they arguing over whose throw-in it was, or did Shearer try to stop Roy taking it quickly? I just remember Roy throwing the ball at Shearer's head. I laughed. It was one of those things that was reflexively funny. Like Lee Bowyer doing charity work. Or David Beckham meeting Nelson Mandela.

Then came the stand-off. Ugly words cast about. Roy told me later that Shearer called him a prick. Which he'd been called a thousand times before, by the way. You'd want to try walking up Corporation Street with him in the week of a Manchester derby. But there was something about the way Shearer said it – the smugness of those cool blue eyes, the sneering curl of his mouth – that rendered Roy like a live grenade rolling around on the deck of a ship.

Now, in normal circumstances, I'd have looked at his furious red face, with its popping eyes locked unblinkingly on the backpedalling Shearer, and thought, 'Dylan!' Except Roy never needed the pseudo-poetry of the most bewilderingly overrated artist of the twentieth century to stoke his feelings about the most bewilderingly overrated footballer of the twentieth century.

He was going to thump him. Nothing surer.

Let me just say here, I abhor violence in, well, most of its forms. Yes, I'd shown my teeth once or twice to Ole Gunnar Solskjær, most recently in Heaton Park, when he was so startled by my lunge at him that he stepped backwards into the boating lake. But Labradors are a generally peaceable breed. Even Marley – the very worst of us – resisted the temptation to sink his teeth into that simpering dolt John Grogan, although he must have been tempted. Yet there will always be a part of me that will never forgive Gary Neville for interfering with the trajectory of that punch. Roy has always insisted that it was the shove in the chest from Shearer that caused him to undershoot at the last moment, sending his warhead whistling harmlessly past the most supercilious face in football. But I blame Neville, who was trying to steer Roy away with the back of his hand on his ribcage and, *I* think, distracted him. Then, worse still, stopped him from following up with the left uppercut that Roy – from his boxing training as a boy in Cork – would have instinctively detonated next.

Like I said, I was never a violent dog. But whenever I see Shearer on *Match of the Day* now, joshing with Alan Hansen about who would have beaten who to a particular ball back in the day, or baiting each other good-naturedly over their comparative abilities with a five-iron, Gary Neville pops into my head and I think, well, there's one thing that Jaap Stam *did* get right.

Roy was visibly upset when he arrived home in the early

hours of the morning – even when he knew that I was fine with it. He understood my feelings about Shearer and anyway, I'd kind of written off the season. From as early as the second week in September, I could see that Arsenal were going to win the league and that United's interest in Europe wouldn't survive too far into the spring. My mind had already turned to life after Alex Ferguson. And so, apparently, had Roy's.

'I'm packing it in,' he said.

I was lapping water from my bowl in the laundry room when he said it, his forehead pressed sorrowfully against the frame of the door. Like Ole Gunnar Solskjær picking himself out of the green-tinged waters of the Heaton Park lake, I could have drowned in that moment.

'What!?' I said, choking the water down.

'I'm serious, Triggs. I'm going to retire. From obviously football.'

'Why? Because of Shearer?'

'Not because of Shearer. At the end of the day . . . it's down to me.'

'Look, you're frustrated,' I said. 'The new signings haven't worked.' Apart from van Nistelrooy, I should have added.

'Too right I'm frustrated. Too fucking right. I'm just tired of letting people down – people who've maybe defended me in the past . . .'

I took that as a reference to me. I didn't feel let down, though. That was the truth.

'I was sitting on the bus, obviously on the motorway home, thinking, 'Give it up, Roy. You've got to stop hurting the people who love you. You've got to stop hurting yourself.'

God, I thought, this is all a bit over the top.

'It was only Shearer,' I said. 'I doubt you're the first person who's ever thought about punching him in the face.'

He smiled. He'd give me that one.

'Yeah, no, obviously I didn't do myself too many favours

there,' he said. 'Let myself down – blah, blah, blah. But it's not just that, Triggs. It's more than that. I've lost the argument – too many players in the comfort zone. Happy with what they've got. Going with the flow. Dead fish. I'm blue in the face saying it. Their cars, obviously their mansions – blah, blah, fucking blah. I just think – end of the day – leave them to it.'

'You might feel differently after a night's sleep.'

'I don't think I will, Triggs. I don't think I will.'

And with that, he went to bed.

He didn't sleep. I didn't sleep either. I lay in the laundry room listening to him above me, turning in the bed like a rotisserie chicken. The following morning, not long after seven o'clock, he suddenly materialised at the bottom of the stairs, washed, shaved and dressed, and told me he was going to Carrington to break to the news to Alex Ferguson.

To this day, I still wonder why he invited me along. Was it, as he claimed, just for the drive? Or was it – am I so arrogant to wonder? – for my counsel? Or was it simply to bring a little bit of home with him, to demonstrate to his boss that he no longer considered the training ground his workplace?

I didn't know.

Ferguson was late. We sat in the car for more than hour, neither of us saying much. I tried to distract him by telling him about a documentary I'd watched a couple of days earlier about the massacre at El Mozote. He made noises like he was following the story – 'El Salvador . . . I'm listening . . .' – but I caught the look in his eye in the rearview mirror and I could tell he wasn't.

Eventually, Ferguson arrived. He was clearly surprised to find Roy's car parked there on a Sunday morning.

'Back in a minute,' Roy said, then he got out and I watched him through the rear window walk purposefully to where Ferguson stood with a perplexed look on his face. Through the soundproofed windows, my ears couldn't bridge the distance between us. But I followed the conversation as best I could through the language of their faces and bodies.

Roy was especially animated, using his hands to semaphore some point. Ferguson turned his palms upwards in a placatory way. Roy semaphored more wildly. Ferguson nodded in apparent agreement. Roy continued to talk, though less demonstratively now. Ferguson placed a mollifying hand on his shoulder. Roy stopped talking and folded his arms. Ferguson said something and took his hand back. Roy shook his head, then looked away. Ferguson cocked his head at ninety degrees and sought Roy's eyes. Roy shook his head, his arms still folded, then he was suddenly walking back to the car.

Ferguson shouted something after him that I didn't hear, then he caught my eye through the rear window of the car. If he could have spoken to me in that moment, I think he would have said, 'Have a word, will you?'

Nothing was said during the drive back to Hale. But that afternoon we went for an hour-long walk and Roy opened up to me. I was glad of the walk as I was feeling a bit stiff in my joints and I wondered was I suffering from hip dysplasia or even a touch of early onset arthritis.

'The manager thinks I'd miss it,' he said. 'Obviously football.'

'You don't think you would?' I asked.

'Not the aggravation! Not that part of it. Always driving, driving, driving. You know. Can't go on like that.'

'You're tired.'

'More hollow. Emptied out.'

'You've been taking too many things on board.'

'Maybe. Maybe.'

'So how did you leave things? With Ferguson?'

'He told me to obviously have a think about things. Maybe sleep on it. Thinks it's maybe a knee-jerk reaction.'

'But your mind is made up?'

'Listen, I don't have to restate my respect for obviously Alex

Ferguson. What he's done at the football club — obviously phenomenal down through the years. But I can't keep doing this forever. And the more I think about it, the more I realise that maybe now is the time to go. Obviously the manager's leaving at the end of the season. I think I've spoken in the past about that bit of maybe complacency that's set in — players maybe not wanting to take that next step . . . Triggs, why are you limping?'

'Limping?'

'Yeah, you're limping.'

I think I mentioned a moment ago that I felt a certain stiffness in my joints, although I was surprised that it was noticeable in my gait.

'Might have a touch of hip dysplasia,' I said.

Roy scoffed at this. 'You haven't got hip dysplasia, Triggs.'

'Might be a touch of it. We're prone to it, you see.'

'Triggs, you haven't got hip dysplasia! Jesus Christ!'

On we walked. God, he was tetchy. I waited until he'd calmed down, then I said, 'You can't retire — you've only just turned thirty.'

'Cantona retired at thirty-one.'

I knew he was going to say that.

'What will you do?' I asked.

'Anything. Maybe travel.'

'Travel?'

'Yeah, travel. On about, you know, great quotes . . .'

'Quotes?'

'I read this one the other day. I think it was, "The world is a book and those who do not travel read only one page".'

'So what are you going to do — hike the Mojave Desert?'

'There's loads of things I could do. It might not even *be* travel. I might sign for Celtic.'

'Celtic? Jesus Christ!'

He laughed. 'I've always been a Celtic fan.'

'Well, if you've lost your appetite for competitive football, that's the place to go, I suppose.'

We had stopped at the little bowling green next to the Britannia Ashley Hotel. Through the black vertical railings, we watched the silver-haired men and women in navy slacks and soft white shoes send their balls turning along the buzzcut grass with great theatrical sweeps of their arms.

'Maybe I could do that,' he said.

I laughed. I think he wanted me to.

'Seriously, Triggs. I think I could definitely bring something to that game.'

The players studied the lie of the green with long, languorous looks, like a sculptor trying to understand the spirit of his stone before he takes his tools to it.

'I think the pace would probably suit Veron more than you,' I said.

'Oh, no, everyone would have to seriously up their game if I was to join. Can you imagine me out there, Triggs? *You're not doing it anymore! Where's your hunger? Where's your fucking pride? You've got your old age pension and your Ford Ka and your timeshare apartment in Southend-on-Sea. But you've forgotten the hard work you had to put in to get your old age pension and your Ford Ka and your timeshare apartment in Southend-on-Sea.*'

God, he was funny when he sent himself up. It was a shame, I thought, that the public got to see it so rarely.

A certain lightness had entered him. All he'd really needed, I realised, was to vent. I was happy that I was there for him. We turned and walked back to the house, my joints, admittedly, feeling a little looser. The phone was ringing when we stepped into the hall. Roy picked up the receiver, listened, then said, 'I'll be here. I know you're going to have a go at maybe changing my mind. I think it's only fair to tell you that I don't think it's going to happen.'

When he dropped the receiver back in its cradle, he told me that Alex Ferguson was calling around the following day for a chat. And from the way Roy took the stairs two at a time, I knew that by this time tomorrow he'd still be a Manchester United player.

*'Listen,' he says, his voice emerging thin and weary through the radio speakers, 'I can't control obviously whether the fans chant 'Keane out!', whether they boo the players, whether they cheer the opposition, as they did with Barnsley today. Obviously it's not nice. You'd rather it didn't happen. But – as I said – it's outside of my control.*

*'I do have sympathy for the fans. Obviously disappointed. We've not played well today. Two down at half-time, we were chasing the game in the second half. Maybe left ourselves a bit open at the back. Then the third goal went in – obviously the killer.*

*'Listen, I'm not going to make excuses. We know we need to do better. In football, you have to deal with setbacks. I'll take it on the chin. As I said, I know the supporters are disappointed, but I hope they'll get behind the team and travel to Hull with us next week. And, whatever they think of me as a manager, that they'll give their support to the players, because they're doing their best.'*

It was just before Christmas that events took what the great novelists call a turn.

I'm not going to tell this story in that self-exculpatory voice that most footballers use in their autobiographies to explain away everything from flipping a Porsche on a motorway at three o'clock in the morning to having sex with a girl in a hotel room with a few teammates looking on.

No, I'm going to make history here. I'm going to say three words that you won't have read in this juxtaposition before in the autobiography of anyone connected with the game of football.

I . . . behaved . . . appallingly.

I was wrong. I was disloyal. I dishonoured my breed. I look back on the end of 2001 and the first few months of 2002 and feel nothing but shame and an aching remorse.

Nothing had changed my view that United weren't going to win anything that season. They lost twice to Deportivo La Coruña in the Champions League.

'Tell Veron not to let Juan Carlos Valeron settle on the ball,' I said, 'and tell Wes Brown to try to anticipate Diego Tristan's runs, because he's quick,' but Roy and I might as well have been talking to ourselves.

Arsenal, Chelsea and Liverpool turned them over without any real difficulty in the league. Veron gave the ball away sloppily in an attacking position for Jimmy Floyd Hasselbaink and Eider Gudjohnsen to one-two their way down the pitch to score for Chelsea. Barthez's attention-deficit issues, meanwhile, were becoming a problem – he gifted Thierry Henry the two goals that gave Arsenal all three points and United fell away to sixth in the league.

I thought, okay, that's that then.

One of the few high points in that autumn of unrelenting gloom was that Ireland had qualified for the World Cup finals. The back of the job was broken on the first day of September, when they beat Holland 1–0 in Dublin. I didn't watch it – again, it was my difficulty with the colour orange – but I did catch a shot of Roy and Mick McCarthy's horribly awkward handshake after the final whistle and I was again filled with foreboding about how this episode was going to end. You didn't have to be an expert reader of human signals to see how their little marriage of convenience was holding up.

But it suited everyone to ignore what to me was just common sense. You can't share joy with someone you don't like. It just doesn't work.

The job was finished off with victories over Cyprus, then Iran in a two-legged play-off, the second instalment of which Roy chose to miss. He had an ongoing problem with a knee that required painkilling injections and bouts of rest and it was decided – by whom would later become the subject of international intrigue – that Roy could be excused the trip to Tehran for the second leg.

So that's the backdrop to the story.

Idina, by the way, had given in to her sister's urgings and met Hugh. By now, in fact, he was a regular fixture in her life. Hugh was a great guy – a former policeman, a widower, with great grey sideburns that looked about twenty-five years out of their time and a smile that suggested he found the entire world just a little bit ridiculous.

The first leg of the playoff with Iran was over – Ireland won 2–0 – and I was thinking of calling it a night. Hugh was staring at me, a little in awe, I thought.

'Uncanny that,' he said.

'See?' Idina said. She had an unlit cigarette between her lips and she spoke through one side of her mouth. 'People don't believe me when I tell them. But she recognises him, Lover.'

She called him Lover, too, even though I never picked up on any overt sexual signals between them.

'Oh, she does that,' he said. 'Gave a yelp or a bark or a huff every time Roy were ont screen. That were amazing.'

You thought that was amazing? I thought. You should have seen me two days ago telling him to be aware of Karim Bagheri's speed on the countercharge.

'Do you know who'd have loved a dog like that back int day?' he said.

'Who?' Idina said, touching the flame of her lighter to her next cigarette.

'Esther Rantzen – that's who.'

Hugh had a point, by the way. It's something I've been guilty of perhaps underplaying in this autobiography, but my ability to even see television in the same way that humans do was – as he said – amazing. You probably already know that the image on a television screen, while appearing to be continuous, is actually being updated and redrawn at a rate of about sixty times per second. But because the human eye has a slower flicker perception rate than the rate at which the picture is changing, it creates the impression of continuity. The canine eye has a faster flicker resolution rate than the human eye, which is why the vast majority of dogs appear so uninterested in television – all they can see is colours flashing at irritating intervals. But then, you've probably all heard stories about dogs who not only sit and watch television but have preferences for certain programmes – sports, soaps and, dare I say, documentaries. Slow flicker perception. That's what it is.

Anyway, I'm way off the point again.

Ireland had beaten Iran and I decided to let Idina and Hugh have the television. I slewed off the sofa and started making my way out to the kitchen. Hugh took up the remote and started flicking through the channels.

'Wait, wait – go back,' Idina said.

'What were it?'

'Go back one. No, two. There you are!'

'Oh, aye, I love this show.'

'That's who she's named after.'

'Who?'

'Triggs. That's who Roy named her after – he told me that himself.'

Not surprisingly, they had my interest. I turned around. The programme, it turned out, was *Only Fools and Horses*, a television sitcom that I knew Roy enjoyed, centred on two brothers working as casual traders in recessionary London and the various jams, stews and muddles they became embroiled in along the way. The character to whom Idina was referring was a simpleton in a powder blue suit who was telling some people in a pub that his father had died a couple of years before he was born – an impossibility, clearly, given the length of the human gestation period from the point of conception, wherein, I suspected, the humour lay. The idiot's name was Trigger, foreshortened by his friends – I noticed with horror that chilled me to the marrow of my bones – to Triggs.

No, I thought. This . . . This couldn't be.

'If dog's so smart, why's he gone and named her after a bonehead like that?'

Couldn't have put it better myself, Hugh. Couldn't have put it better myself.

I sloped out to my basket in the kitchen, hurt, embarrassed, my shoulders slumped, as unhappy in that moment as I had ever been.

Being generous by nature, I tried to offer Roy the benefit of the doubt, of course. I lay in my basket, thinking Idina may have been simply mistaken. There's another Triggs surely. An explorer. A poet. An inventor. But no. Deep down, I knew I was named after that halfwit road sweeper, just as surely as I knew that I'd been the butt of a joke to which everyone in Manchester was privy but me.

Is that why Ryan Giggs always regarded me with a smirk on his lips? Is it why Steve McClaren once laughed in my face when Roy told him my name outside Iceland Foods in the Fallowfield Shopping Centre? Is that why David Beckham looked at me sometimes like he considered himself my intellectual equal?

It all made sense now.

Roy arrived back from Dublin the following day, as happy

as, oh, I don't know, say, Coleen Rooney in a shop? He tried to interest me in the details of the match during the drive back to Hale. 'We agreed if it was a positive result,' he said, 'that I wouldn't travel for the second leg. Two-nil is *obviously* positive.'

And I did something that disgusts me to this day. I ignored him – just stared out of window, counting off the exits on the M56, thinking I'd rather be in any other car on this stretch of motorway right now than this one. Roy, I think, presumed I was tired or just not in the mood for conversation.

This is where my shame deepens. Because I kept it up. Not the silent treatment. You can only maintain that for so long before you're required to have it out. Instead, I was caustic with him. Oh, I could do passive aggressive like no female in the world, on four legs or two.

He'd say, 'Triggs, is there something wrong?' and I'd feel my stomach curl in on itself at just the mention of the name.

So then it'd be, 'Wrong? Why would there be something wrong?'

'It's just, I don't know, you don't seem yourself.'

'Oh, I'm very much myself, Roy. This *is* me.'

There was one lunchtime he came home from training and mentioned that he'd had a chat with van Nistelrooy about his need to work on his link-up play. 'I gave him that quote,' he said, 'I think I might have mentioned it maybe once or twice in the past – *there's no i in team.*'

'No,' I said, under my breath, 'but there's four in platitude-quoting idiot.'

'What was that, Triggs?'

'Didn't say a word, Roy.'

Me!? I know. Try as I might, though, I just couldn't get my head around it. Did he really consider me stupid? I kept thinking. Had I not had a generally improving effect on his life?

Of course, he had no idea why our friendship had seemingly cooled. But Roy — loving, generous, loyal, funny, sensitive, misunderstood, vulnerable Roy — never stopped making the effort.

There was one afternoon, I was watching a Biography Channel special on the life of Erik Weisz, the Hungarian-American magician and escapologist better known to the world as Harry Houdini. Roy joined me on the sofa, mussed my coat and tried to pick up the thread of the programme.

'The lad Houdini,' he said. 'I've heard of him, Triggs.'

I didn't respond.

'So how did he die in the end?'

You may or may not know that it was a burst appendix that eventually did for Houdini, the result of being punched in the stomach by a college student whom he'd invited up on stage to test the steeliness of his abdominal muscles.

'A blow to the guts,' I said curtly.

'Did he?'

'Some of us know that feeling, of course.'

I mean, I was a bitch. Even rebuffed Roy's efforts to involve me in United's season. By December, they had the second worst defensive record in the Premier League. They were three points off the top, yet the teams sweating about relegation at the other end of the table were making a better fist of keeping out goals. Roy pointed this out to me while I was enjoying my breakfast one morning — chafing his hands, I remember — clearly soliciting my opinion. And what did I do? Pulled various ho-hum faces, then went back to my polenta and blended corn kernels. Shameful behaviour — from any dog.

Even on our walks, I remained mostly silent. I sulked through December and January, when United began to show surprising signs of turning their season around, winning eleven out of twelve matches and climbing to the top of the league again. It was mainly down to the brilliant form of Giggs and the goals of van Nistelrooy and also Ole Gunnar Solskjær, who was back in both the United first team and my dreams.

('Who am I to shay the manacher is right or wrong? At the end of the day, he hash achieved all he hash in the game. If he wantsh go out and buy a new shtriker, thatsh up to him. All I can do ish take my opportuntiesh when they arrive and – ash I've shaid in the pasht – make it ash hard for him ash poshible to leave me on the bench.' Oh, horrible! Many times I woke up barking in the night.)

There was a feeling – certainly in our house – that United's momentum might be sufficient to carry them over the line by the time May came. We ran into Giggs one freezing morning, walking his two Boxers in Stamford Park, and he was full of it.

'You'd have to say we've done ever so well to turn things around,' he said

Roy was unmoved. Wasn't he always? 'As I think I said after the Southampton match – you know, let's not go patting ourselves on the back just yet. It's obviously a long season.'

The two boxers – who moved in that edgy, freeze-frame way that always put me in mind of Robbie Keane – sniffed at my tender parts while I stared disinterestedly at the skirls of snow blowing across the path in front of us.

'At the same time,' Giggs said, 'you'd have to say our tails are definitely up. Ole and Ruud are scoring goals – it was either Gary or Phil Neville used the phrase the other night – *at will*. Then we've got Diego Forlan, who's obviously about to come in . . .'

Let's leave Diego Forlan for another day – as Alex Ferguson should have said himself.

'. . . and we've obviously tightened up a bit at the back.'

'You're on about tightening things up at the back. We're still conceding silly goals, Giggsy – even in the matches we're winning.'

'I think Laurent's starting to get to grips with obviously the English game, though. Okay, he's maybe not blessed with raw pace, but he's obviously vastly, vastly experienced . . .'

'Oh, he's a player. There's no question.'

'A definite player. And Veron – what can you say? Some of the things he can do with a football. I mean, sublime! Surreal, almost. Okay, he's had his critics since he's come in. He's obviously struggled to come to terms with not having as much time on the ball as he was used to in maybe Italy. And his left peg's for standing on! He won't be happy with me for saying that! But yeah, no, I don't think it'll be too long before he's obviously repaying a massive chunk of that price tag.'

Like I said, I wasn't really following the conversation. But then I looked up and just happened to catch Giggs's eye and he said, 'Wotcha, Dave!', the catchphrase of the television Trigger, who I realised now was known the length and breadth of England as an instant synonym for a certain kind of simpleminded idiocy.

Giggs suddenly jumped backwards. So did his boxers. 'Has she just growled at me?' he said.

Roy shot me a look of admonishment. The man who almost broke Alfie Haaland's leg. The man who stood on Gareth Southgate. The man who took out Gus Poyet. Like *he* was in a position to judge me.

'I don't know *what's* come over you, Triggs,' he said.

'Obviously, sorry, Giggsy.'

'If that were on the field of play,' Giggs said, 'that'd be a straight red, no question. *You* know that better than anyone, Keaney.'

'Alright, Giggsy, don't go fucking on about it.'

We drove home in silence.

I continued to brood, even when Roy arrived home one day early in February and told me that Alex Ferguson had changed his mind about retiring.

'Reversed his decision,' he said, unable to suppress a smile. 'I think he'd have missed the game. Couldn't picture him at Haydock or Kempton or wherever else there is while we were doing our stuff on obviously a Saturday or a Sunday afternoon. Or playing his fucking piano. I think I might have even said that in the past. Yeah, no, it's good. Listen, it's good for the football club. Although that's obviously Yorkie fucked.'

I just went right on watching television – what kind of a cur *was* I? – just as I went on moping through the early weeks of spring, as United slowly surrendered winter's gains, yet surprised me by reaching the last four of the Champions League. I was still following events. Clearly, I still had *some* sense of my responsibilities. I just wasn't communicating any of my thoughts to Roy.

With or without my help, they beat Deportivo La Coruña at home and away in the quarter-final – a good gauge of their improvement since the autumn, when they'd lost to them twice. But progress came with a heavy forfeit. Roy tore his hamstring in the first leg. And still I continued to subject him to the tyranny of my silences, even after watching him on television being carried from the pitch in a humiliating king's chair, even as he limped about the house on one leg, crushed and desperate for a word of consolation from me. I remained hard to him.

In the semi-final, United were drawn to play Bayer Leverkusen, a team from a small factory town in Germany who, I knew, just about everyone was underestimating. I'd seen quite a bit of them that season. They were a flaky sort of team. I watched them that spring concede four goals against Arsenal and four against Juventus, even in winning their second phase group, and, of course, they went on that season to throw away the Bundesliga from a winning position.

But they were technically good, as you'd expect of any team coached by Klaus Toppmöller, a former Kaiserslautern centre-forward whose training, and perhaps true calling, was as an architect. He had good players. Michael Ballack, if permitted, could control a match from the middle of the field. They had Yildiray Baştürk's inventiveness and the non-stop running of Bernd Schneider. And I always thought Oliver Neuville was rather underrated as a striker.

The key to beating Leverkusen, as Arsenal and Juventus had already demonstrated, was to harry them in their own half and not allow them to play their composed possession game. They much didn't like pressure – as they proved that year by finishing second in all three races in which they were involved. But if Roy was missing, I wondered whether Nicky Butt was capable of exerting the kind of pressure required to prevent Ballack from running the match. And from watching United that spring, I was beginning to have real doubts about Ruud van Nistelrooy's fitness. After the season and a half he'd just had, he looked bone tired.

Absolutely none of these thoughts did I mention to Roy, by the way, even as I watched him struggle desperately to get fit in time for the first leg. I was thinking, Hey, I'm just an idiot, remember? Why would anyone listen to what I have to say?

I felt that United needed the breathing space of a two-goal lead to take into the second leg in Germany. But they were atrocious that night. Ballack was allowed to run the game in much the way I feared and United were fortunate to get away with a 2–2 draw. Roy wasn't fit enough to start and made only a late cameo, Beckham was missing after breaking his toe against Deportivo La Coruña and Gary Neville was carried off with an almost identical injury in the opening minutes of the first half. And their nerve seemed to fail them. Without Roy, the forward momentum was missing. With Veron filling in for Beckham, Phil Neville coming on for his brother and Giggs constantly cutting inside to try to offer United something that was missing in the final third, there was no real penetration. And I was right about van Nistelrooy. He missed three good chances and looked out on his feet long before the end.

I still thought United were more than capable of winning in Leverkusen. I think Roy was of the same mind, certainly from the resolute noises he was making while stacking the breakfast things in the dishwasher on the morning he left for Germany and in the fifty minutes we were delayed on the way to Cheadle by a truck that had shed its load.

'I think I said it before the first leg,' he said. 'No disrespect to Leverkusen, but we're a better team than them, no question. But we stood off them in the first match, let them play their obviously patient possession football. We can't afford to make that mistake again.'

And I just sat there, listening to the smart-alecky chat of the two breakfast show presenters and the intermittent traffic updates, a silent backseat passenger in every way. Believe me, my behaviour embarrasses me now. I had some thoughts that I could have shared with him. And not all of them involved giving Laurent Blanc the incorrect terminal number. No, I had ideas about ways in which they could have hurt Leverkusen. But then, would it have changed anything? Would they have been any less flat than they were that night?

Roy put them into the lead, from a beautiful pass by van Nistelrooy. He was magnificent that night. And watching him through the pea soup fog of Idina's living room, I won't deny that I felt a swell of pride as he railed against the inevitable. But then I thought about that moron in the donkey jacket, pushing his brush head around Peckham Market, and my feelings became dark and discoloured, like the woodchip paper that was curling off Idina's walls.

Neuville equalised — I'd had some thoughts about him that might have made a difference — and you knew that that was that.

When he returned home, there was a sense of weary resignation about Roy that his smile failed to sift out. In fact, he seemed so unusually and horribly reconciled to it that I told myself to snap out of it. He needs you, I thought.

The following week, United were due to play Arsenal, who were five points clear in the league and required only a draw to make it theirs. I thought, Grow up, Triggs. What does it matter what he calls you? The important thing, surely, is how you feel about each other. I thought, take that olive branch that he's been offering you. Tell him he should play deep tonight – almost in a sweeper role – to protect Laurent Blanc from Freddie Ljungberg's pace. But I couldn't even bring myself to do that.

So Arsenal won 1–0 to become Premier League champions at Old Trafford. But it was a few more days before my shame was really complete.

I was in the laundry room. Can't remember what I was doing. Feeling sorry for myself, probably, since that had become almost my full time occupation. I heard laughter coming from the living room, then Roy's voice, saying, 'Jesus Christ, that's funny! That is fucking funny.'

At first I wondered had he seen David Beckham's new mohawk hairstyle. I padded into the hall and canted my head around the door of the living room. He was watching – I couldn't believe it – Only Fools and Horses. And there, filling the screen, was my namesake, telling anyone's who'd listen that he'd had the same broom for twenty years, although it had had seventeen different heads and fourteen different handles.

Roy seemed to find this hilarious.

He sensed me standing there, just out of his line of regard, and called to me over his shoulder. 'Triggs, come in here,' he said.

'No,' I said, 'I'm fine thanks. I'll go and watch one of the other televisions.'

'Come in here,' he insisted. 'This is the lad I named you after.'

I was lost for words. What was he doing, rubbing my nose in it?

I stepped dumbly into the room – maybe I *was* like him after all.

'Do you remember Brian Clough? Cloughie, who I told you about? He had a dog – obviously a Lab as well – called Del Boy, after that lad there. David Jason. So I named you after – see the fella there in the donkey jacket?'

I didn't look. Didn't need to.

'Why?' I said.

I'd wanted to ask that question for months, but he just shrugged like the answer didn't require any thought.

'Because he puts me in good form, Triggs. Like you. Doesn't matter how shitty the day's been. How obviously frustrating. Doesn't matter what's going on at obviously the football club. I come home and I see you and I just smile.'

Well my heart ran over. I couldn't have formed a word even if I could have thought of one in that moment. He patted the Italian leather beside him. 'Come up here and watch it with me, Triggs.'

'I . . . haven't been myself,' I said.

'What?'

'For the past few months. I've been . . .'

'Listen, we all go through it. *A person needs a little madness or else they never dare cut the rope and be free.*'

I jumped up beside him. The leather wheezed under my weight. He put his arm around me and I sat in the loving crook of his elbow, thoroughly ashamed of myself, but determined never – ever! – to let him down again.

# 13.

# 'Stick the World Cup up Your Bollocks'

IN 1975 OFFICIALS IN HAICHENG, IN LIAONING province in North Eastern China, were so concerned by the strange behaviour displayed by the city's domestic animals – specifically dogs, who refused to sleep, paced in compulsive little patterns and whined as if in pain – that they decided to evacuate the city. This was something I saw once on Discovery. Ninety thousand residents were ordered to leave their homes. A few hours later, a massive earthquake, measuring 7.3 on the Richter scale, shook the city like a snow globe, destroying ninety percent of its buildings. But the death toll was unnaturally low for an earthquake of that magnitude. Only thirteen hundred people died – thanks to dogs and their ability to detect shifts in the mood of the Earth to which humans are insensitive.

Clever people, the Chinese.

Admittedly, the sequence of foreshocks that rippled through the earth under the city in the days before the quake might have also persuaded them to get the people out. But it's a fact that ever since that day, dogs have been a part of the country's national earthquake warning system.

Any human who still doubts that the stress-related behaviour of dogs can predict major seismic events should have seen me in the weeks before the World Cup, in the early summer of 2002. I barked. I mewled. I plied back and forth in tight figure eights. I even asked Roy straight out not to go, after spending two or three days trying to subtly steer him into making the decision himself. On the walk into Hale, I pointed out that his legs looked a little heavy. Which was true.

'Is it your hamstring?' I wondered. 'I did worry that you might have rushed back for the Bayer Leverkusen match.'

'The hamstring's fine,' he said.

We walked on into the village. Roy had some business to do in Oddbins. When he stepped outside, I said, 'You just don't look like you're walking comfortably. Is it your knee maybe?'

He laughed. 'Triggs,' he said, 'I know what you're trying to do.'

'What do you mean?'

'I know you don't want me to go to the World Cup.'

'It's not that I don't want you to go to the World Cup.'

'You're on about you don't want me to play for Mick McCarthy.'

'Exactly.'

'And Mick McCarthy is managing Ireland at the World Cup.'

'Yes.'

'So you don't want me to go to the World Cup.'

'Okay then, I don't want you to go to the World Cup.'

He reached down and stroked me. 'Listen,' he said, 'me and Mick are fine. As I think I've said maybe once or twice before, we're on the same page of late.'

Yet all I could think about was that impression of them on the field in Dublin after the win against Holland. The undertow of status anxiety betrayed by Mick's body language. The contempt that Roy's posture failed to conceal, already turning away from the fact of their handshake, his eyes glazed over.

Now, before the tournament started, they were going to

spend a week together on a tiny crumb of an island in the Pacific called Saipan. Easy to see the flaw in the idea now. I saw it *then*. I saw it the previous September. I saw it in the summer of 2000, the day that Mick came to the house and didn't drink his tea.

Roy thought Ireland could win the World Cup. Of course he did. At the most – the very most – it meant winning seven football matches in the course of a month. What was so difficult about that?

I remember Roy expressing this in broadly similar terms to Paul Scholes a day or two after the league season ended. Roy had driven to Carrington to deliver a bottle of wine to Laurent Blanc as a thank you for turning him on to the physiotherapist in France who fixed up his knee that season, and he took me along for the drive. I was relieving myself against the wall of the Academy building when Paul happened by.

'Alright, Keano?'

'Alright, Scholesy?'

Paul always had a sort of scrubbed aspect to him that made you think he'd just climbed out of a hot bath.

'When are you off to obviously the World Cup?' he wanted to know.

'Next week,' Roy said. 'You?'

'Same.'

'How do think England will do?'

He shrugged. 'Yeah, no, it's a tough group. I think I'm on the record as saying that it's a lot tougher than a lot of people maybe think it is. I mean obviously Argentina are going to be top notch, with the likes of Hernan Crespo and Gabriel Batistuta, who can definitely hurt you – obviously scintillating on their day. Sweden are a good side – ever so hard to beat and you'd have to say vastly experienced. That's obviously well highlighted. And anyone who underestimates Nigeria in this World Cup will do so maybe at their peril. I don't think there's too many teams will relish playing them – put it that way! What about you, Roy, how do you think the Republic of Ireland will do?'

Roy didn't even blink. 'I think we can win it.'

Well, Paul was very noticeably shocked – and this was a man who spent four hours of every working day in his company, remember.

'Seriously,' Roy said.

'Yeah, no, fair enough. Who've you got again? Germany, is it?'

'Germany, yeah.'

'Who are maybe not the force they once were, but you can obviously never count them out. That's been documented many times I think over the years . . .'

'Cameroon.'

'Cameroon, who've got Samuel Eto'o, who's a supreme athlete – you'd have to say phenomenal – and obviously an out and out poacher.'

'Then Saudi Arabia.'

'Which is next to Dubai – that's all I know about them. At the same time, no disrespect to them. Yeah, no, you'd have to fancy your chances of getting out of the group.'

'Scholesy, I'm being fucking serious with you. I think we can go and win it.'

Blanc wandered over to where we were standing, a Gauloise glowing between his fingers. He was the first footballer I ever saw smoke a cigarette. I thought it rather suited him.

'I think Roy makes a very good point,' he said. 'I think there is not one outstanding team in this World Cup. It is open. Maybe the most open of all.'

He was a smart man, Laurent Blanc. I was sure he must have been a good footballer once.

Roy handed him the bottle, which was the reason we'd been to Oddbins. Blanc spun it round one-handed to look at the label – come on, he was French – and Roy took offence at the insinuation. 'It's a fucking top notch bottle that,' he said.

'*Oui! Oui!*' Blanc said, holding his other hand up like he was swearing an oath, wisps of noisome tobacco smoke still curling from between his fingers. 'I love Bordeaux. Is my favourite wine. Like you say, Roy – top, top notch.'

It was the first convincing demonstration of defensiveness I'd seen from the man all season.

'I'd better go,' Scholes said. 'Got this party tomorrow, to be fair.'

'What party?' Roy said. God, he was in crabby form that day.

'Yeah, no, Becks is having a party. Him and Victoria. Gucci and Sushi is the theme. It's, like, a pre-World Cup thing for the England players. I expect that's why he's not mentioned it to you.'

'Let me get this straight. You're having a party – before you even *go* to the World Cup?'

'Yeah, no, they're really pushing the boat out and all. Marquee, all that. Got caterers in, like proper sushi chefs. Quality. The things they can do with them knives – seen it before, that place in the Arndale Centre – you'd have to say tremendous. Possibly even sublime. White tie. Best of champagne. Then they've imported, like, sixty thousand orchids – supposed to be quality flowers – to give the place the whole oriental vibe . . .'

Throughout all of this, I was trying not to look at Roy's face, for fear of laughing. That thing about Scholes being the quiet man of the United squad? It wasn't true. Oh, he could talk.

'Becks is thinking of maybe dressing up as a Samurai warrior, but don't say owt because it's a surprise. And they've got, like, four hundred coming, you know? I think Elton John's going to be there, although I think I've said in the past that I'm not much bothered about his music. Obviously Sven as well. Mick Hucknall always shows his face at these things, don't he? Hats off to him, he's had phenomenal success. Lad from Denton. Must have to pinch himself sometimes. I think Becks said Robbie Williams was going to be there as well.'

Roy had to go. Which I agreed was an excellent idea. You could almost hear the agitation in him coming to a seething boil. I don't even remember if he said goodbye or good luck, just that very, very shortly after Robbie Williams and Elton John's names were invoked – and Russell Watson! How could I forget Russell Watson – we were back on the A6144, and Roy was muttering, 'Sushi. Jesus Christ.'

'*And* Gucci,' I said, in a devil's advocate kind of way.

He shook his head. 'Parties. Robbie Williams. Another quarter-final exit for England – you watch. Jesus, Becks doesn't even know if he's going to be fucking playing yet. He'd be better off putting his head down, concentrating on getting over obviously his injury.'

He was right, of course.

That's not to say that the party was just an exercise in pointless vanity. No, the reason for it was to raise money and awareness for – what was it again? Isn't that awful? I've forgotten.

'That's how you know you've been at a good awareness-raising party,' as I heard one horrifically hungover Premier League player – I'll spare his blushes by not naming him – tell Roy from the passenger seat of his Maserati on Lower Mosley Street one morning years later.

By now, of course, the Beckhams were so addicted to themselves that they just had to be the centre of attention.

'Have you heard this one?' another player – again, no names! – told Roy around that time. 'When Beckham had his metatarsal x-rayed, he's asked if they were paying him anything for image rights!'

That was a joke that did the rounds of Carrington.

Had I been David Beckham's dog, I'd have told him to forget about the party and just concentrate on his recovery. But I wasn't – mercifully – David Beckham's dog. I was Roy Keane's dog. And I had my work cut out as it was.

I asked him one more time not to go to the World Cup. It was a couple of days later, about an hour before he drove me to Idina's house in Cheadle. There was something on the television about Niall Quinn's testimonial match the day before. It raised more than a million pounds for various children's charities, but the biggest talking point was that Roy had been a no-show. Look, don't ask me why. I don't even remember it being mentioned in the house. But the anxiety began to rise in me.

'You're making a huge mistake,' I said.

He was packing various bits and pieces into his leatherette flight bag. 'Triggs,' he said, 'this is my last chance to play in the World Cup. Obviously measure myself against the best players in the world.'

So I said nothing more. And off Roy went to Dublin for a final friendly match against Nigeria, determined to follow the narrative to its abject end.

I couldn't settle in Idina's house. I shuttled from room to room. I sat down. Got back up. Sat back down again. Comfortable nowhere. 'What's upset *her*?' I heard Hugh say one day. 'Summat's clearly up.'

'I really don't know,' Idina said. 'She's not herself – that's as much as I do know.'

'It's like she's distressed or summat.'

'She's been like that for three days now.'

'Is she missing *him*?'

'I don't think so. She's always fine. How many times has *he* been away in the last year?'

'Well, you can't have her barking like that int house, Dina. Send you mad, that would.'

It was news to me that I *had* been barking.

Idina knelt to my level, took my face in her hands and said,

'Shush. Shush now, Lover. If you don't stop barking, I'll have to put you out with the other dogs.'

I made a conscious effort to at least stop barking, sublimating it into a low and far more occasional yowl that I expect was no less annoying to listen to.

It was a day or two later, in the late afternoon, that Hugh called in with some news that did silence me.

'You'll not have to put up with it for much longer,' he said. 'He's only on his way!'

'What's that, Lover?'

'He's coming home.'

'Who's coming home.'

'Roy Keane, that's who.'

He showed her the back page of *The Star*. Idina's lips parted, so great was the shock, and the cigarette that had been burning between them dropped to the floor in an explosion of sparks.

'What's happened?' Idina said.

'He's not happy wut set-up apparently.'

'In Japan?'

'No, they're not in Japan yet. They're on this island. Sampan or summat. They've had a row at training and he's told one or two to F-off . . .'

This is how I followed what was unravelling on that island nine time zones away – through snatches of conversation whenever Hugh popped in and whatever information I could glean myself from the television and radio when they were on.

'Says here he were unhappy that goalkeepers were resting at end ut training and there were a row. He's sworn at one or two. Oh, this is interesting – says there were understood to be underlying tensions about condition ut training pitch and non-arrival of equipment such as footballs and hydration drinks.'

It suddenly made sense to me. Maybe not the same sense it made to everyone else. The pitch. The footballs. The drinks.

They were just in our kitchen a proxy for his feelings about Mick, which I had seen that day as clearly as humans can see colours. He'll have wanted to go home from the minute he arrived – I knew that as well as I knew him. But he needed an objective correlative for walking away.

'He's called this guy here a . . . Oh, Dina, I won't even say word.'

'Go on, say it.'

'He's called him a bollocks. And that's swearing. Then he's gone to Mick McCarthy's hotel room – according tut piece here – and told him he wants to go home. Says they've called up Colin Healy now.'

'Who's Colin Healy?'

'I've no idea.'

I didn't either, by the way.

Idina turned her head to me. 'Shush, now. Come on, shush, my love.'

Hugh was suddenly looking at me then with an expression of wild surmise. 'Here, you don't think . . .'

'What's that?'

'You don't think she *knows* summat, do you?'

'What do you mean?'

'Well, they say that, don't they? Dogs have got extrasensory powers. I knew a fella worked int dog unit. You wouldn't believe stories he told me about how tuned-in some of them are and what they can pick up on.'

'Do you think?'

'Well, it's like we keep saying – summat's up. The barking. Can't sit still. Hasn't eaten in – how long's it been?'

'She's eaten bits and pieces.'

'But not proper – since *he* left really, in't it?'

'Since the day he dropped her off, that's right.'

Hugh stroked my coat, then I felt his hand migrate to my chest. 'Feel that, Dina,' he said.

'What?'

'Her heart. It's racing. Have a feel.'

He guided her hand to the area.

'Oh, it is,' she said. 'That's not right, is it?'

'I think we should whip her downt vets – bit lively and all!'

'I'll get my keys.'

Fifteen minutes later, we were sitting in the veterinary surgery above Di Luca's Tropical Fish Sales on Councillor Lane. The vet – a woman with spike heels and a permanently outraged expression – ran through a perfunctory catechism of questions with Idina.

'Does she have any allergies?'

'Not that I know about.'

'What have her stools been like?'

'I'm not sure as I've seen any. She's not been eating, see.'

'Has there been any change in her environment recently.'

'Well, yes, because she's not my dog, see. I run a boarding kennels. You'll not know that because you're new. So I'm only looking after her.'

'A boarding kennels?'

'That's right.'

'Well, surely if you run a boarding kennels, you'll know that this isn't unusual behaviour for a dog to be exhibiting. Presumably, you've had animals before who've had difficulty settling? Dogs suffer from separation anxiety, just like humans.'

Idina turned her head to Hugh, sitting beside her. With her eyes she seemed to urge him to speak.

'Well, we did wonder,' he said, 'if her agitation – and she's clearly agitated, even now – had owt to do with what's been int papers.'

'What do you mean?'

'Well, we didn't like to say owt, but she's Roy Keane's dog, see.'

'Who?'

'Roy Keane. He's a footballer and that.'

'I don't follow football.'

'Well, it's all overt papers this morning. He's had a massive row. Oh, something and nothing. He's coming home fromt World Cup – that's it all and all about it!'

'Sorry, I'm struggling to see how any of this is relevant.'

Idina rushed to his aid. 'Because they say – don't they? – that some dogs know when their owners are coming home. There's been studies done on it. TV programmes. I've seen it myself at the kennels. There's some dogs, they'd be nearly jumping out of their skins, like they know they're about to be collected.'

The vet twisted her mouth into the approximation of a smile. 'I think a far more likely explanation is that she's simply making strange, as dogs often do when they're taken out of their comfort zone.'

'But she's been with me lots of times. Shush, Triggs! Come on, shush now!'

'Like I said, I've examined her. Physically, there *is* nothing wrong with her. It's just stress owing to the change in her environment.'

'What would you recommend we do?'

'Recommend? Plenty of TLC, I'd say. Music can also help. But do stop worrying. Dogs *are* very adaptive. She'll settle in her own time.'

Outside, Idina scrabbled in her bag for her cigarettes like they were vital oxygen-givers. Hugh shrugged impotently. 'That's us told.'

I was suddenly drawn towards a black Peugeot 206 that was parked illegally in a loading zone with its hazard lights flashing. There was no one in it, I could see, but the front driver's door was open. It was the radio, I realised, that was drawing me in.

A voice said, 'Republic of Ireland captain Roy Keane has decided he wants to remain part of Ireland's World Cup squad after all. The Manchester United midfielder told manager Mick McCarthy that he was quitting the team following a bust-up over training facilities at the squad's pre-tournament base on the Pacific island of Saipan. However, overnight, Keane appears to have had a change of heart and informed McCarthy of his decision just minutes before the deadline for the submission of the final squad names to FIFA . . .'

*Somnolence is my default state these days. Which is part of the deal with getting old. All that energy you expend when you're a young dog, a day arrives – if you're fortunate enough to live that long – when you have to pay it back.*

*My days are essentially defined by sleep, with occasional bouts of wakefulness. And I'll do it anywhere, even here in the car, where before I never could close my eyes without the motion making my stomach sick.*

*'There's supposed to be one or two nice walks out this direction,' he says. In more ways than one, we're still trying to get the lie of the land in this part of the world. 'Mostly flat. Obviously, neither of us is getting any younger. I think I've aged ten fucking years since the start of the season. There's grey hairs on my head that weren't there a week ago!'*

*He chuckles to himself. Ipswich lost 1–0 at Hull yesterday. They're subsiding back down the table again. I wish there was something I could do. Something I could say. But those days are gone.*

I felt helpless. Looking back now, I know that's where the agitation came from. I was used to directing events. Here I was, nine time zones and eight thousand miles away from him, disconneted from his thoughts, just as he was from mine. I sat on the back seat of Idina's Ford Fiesta, Hugh's staying hand on my ribcage as if trying to smoothen out my uneven breathing, and I tried to imagine what could have changed his mind.

'What time's he likely to be home then?' Idina wondered. They hadn't heard what I heard and were half a day behind the news. 'How long is it from Japan?'

'Well, he's not coming from Japan, is he? He's on that island. Be two or three flights that.'

'Two or three?'

'At least. You're looking at twenty-four hours, I should think.'

We arrived back at the house. It was lunchtime for the kennelled dogs. I followed Idina outside. Sensing my anxiety – the air was rinsed with it – they barked at me through the steel mesh of the communal play area while Idina organised their food. I stayed close to the house. I went back to shuttling back and forth, this time on the lawn, compulsively turning conjoining circles on the grass, picturing in my imagination Roy in his room, torn between what he wanted and what was expected of him.

There was a roar. Hugh was shouting from the kitchen. 'Dina! He's staying, Dina! Come and see this!'

Idina came scuttling past me into the house.

Roy's decisions often represented the brokering of an uneasy peace between heart and head. This one wouldn't hold, I knew it. I could only guess at the colour of Mick's thoughts. His captain was going home. Now he was staying. Another chip out of his authority. Another accommodation. Another compromise.

I went on tramping those figure eights until eventually, inevitably, sleep-deprived, hungry, emotionally squeezed-out like an old dishrag, I lay down and did something that I hadn't done in God knows how long – I went to sleep.

I woke with the very definite sense that I had missed the best part of a day. It turned out I had been unconscious for twenty hours unbroken, although I had a dim sleep memory of Hugh carrying me indoors, kind hands caressing my coat and hushed whispers of, 'Must be exhausted, poor thing.'

I woke to the sound of his name being spoken. Roy. Yes, Roy. That's no problem, Roy. I looked up. Idina was making a pot of tea with the cordless cradled between her shoulder and neck.

'I'll be here,' she was saying. 'No, don't be silly. I'm not going to need to go out. I've got everything in, Roy. You just mind yourself, do you hear me? I'll have her ready when you come.'

My two ears loomed. Idina rushed, hips swinging, out of the kitchen and into the living room, which was soon filled with television noise. Still faint from sleep, I lolloped in after her and lay down at her feet, both of us watching.

It didn't come on straight away. That only happens in movies. India and Pakistan were, as it happened, threatening to destroy each other with nuclear weapons, so the story, understandably, wasn't the lead headline on the BBC news.

Eventually, it came on.

'Republic of Ireland captain Roy Keane will play no part in next month's World Cup finals in Japan and South Korea after directing what was described as a foul-mouthed tirade against manager Mick McCarthy at a team meeting on the Pacific island of Saipan. The Manchester United captain was sent home from the team's pre-World Cup training base after verbally abusing the Irish team boss, who challenged him over criticisms he made about aspects of Ireland's preparation in a newspaper interview . . .'

A newspaper interview? What newspaper interview? My mind could only speculate. Want to know what I thought? Well, knowing Roy as I did, my guess was that he was furious with himself for changing his mind about going home. So he did an interview – with either Tom Humphries or Paul Kimmage, the two journalists he tended to talk to. And whether he realised it or not, by doing so he was asking the manager to make the decision for him – to put him out of his misery.

Look, I know that's not how Roy saw it. He had his way of looking at the world and I had mine. He was a human and I was a dog, let's not forget that. But three years later, when he left Manchester United, wasn't the *modus operandi* the same? A furious row at training over his perceived slackness of the operation, followed by an interview with the media that implied criticism of the manager, followed by an argument with the manager, followed by banishment by mutual agreement.

Of course, Mick – with his status anxiety and his simple workingman's pride – was never going to do anything else except what he did, which was to gather everyone together and confront him. They both got what they wanted, subconsciously at least – the end of the stress that comes with pretending that you're happy when you're not. That's the way I saw it anyway.

Not that I cared anymore. Idina could see the change in me immediately. I had quietened right down. I just wanted him home now, just as I never wanted him to go away.

Hugh popped around later with a copy of the *Manchester Evening News*, which contained a precis of what Roy was supposed to have said to Mick – or rather, a version that the media agreed upon. I had a look at it over Idina's shoulder and I had to laugh. With all the swearwords asterisked out, it looked like the night sky at Guy Fawkes Day.

'You can't speak to your boss like that,' Hugh said. 'Look at alt these things he's called him.'

Some of them I actually recognised from conversations that Roy and I had had about Mick.

'But why did the other fella have to go and provoke him?' Idina said.

A neat enough summation, I suppose, of the argument that was raging at that point in every home and workplace in Ireland.

TRIGGS: THE AUTOBIOGRAPHY OF ROY KEANE'S DOG

Roy turned up the following day. I heard the car door slam and then I found myself suddenly staring at him along the length of Idina's hallway. His face erupted into a smile at the very sight of me and I abandoned myself to the moment. I ran and jumped at him and he caught me in a headlock and wrestled me lovingly and I barked and he laughed and I may have even licked his face. He'd obviously been at the after shave samples in the duty free at Heathrow.

'Was she okay?' he asked Idina.

'Oh, she's a smart one, that one,' was all she said.

Then we drove home, the nose of the car separating the sea of journalists and photographers lapping around the front gate. There were camera flashes. Questions shouted through the glass.

It was good to be home.

We entered the house through the double-door garage. Without a word, Roy disappeared upstairs. I listened from the hall. The taps in the bathroom ran. The toilet flushed. I heard him kick off his trainers. Wardrobe doors opened and closed. He came downstairs. He'd changed his clothes. His new outfit – jeans, trainers and a roundnecked sweatshirt – suggested a teenage mugger, but I said nothing. Just smiled. Because I knew what was coming next.

'Are you ready?' he said.

I waddled happily towards the door. Then we were striding through the gates and through the world's media like two predatory fish parting a school of tuna. We descended Bankhall Lane, taking the road, not the path, with dozens of bodies shuffling desperately behind us, alongside us, in front of us – the sound of shoe leather scuffing the road – pushing recording devices and camera lenses in our direction. And shouting, all at the same time.

'Any regrets, Roy?'

'Are you happy to be home?'

'Do you have a message for Mick and the lads?'

'What's the dog called, Roy?'

'Triggs,' someone – a veteran, I expect, of one of our earlier walks – said, and I saw quite a few people write it down. I probably had an idea then of how big this thing was going to be.

I tried to follow Roy's lead in always maintaining eye contact with one member of the pack, just to let them know that we weren't prey here. I admit, he was a lot better at it than I was.

Down Bankhall Lane we strode, until we reached our little stile. Roy went over it, I went under it and, for reasons I can't explain, the crowd chose not to follow us down the narrow, muddy path that led to the Bollin.

Five minutes later, Roy was sitting on a rock and I had settled my chin on his lap, the gentle murmur of the river's current like balm to my soul.

'You were right,' he said.

I didn't respond. It was nice to hear him say it but the last thing he needed was me telling him I told you so. Humans and dogs often reach the same conclusion, but that doesn't mean they arrive there via the same route.

I tried to keep the conversation light. 'Stick your World Cup up your bollocks?' I said.

It was a line I remembered from his tribute to Mick. I could hear him delivering it in that high pitch of his.

He laughed. 'I meant to say, "Stick your World Cup up your arse, you bollocks," but, well, I was on a bit of a roll!'

It was interesting. It seemed to me that his anger with Mick had dissipated. Nothing like getting it off your chest, of course. Hard to think of any bases he neglected to cover if the account in the *Manchester Evening News* was accurate. Now his anger seemed to be directed at Niall Quinn and Steve Staunton, who'd sat alongside Mick at his press conference looking obligingly traumatised by what they'd just overheard over dinner in the Chinese restaurant.

Steve said he'd never heard anything like it in all of his years playing football. Niall said something similar. Niall had played in how many Manchester and Tyne-Wear derbies? Staunton had played for Liverpool against Everton, for Aston Villa against Birmingham – had they really never heard a man being called a cunt or a bollocks before?

'Sitting there,' he said, 'like two innocent children – *never heard the likes of it.* Open your ears next time you're taking a fucking corner kick. Jesus . . .'

His voice trailed off. I felt almost weightless with happiness at having him back.

'They want me to do an interview,' he said. 'For Irish television. Lad called Tommie Gorman. Thinking of maybe doing it.'

'Why?'

'Put my side.'

'Haven't you done that by coming home?'

'There's a lot of things being said back home. Traitor – blah, blah, blah.'

'Traitor?'

Dogs have no concept of nationalism. With us, it's just species and breed.

'I don't understand how that constitutes treachery,' I said.

'Ah, turning my back on my country – blah, blah, fucking blah. Anyway, I think I'm going to maybe do the interview.'

'They'll probably ask you to go back,' I said.

'Go back?'

'To Japan.'

'I'm not fucking going back.'

Over the days that followed, the argument became complicated by the search for a form of words that would suffice as an apology for Mick, but not represent a climbdown for Roy and would deliver him back to the World Cup finals. Take it from me, he was never going back. The Saipan Affair, as it became known, might have rent Irish families in two, but there was so much less to it than met the eye. To a dog's eyes, it was a simple hierarchical dispute. Two alphas who didn't like each other and who discovered, on a tiny island in the middle of the Pacific, that they just didn't have it in them to go on pretending.

We sat there for half an hour, then we picked ourselves up and – backs straight, heads up – made our way up the steep bank, across the golf course and back into the yattering maw of the waiting paparazzi.

Oh, and Ireland didn't win the World Cup that summer.

# 14.

# Wag!

MEMORY, UNLIKE A GOOD DOG AT YOUR SIDE, IS a notoriously unreliable adjutant. I'm conscious in writing this memoir that my recollection of events is at times, well, perpendicular to Roy's own account in his 'brutally honest' (*The Irish Times*), 'brutally frank' (*The Sun*) and 'brutally revealing' (BBC Sport) autobiography. Readers who place *Keane* and *Triggs* side by side to compare accounts of essentially the same life shared will learn nothing except that memoirs are just an account of what was true for you at a particular time. Which is why celebrities have so many cracks at it these days. Wayne Rooney's already had two goes, I think. Dwight Yorke's ex, I hear, is up to five now.

If journalism really is history's first draft, then these things are its second, no more definitive an account of what really happened than Ashley Cole's explanation of how photographs of him in his Y-fronts made it into the mobile phone of a woman who wasn't his wife.

That's the nature of perception, I suppose. And I'm a dog – I can't stress that enough times. There might be a seventy-five percent overlap in our genetic codes, but I've been around the track enough times to know that humans have modes of thinking that I could never fathom. And – let's be honest here – vice versa.

I knew all about Roy's book. Of course I did. Eamon Dunphy

had been a regular visitor to the house that spring. I must say, I rather liked him, much as that will disappoint some readers. He was a gregarious sort of character with a big, generous laugh and, yes, I took to him immediately. The interviews were conducted mostly in the study, but occasionally over tea or coffee in the kitchen, with me struggling to follow the torrents of conversation from the other side of a closed door.

The way it seemed to work was that Eamon would coax and urge, then Roy would share, his voice alternately ascending and descending in pitch, according to the seriousness of the subject. I asked Roy to keep my name out of it, which he mostly did, apart from a couple of references to how much of a support I'd been to him – which were greatly appreciated – and the line, 'Unlike humans, dogs don't talk shit,' which Eamon loved and insisted had to go in.

To be honest, I wasn't altogether comfortable with the attention I'd been getting. The television exposure we'd enjoyed that summer meant I couldn't go outside the door now without being recognised. Passers-by hailed me rather than Roy. It'd be, 'Alright, Triggs? Taking Keano for a walk again, are we?' or some variation on that theme. Roy loved it.

'You're more famous than me now,' he'd say.

Once, a white van with lettering on the side advertising 'painting and decorating solutions' slowed down on Langham Road and a voice from inside shouted, 'Triggs, what are you doing with that Manc bastard? Does he know you've got a season ticket for City?'

Roy laughed so much at that one – 'Hats off,' he said, at the sheer inventiveness of it – I thought he was going to cough up a lung. I laughed along, too. God knows, we'd had few enough reasons to laugh that summer.

I suddenly had a huge following. There were letters. There were cards. There were even marriage proposals. There are some very odd people out there, by the way, although you learned to spot them, generally from the green ink. Strangers, who'd seen the way Roy and I were around each other on television, would spill their hearts, their secrets, their problems out to me – for a while, I must have been Britain's most popular agony aunt. The sad, the lonely, the bereaved, the broken-hearted, the confused, they all wrote, just looking for an ear, their letters typically beginning with the words, 'I can't believe I'm writing a letter to a dog . . .' and often ending, after ten or twenty heart-rending pages, with the line, 'I don't expect you to write back.'

Which was very understanding of them. Regrettably, I was just too busy.

And still it kept on coming. There were presents. Squeak toys. Pull toys. Chew toys. A voodoo doll of Mick McCarthy that both Roy and I felt a little uneasy about handling. There were collars and leads, even though we didn't go in for them anymore. There were water bowls monogrammed with my name. There were His and Hers matching bath towels. Two pairs of baby-sized Diadora trainers that matched Roy's and fitted my paws perfectly. Someone sent me a darling little raincoat with the words 'I'm Proud to be Irish' on the back, although Roy and I could never figure out whether it was a gesture of solidarity or an underhanded comment on him, so I never bothered wearing it.

Then there were the notices I was garnering, which, from memory, included this one from *The Guardian*: 'There's no doubt, watching their body language, that Roy Keane and his dog Triggs enjoy a very loving symbiosis. You can see it in the way they walk in perfect lockstep with each other and in the little smiling glances they occasionally share, as if privy to a joke of which none of the attendant paparazzi are aware.'

And this one from the *Manchester Evening News*: 'It's nice to know that Roy Keane, who once famously admitted that he didn't have the phone number of a single Manchester United team-mate, has at least one close friend. Triggs, his obviously dearly-loved Labrador Retriever, has been a kind of emotional crutch to the United captain in the wake of his explosive row with Ireland manager Mick McCarthy on the eve of the World Cup. To the point where, it doesn't seem unreasonable to ask, is Roy walking the dog, or is the dog walking Roy?'

Very perceptive, that one.

And this one from *The Times*: 'If anyone has a secure line to the thoughts of the most complex figure in football today, it's the four-legged Labrador Retriever who has been his constant companion throughout the summer. They set off for their twice-daily walks through Hale like two boys together.'

Boys? There it was again. What were they doing on the subbing desks in these papers? A male adult Labrador would have been about fifteen pounds heavier than I was at that time, thank you very much.

You see, that was the two-edged sword of fame. And I knew from very early on that I didn't want it. I'm not saying I wasn't flattered to see myself described as 'Roy Keane's ever faithful hound' (*The Star*), 'the Manchester United captain's rock and support' (*Irish Independent*) and 'the most famous dog in football since Pickles, a mongrel who dug up the stolen Jules Rimet trophy in 1966' (*The Daily Telegraph*). But I had no interest in carving an identity for myself independent of him. Oh, I could have got myself an agent. Among the letters and gifts and – I kid you not – women's underwear that arrived, there were offers of book and movie deals, endorsement opportunities and television ads for everything from tinned food, which I didn't even eat, to a brand new flatscreen television model that was in direct competition to the Mitsubishi Black Diamond one that Mick McCarthy was advertising at the time. There was even a dog shampoo company that wanted me to star in a parody of David Ginola's L'Oréal ad. I think David Baddiel was going to do the voice.

We did think about that one. It sounded like it could be a laugh. But in the end, I turned everything down. I suppose I just had a very acute sense of my place – and that place was at Roy Keane's trainer-shod feet, wherever they should take us.

An observant eye will have noticed how, after our first two or three walks, when I jumped about playfully, admittedly excited by the attention, I began to tone down the act a bit, keeping my eyes lowered and reverting to playing the humble chatelaine, which is probably where a lot of the misconceptions about me being a weak and submissive animal came from. I mean, she's Roy Keane's dog – what else was she going to be, right?

Hah!

No, I realised with a selflessness that would be very much typical of the Labrador mindset that none of this was about me. Even with my name on the lips of hundreds of millions of people across five continents, it was never necessary for Roy to remind me that I was here for him. I was here for Roy Keane.

That was the reason I asked him to let me read the galley proofs of his book. Look, I'm not saying I would have told him to tone down what he said about the business with Alfie. I might have forewarned him that saying he'd waited three years to do what he did – and especially the line, 'Take that, you cunt' – was going to land him with an FA disrepute charge. Or maybe I wouldn't. Roy had already served a suspension for it, after all. Notwithstanding the little white lies that the pundits indulged in when they spoke about these things ('Oooh, he's mistimed it badly, hasn't he? I'll tell you what, though, I know him – and he'll be furious with himself for that one!'), I thought it was accepted by everyone that Roy had set out to deliberately injure Alfie. Isn't that why the FA banned him for three matches? It wasn't for poor timing, was it?

The deadline for the book was tight. In the end, Roy didn't bother showing me the pages. Perhaps I could have pushed it with him. But looking back, after the year we'd just been through – and I was still feeling an enormous weight of guilt over the *Only Fools and Horses* business – I was more concerned with drawing a line under the past and getting on with the new season.

I was excited. United had spent nearly £30m on Rio Ferdinand and I tended to agree with Roy's assessment of him as 'a definite player – a top, top centre-half, who can obviously play a bit as well'.

It was about time the club got serious, I thought.

They started the season shakily. Overcame Zalaegerszeg in a Champions League qualifier after losing the first leg in Hungary, narrowly beat West Brom, then drew with Chelsea, before the first extracts from *Keane* appeared in the *News of the World*. Well, I knew there was going to be trouble from the moment I saw the headline. 'Take That', etcetera. But I said nothing.

It was a day or two later, while we were engaged in a bit of roughhouse play in the back garden, that Roy brought it up out of nowhere.

'Been charged,' he said.

I was play-biting his exposed forearm at the time. I feigned surprise. 'Charged?'

'Bringing the game into obviously disrepute.'

'Oh.'

It was easier to ignore what was weighing heavily on my mind and no doubt his: that I'd offered to throw my eyes over the manuscript, but then, unusually for me, hadn't followed through.

'Stuff I said about Alfie,' he said. 'Fucking clown.'

'What kind of a ban are we looking at?'

'Three, maybe four games.'

This was trouble we didn't need, and I admit I felt awful in that moment. Not reading the book had been a dereliction of my responsibilities to Roy. I worried about him all that week. He did everything – made scrambled eggs, set the video to record *Top Gear*, picked food debris from the dishwasher's filter cup – with his face set in a hard expression of defiance. And after a break of a few weeks, we had company on our walks again, a tighter little clique of journalists and photographers this time, scuttling after us down Bankhall Lane, shouting, 'Any regrets, Roy?' and 'Do you have anything to say to Haaland?'

Except it wasn't fun like it was before. The novelty had worn off after a long summer of it. And I sensed a more general fatigue in Roy. His knee was still at him. His hip was at him, too – as was mine, by the way, though I didn't like to mention it – and he was going to need an operation. But he was fed up as well. Everyone, I suppose, has a threshold of trouble.

As the following weekend approached, I got a sense of things coming to a head. Dogs have an innate feel for it – you'll have gathered that by now. And, look, I'm not going to deny that I heard Bob Dylan's voice in the house that week because I did. Again, without wishing to labour the point here, the slipshod organisation, easy marks and missed opportunities in his songs were things that the perfectionist Roy would normally have hated, but he always found it in himself to suspend his critical faculties when it came to music.

United were playing Sunderland and everyone was greatly exercised by the fact that it was the first time Roy would come face to face with Niall Quinn and Jason McAteer since Saipan. Like Roy even cared. But Quinn *did* care. He tried to pre-arrange a handshake with Roy on the pitch before the match – who the hell did he think they were, Yasser Arafat and Yitzhak Rabin? – but Roy was having none of it, and that just added kindling to the situation.

It wasn't a live televised game and I spent the afternoon in the laundry room, tending to a sweet potato that I'd plucked from the vegetable tower, with a small knot of apprehension hardening in me. I found out from the news that Roy had been sent off for elbowing Jason McAteer in the face off the ball.

I saw it later on *Match of the Day*. Looking back, I blamed Alex Ferguson for not substituting Roy. He was coiled so tightly – he gave poor Phil Neville an angry shove at one point – that you just knew how it was going to end when Jason started writing with an imaginary pen and saying, 'Put it in your book, Roy. Put it in your book.'

So Roy was sent off again. Quinn watched him trudging off the field, full of self-disgust, and decided that this was the ideal window for *that* handshake, misjudging the situation like he tended to misjudge most things, crosses included.

'Fuck off!' Ferguson told Quinn.

The words may have slipped my lips, too.

So for Roy, it'd be three more matches missed on top of whatever the FA were going to give him for the Haaland business. He arrived home in the early hours of the morning, two placatory hands in the air, not upset, not angry, just worn out.

'Fucking Jason,' he said, almost as an exhalation, kicking off his trainers and throwing his car keys on the free-standing island.

The thing was, he liked Jason. We both did. There was an uncomplicated quality to Jason's happiness. The idiot act, by the way, was just cabaret. He was smart and – Roy and I both agreed – a far better player than he gave himself credit for.

It would have been an insult to both our intelligences to pretend that this was about Jason mouthing off, though. Roy needed a break. I felt that very strongly. And, as it happened, Alex Ferguson did too.

'The manager thinks I should maybe get my hip done,' he said. He opened the fridge door. He was going to heat some milk for himself.

'When?'

'Straight away. I'm going to get three matches for hitting obviously Jason – fucking stupid, shouldn't have let myself get sucked in, even though he maybe had it coming to him at the end of the day – and then four, maybe five matches for the book. You're looking at the best part of two months.'

'Makes sense then.'

'Listen, as I said, one way or the other, the hip's going to have to be done. Might as well be now.'

So that is how Roy and I came to watch almost the entire first half of the 2002/3 season unfurl from the living room sofa. We both enjoyed the time together, if not the football, which was some of the worst I'd ever seen them play. Two wins from their first six league games had them down in ninth position in the league, their worst start to a season, someone pointed out, since the club was last relegated.

'He'll be loving all of this,' Roy told me one squally afternoon on the Rappax Road that autumn. He was picking up after me at the time, wearing a plastic sandwich bag like a glove to pluck it off the ground, then turning the bag inside out to capture it inside, a ritual performed with the same expression of barely contained outrage he usually wore when he was within tackling range of Patrick Vieira or Emmanuel Petit or Lee Bowyer or Danny Murphy.

'Who'll be loving all of this?' I wondered.

'The manager. Everyone writing him off. Writing obviously the team off. Saying they've maybe had their day. End of an era. Blah, blah, blah.'

This was true. A shareholder had stood up at the club AGM

and said that Ferguson should be sacked. And at the same time, Arsenal looked so good – they always did during Roy's enforced absences, did you notice? – that Arsene Wenger started positing the idea that they might go through the entire league season without losing a match.

I'll be honest, it did cross my mind, too, that Ferguson might have been wrong to go back on his plans to retire. The team seemed to be a testament to his diminishing powers of judgment. Laurent Blanc was still there and still a liability. Juan Sebastian Veron had improved, but now he was being pushed from position to position and I still didn't believe he was suited to the hard-working demands of the English game. Diego Forlan was a striker who hadn't scored in twenty-six games – do I need to add to that? I was even having doubts about Rio Ferdinand, which I kept to myself because I'd decided to remain upbeat for Roy's sake, especially in the weeks after the operation.

It was about two-and-a-half weeks before he threw away the crutches, then we started our walks again, just the two of us, the way it used to be – short distances at first, then adding a hundred metres or so every day. At the beginning it was, 'See can we make it to the bridge over the railway tracks!', but then before too long it was, 'The clock tower and back, Triggs! Let's try and take five minutes off obviously yesterday's time!'

I felt like I was a young dog again, helping him through the early, halting steps in his recovery from his cruciate injury. This time, though, there was no doubt about him playing again and he stayed positive. There was a lot of talk about Vieira getting away with murder – 'no one's asking any fucking questions of the lad' – which was always a sign of where Roy's attitude was at.

That's why I kept my view that Ferdinand was slow and a bit too casual to myself, even as Nicholas Anelka cut him to pieces in the Manchester derby that November. The entire United team was bad that day. All you'd have heard if you'd stood outside our living room door while it was on was Roy and I groaning in close harmonies.

Roy said Ferguson sat them all down afterwards and told them they were a disgrace to the club. Something like that.

'Listen, they know,' Roy said. At the time he was peeling back the lids of my eyes with his thumb. I'd become somehow convinced that I had corneal dystrophy, a condition to which Labradors are particularly prone. 'They don't need obviously the manager to tell them that that level of performance isn't good enough for Manchester United Football Club. They know. I think I've said quite a few times of late – there's no fucking aggression about them. When was the last time you saw a team scared to be playing Manchester United? They all fancy their chances . . . Triggs, there's fuck-all wrong with your eyes.'

'Are you sure?' I said.

He let go of my lids.

'Like I said before . . .'

'Did you look for greyish white lines on the corneas?'

'Triggs, there's nothing wrong with them.' He laughed then. 'What was it you thought you had last week?'

I looked away. 'A luxating patella,' I said.

He laughed again. 'A luxating patella! Jesus Christ! And I won't even try to pronounce what you told me you had when I took you to the vet a month ago.'

It was osteochondritis dissecans, but I said nothing.

'Isn't it funny how you always get these things, Triggs, when I'm out obviously injured as well?'

I knew what he was getting at. Look, I was a smart dog. Of course I'd considered the possibility that at least some of my illnesses were sympathetic in nature.

Ferguson's talk seemed to work. Didn't they always? In

three consecutive league matches that November and December, they beat Newcastle, Liverpool and Arsenal. Roy was already straining at the lead to get back, especially when we watched Phil Neville destroy Vieira in the first week of December. He was outstanding that day, like someone had transplanted Roy's brain into his head and his heart into his chest cavity.

'That shove you gave him seems to have done the trick,' I said.

Roy laughed. 'What can you say about that performance? Obviously tremendous. The Fireman, the lads call him, because that's what he does when he's on top, top form – runs around putting out fires.'

Roy and I, we were a team.

*He's cleaning out the gutters. I'm standing at the foot of the ladder, looking up at him throwing down handfuls of leaves wet with rainwater and little cakes of mud with tufts of grass attached. I hold my nose to one and have a sniff. He turns his head and looks at me down the length of his back.*

*'Triggs,' he says, 'that's muck.'*

*Then he's quiet and I know him well enough to know that he's enjoying some private, gallows joke about his team's defending also being muck.*

*Ipswich lost 4–1 to Norwich yesterday. It was on the radio this morning. Norwich skipper Grant Holt bagged a hat-trick as the Canaries deepened the problems of their East Anglia rivals . . . and blah, blah, fucking blah, as Roy might say himself.*

*He plucks a tennis ball from the trough and throws it casually over his right shoulder. I watch it bounce once, twice, three times, trying to snap at it as it describes a series of ever-shortening arcs. Then it stops bouncing and starts rolling, away from the house, down the slope of the front driveway, and I chase after it, barking and attempting to catch it in my teeth, but succeeding only in nudging it with my nose, adding to its momentum.*

*The front gate brings its life to a dramatic end. It hits it hard, rears up, then dies in a series of little bounces. I bark twice, then assume a play position, my chest flat on the tarmacadam, my rump raised in the air.*

*For his entire football career, Roy worked with very talented footballers – the exceptions I have mostly covered – who shared his ambition. He could persuade players to do anything. All it ever took was a word. And sometimes only a look.*

*But there's no van Nistelrooy at this club. No Giggs. No Cole. No Beckham. No Scholes. No Schmeichel. No Neville. No Butt.*

*These are Championship players. Most of them will only ever be Championship players. As he learned at Sunderland, you can persuade them to play above themselves only for so long. And then what do you do? Kick the tactics board? Start transfer-listing some to encourage the others? Shout louder?*

*I have no answers for him and that's why my heart is in a permanent state of breaking. I turn my head sideways, take the ball between my teeth and trot back to the house.*

Laurent Blanc was a modest man. But then, as I think I've mentioned, he had a lot to be modest about. At the same time, Roy liked him – 'two good feet, obviously a tremendous footballing brain and a great character in the dressing-room' – so I learned to just bite my tongue whenever his name came up.

He was going to be gone at the end of the season anyway.

But there was one day during the autumn of Roy's recovery from his hip surgery when a chance meeting with the man I held partly responsible for costing United the league, and the Champions League the previous season, was to define what would be the third and final phase of Roy's career.

There we were, limbering along Ashley Road one mild Tuesday afternoon when we ran into him, feeding coins into a parking meter outside Pizza Express. It was, "Allo, Roy. 'Allo, Triggs,' and, 'Alright, Laurent?' and very quickly they settled into a conversation about Roy's hip and how it was healing.

'You are how old?' Blanc wondered.

'Thirty-one,' Roy said. 'Obviously thirty-two my next birthday.'

'You are in tremendous shape,' he said and his eyes made his meaning, tracing the hard outline of his pectorals through his long-sleeved T-shirt. Roy had maintained a regimen of daily exercise throughout his recuperation. 'But this I must say to you – you must take things a little bit easier.'

Roy laughed at the idea, while I just thought, 'Yeah, that'd be right, coming from you, Laurent.'

'Roy, I am serious. For me, you are the best player in England. At what you do – *comment le dites-vous*, box to box, yes? – you are the best in the world. *Sans doute*. But if you continue playing the way you have been playing – with your hip – you will have perhaps two years left. If you become more clever in how you use your energy, you can play for four, perhaps five.'

I watched Roy weigh this up. 'Yeah, you maybe have a point there,' he said.

I started sniffing at a discarded crisp packet with a big-deal look on my face.

'Of course, you must also stop this,' he said and he made a sort of chopping motion with his elbow that I took to be a reference to him cuffing Jason McAteer around the ear. 'You are invaluable (*enn-valu-obluh*) to Manchester United when you are on the pitch. You are worth nothing to Manchester United when you are not.'

It was all a bit stating-the-obvious to me, even if the French accent lent the words a more meaningful connotation than they perhaps deserved. I was sure that must have been a large part of Cantona's charm, too. But Roy was clearly moved by what he'd heard. He picked up some cubes of beef in the butchers for a stew, then we puttered back to the house, with Roy talking the whole way about Blanc and what a 'top, top professional' he was and how he'd 'proven himself at obviously the highest level of the game' and how his preparation for matches was 'phenomenal'.

It wasn't jealousy. I just didn't think he'd said anything that I was incapable of coming up with myself. But I swallowed down my feelings – Labradors are the dictionary definition of the term altruism – and accepted that sometimes we need to hear different voices in our ears, even if they're saying the same things.

As I've said more than once in these pages, it wasn't about me. My priority was Roy and getting him back playing football again.

At the beginning of December he drew a ring around Boxing Day on the calendar – away to Middlesbrough – as the date of his return. I think it would be fair to say that we both wished Christmas away that year. Then off he went to face Middlesbrough, with a final injunction from me: 'Watch those balls through to Alen Boksic. He might be getting on in years, Roy, but he's still quick.'

United were beaten that day, and beaten badly. The details – including those of Boksic's opening goal in the 3–1 defeat – are of academic interest only. The point is that it was another of those days that were like a cold shower. The players gave themselves a good shake, then went back to the perfunctory business of putting away the Birminghams and the Sunderlands and the Southamptons and the West Bromwich Albions – the humdrum work on which their success was founded.

There was another meeting in Alex Ferguson's house, between the defeat to Middlesbrough and the victory over Birmingham two days later. Another of those line-in-the-sand get-togethers he occasionally hosted when he felt like the players needed a collective roust – my first, as it happens, since I'd shown Ole Gunnar Solskjær the size of my incisors four Christmases earlier. And though he continued to plague my dreams on an intermittent basis – 'Ego doesh not come into it! At the end of the day, itsh about the team!' – I said yes when Roy asked if I fancied coming along for the drive. He liked having me around – that was hardly a secret.

'Do you think you'll be okay – obviously around Ole?' he asked, as he sought a parking space between the Bentley Continentals and the Aston Martin Vanquishes and the Lamborghini Gallardos and Gary Neville's Prius, which was still running fantastically well, I'd heard in dispatches – its fuel efficiency, you'd have to say, sublime.

'I think I can control myself,' I said.

'Are you sure?'

'I think so.'

'He's a good lad, Triggs, as I think I've said on maybe one or two occasions in the past. Obvously still banging them in as well. Doesn't miss many – look at his record.'

I dropped out of the car onto the cobblelock, which I couldn't help but notice was of the same herringbone design as ours. I remembered Ferguson admiring it. And that's when I spotted Ole, out front, demonstrating in mime a goal he once scored for a clearly enraptured Ruud van Nistelrooy.

'The ball bounched up invitingly,' he was saying, 'and I think to myshelf, okay, technique ish everything in momentsh like thish . . .'

'Maybe I'll wait in the car after all,' I said.

But Roy wouldn't hear of it. 'Come on, Triggs, you've seen him how many times before on television? Obviously the Baby-Faced Assassin. And you've never had any problem with that.'

My nightmares were perhaps the only secret I ever kept from Roy.

I walked with him towards the house, hiding behind the

moving shield of his legs, and aimed a peremptory, side-of-the-mouth warning growl in Ole's direction as we passed – for which Roy was forced to apologise.

'I think it might just be your smile,' he said, steering me through the front door with a firm grip on my withers.

Ferguson greeted us in the hallway with a, 'Happy New Year,' and a, 'Ah, you've brought Triggs,' and I remembered hearing many times about his extraordinary head for names. He had them all on instant recall, the wives, girlfriends and children of the players he had, and the players he had designs on, youth team players, kids that the club's extensive network of scouts were keeping tabs on, their mums and dads, brothers and sisters. And now pets? You couldn't but be impressed by a man like that.

Imagine, if you can, the excitement that rose in me when he turned to Roy and said, 'Put her out the back garden, Roy – my wee fella is out there.'

Now, I must confess something here. I've never been what you might call a social animal. Humans, I liked. Some of them I liked very much. But meeting other dogs held little or no interest for me. Oh, I could breeze through the social mechanics involved – sniffing each other's odours, declining an invitation to play with a flash of my teeth – but generally speaking, I could take them or leave them.

But this was different. This was Alex Ferguson's dog Knox, he called him. What animal wouldn't want to meet Alex Ferguson's dog? Sure, he was still a relative pup at two – or fourteen, whatever way you chose to calculate these things. But I've always thought that people who refer to dog years and human years tend to miss the point. A life is most accurately measured not by years but by the intensity at which it's lived. Actually, I don't know where I picked that quote up. Might have been one of Roy's. But it's as true for dogs as it is for humans.

I couldn't wait to meet him. I thought, Imagine what this animal knows!

I weaved my way through the forest of human legs in the hallway – Rio Ferdinand and John O'Shea discussing the wedding of Billy Mitchell to Little Mo Slater in *EastEnders*, David Beckham throwing back his blonde mane to offer Nicky Butt a sniff of the new Clive Christian that Mrs David Beckham had bought him for Christmas – with Roy forced to run to maintain his handhold on my scruff. In the end he let go and I bounced through the dog flap in the back door and out into the garden – Ferguson may have called it a yard – to find myself staring at an Alsatian-Collie cross. He was lying untidily, like a thrown sable stole, in the doorway of Ferguson's greenhouse, trying to bite his own tail, looking every inch the hopeless dud that he turned out to be in reality.

I couldn't believe it. I was beyond disappointed. Look, I'm not making any claims for myself as a towering intellect, but that was one stupid dog. One of those animals trapped in a perpetual present, his entire world circumscribed by just three urges, which I imagined playing in a continuous loop behind those shallow, expressionless eyes of his: eat, sleep, fuck.

A bit like [*name removed for legal reasons*]. Without the eating and the sleeping, of course.

I sensed his interest in me even before he climbed to his feet and shambled over with a confidence so ill-justified, you had to wonder was he even all there. He didn't bother with the preliminaries, just attempted to board me without fanfare. Christ, I wasn't even ovulating! I turned my head and took a generous bite of his flank and he howled, then staggered back to the greenhouse, whining that I should have told him I wasn't interested before he went to the trouble of getting up.

Pardon my language here, but what a fucking arsehole.

I walked around the outside of the house and found the lounge room window, which was conveniently open, even though it was two below zero outside. Ferguson had a schoolmasterish fixation with fresh air as an aid to thought. I threw my front paws up on the window ledge and watched the humans array themselves around the room, already rubbing their upper arms and their thighs against the punitive cold. Poor Juan Sebastian Veron was kitted out in ski gear – his narrow, goateed face and jug ears, with their giant hoop earrings, peering out from beneath layers of insulation, like a pirate about to tackle the Eiger.

I thought, There's a man who's not long for the north of England.

Ferguson said that nobody in the room needed to be told how poorly the team had been playing recently and it had helped in the past to get everyone together like this to air things out, circle the wagons, regroup.

Gary Neville spoke up. Which was often the way. 'At the end of the day, it's like the gaffer said in the dressing-room yesterday – it's up to us as a team to maybe stop the rot. I mean, it hurts to lose matches like we've been losing them of late. It's obviously not what we've been used to at Manchester United Football Club. And I fully understand the frustration of our fans because we've not been playing well. We've simply not been playing well and it winds me up as much as it does them. I mean, if you'd told me at the start of the season that we'd lose back-to-back matches against Blackburn and Middlesbrough, I'd have not believed you. Flat out. I'd have had to pinch meself. And that's not meant with any disrespect towards Blackburn or Middlesbrough.'

Next, it was Phil Neville: 'Still feels almost surreal. You'd look at those two matches and normally you'd think six points. But they've not read the script.'

Then Ryan Giggs: 'Middlesbrough have become maybe something of a bogey side to us of late. A real potential banana skin. To be fair, even though we've not performed on the day

– that much has been documented – it could just as easily have been 3–1 the other way. Had we converted maybe one or two of our chances.'

'Definitely,' Rio Ferdinand said.

He tended to say that a lot.

'Credit to Middlesbrough,' Nicky Butt piped up. 'For me, they've done ever so well. They've deserved their win, no question. Probably helped a bit by obviously Boksic's goal early doors. The second one was the real killer – even though Giggsy's done tremendously well to get us back into the game . . .'

'Scant consolation,' Giggs said.

'It were some goal by the lad Szilard Nemeth,' Butt said. 'I think he'll probably dine out on that one for a long time to come!'

'And – for me – even though we've not turned up on the day, the lad Queudrue's played out of his skin as well.' This from John O'Shea.

Through the window, I searched the room for Roy's face to find out what he was making of all of this, but he was out of my line of vision. My back legs were sore from standing, so I dropped back onto all fours and followed, as best I could, the sallies of conversation from a sitting position underneath the window.

Gary Neville: 'At the same time, you'd have to say, let's not go beating ourselves up. Seven Premier League titles in ten years, *I* think, says a lot for our quality. And hopefully that can continue. Even though Sheasy's right, we've not turned up on the day of late, sometimes you have to maybe focus on the positives. Like, obviously Ruud's doing fantastically well at the minute – still banging them in. He's been like a talisman, to be fair. I'm trying to think of the expression that Lawro's used on the telly to describe what it must be like to try to mark him . . .'

Nicky Butt: 'Juggling custard.'

Gary Neville: 'That were it! You've got to hand it to Lawro, it's a tremendous expression. But that *must* be what it's like for defenders – I certainly wouldn't relish playing against you, Ruud.'

Ruud van Nistelrooy: '(Laughs).'

Gary Neville: 'Plus, Diego's off the mark now. I think I'm on the record as saying that once he's broke his duck, it'll not be long before he's scoring freely – that's beyond question.'

Paul Scholes: 'Seba's another who's in obviously scintillating form.'

Rio Ferdinand: 'Definitely.'

Paul Scholes: 'You'd nearly have to say spellbinding. He's a player who's been obviously mercilessly targeted in the past by a section of our crowd, even though most of our supporters have been tremendous . . .'

Juan Sebastian Veron: '(Nothing).'

Paul Scholes: 'Like a lot of South Americans who've come to these shores, he's maybe not settled in straight way. But I think he's proving now what a tip-top player he is – his form's been downright amazing of late – and he's richly deserved the plaudits he's been getting. I think he's going to do phenomenally well for us.'

Juan Sebastian Veron: '(Nothing).'

Roy took a breath and silence suddenly fell across the room. It kind of put me in mind of that scene from *Jaws* – which Roy loved to watch – when Robert Shaw tells the public meeting that he'll catch their shark, 'the head, the tail, the whole damn thing.'

'Teams used to play us and they'd be scared before they went out on the pitch,' he said, his voice climbing and rappeling. 'You'd see it in their eyes in the tunnel. Didn't believe in themselves. Be nearly Game Over before a ball was kicked. I don't see that anymore. Every team we play now, they fancy their chances. Even at Old Trafford. It's been going on for nearly two years now and I'm blue in the face saying it. Going out there, thinking, doesn't matter if we concede two or three goals, we'll get four at the other end. But it's not good enough. It's not good enough for this football club.

'But as I said, I'm saying it so long, I'm getting sick of the sound of my own voice. It's no good obviously patting ourselves on the back – you're on about Seba's doing well, Ruud's getting goals for fun, blah, blah, fucking blah. I don't know do some of us need reminding that we won nothing last season. We won nothing last season and, the way we're going, we're going to win nothing this season either. And that's exactly what we deserve.

'Because we've started to believe the hype about ourselves. Fergie's Fledglings. The elusive treble. Double winners. Double-double winners. Three-in-a-row winners. Obviously the money. The mansions. The fucking cars outside that door. And we've forgotten the basics. We've forgotten . . . the basics. How to defend. How to keep possession. How to put obviously pressure on other teams. And I'm including myself in that. We've forgotten how to be clinical. How to put these teams away – your Blackburns, no disrespect, your Middlesbroughs – week in, week out. That's what we need to start doing again. And let's put the past in the fucking bin where it belongs.'

Someone started clapping. Then a general round of applause broke out. Honestly, *I'd* have gone out and played for Manchester United after hearing that little speech.

'Well put, Roy,' I heard Ferguson say, apparently joining the applause. 'Very well put.'


I say this with all due modesty, of course, but of all the Premier League title wins to which I contributed, the 2002/3 one gave me more pleasure than any other. Mainly because it should never have happened. Arsenal looked so good that winter and early spring that it really did feel like the centre had shifted. They were two points ahead with a game in hand and it should have been more.

United chipped away at their lead, though, by doing just what Roy had said – clinically disposing of Southampton, Birmingham, Fulham, Charlton, Aston Villa. Roy was playing a cleverer game, not charging full-bore into challenges anymore – playing more patiently, more intelligently. Van Nistelrooy was – and remains to this day – the greatest goalscorer I've ever seen and some of the best defenders in England were turned into gibbering incompetents that year by the thought of what he could do to them. And there was a general tightening up at the back.

I was holding my end up too, contributing, in my own small way, little insights and observations as they occurred to me. Climbing Arthog Road the night before United played Chelsea that January, for instance, I reminded Roy of Graeme Le Saux's occasional doziness when he was in possession – or Graeme Le So-So, as I used to call him because it always got a laugh out of Roy. Anyway, you may or may not remember – and it's probably not that important anyway – that Roy robbed Le Saux of the ball in midfield that day for Veron to set up Forlan's winner.

Another night that March, he was standing on a chair, changing the light bulb in the laundry room, when I mentioned Leeds United's inability to organise themselves at set-pieces. Two days later, Mickaël Silvestre slipped unseen past the guards and headed in a Beckham free-kick for three more points.

I was very much on top of my game.

I also took a leaf out of Roy's book in making my contributions a bit more, shall we say, nuanced? I no longer charged in mindlessly. For instance, I resisted the urge to tell him what I really thought of Rio Ferdinand, which was that he had no pace and a mind that tended to wander – and God knows, it was too small to be out by itself. Instead, I told him that they could all do with concentrating a bit better at the back. And suddenly they did, including Rio.

Similarly, when Ryan Giggs's form deserted him that season and the crowd was on his case, I pointed out to Roy how long it was since he'd had a week off. So Ferguson dropped him for a couple of games. Giggs came off the bench to score what I still regard as the greatest goal of his career, against Juventus in Turin.

It's amazing how, when things are going well, one week just bleeds into the next. Slowly, inexorably, Arsenal were reeled in. And at the same time United coasted through what might have been a problematic Champions League group to reach the quarter-finals.

All of this was set against the backdrop of Alex Ferguson's disintegrating relationship with David Beckham.

I'm a very intuitive animal, as you know. And I'd picked up on the bad vibes at Ferguson's house that Christmas. I could read it in the signals their bodies were giving off even in the brief minutes I spent peering through the window. There'd been words, I later learned. Beckham had gone to Buckingham Palace for something or other while he was injured and Ferguson was unhappy with him. Then he'd asked for time off to attend his son's nativity play. I expect the kid was a far more convincing Wise Man than his father.

Don't get me wrong, I liked Beckham. I hope I haven't given the impression that I didn't. He was a good man. And a great footballer – some of his qualities were greatly underrated. But I just had these nagging doubts about him that refused to be silenced. I remember hearing that he was collecting signed football shirts for the wall of his pool room and I felt, well, much the same as I would feel when I watched him hugging Zinedine Zidane in the tunnel before England played France at Euro 2004. Blame it on my upbringing, but I was thinking: would Roy do that?

I suppose the lesson is that you can't fight your nature. I understood that better than anyone. One moment I was regaling Roy with the story of the splitting of the atom in a Cambridge laboratory in 1932, the next I was outside the Co-Op Foodstore on Ashley Road with my nose in another dog's shit. We can strive to be who we want to be but, in the end, who we are is who we are. It's as true for humans as it is for any species.

Whatever was going on between Ferguson and Beckham came to a furious head on an afternoon that you probably know all about already. Arsenal put United out of the FA Cup. Ferguson blamed Beckham for Arsenal's second goal. For what it's worth, I did, too – he should have followed Edu's run. But Beckham took exception to being singled out. Ferguson asked Beckham why he couldn't be told anything. Beckham swore at him. Ferguson kicked a boot, which flew up like a woodcock frightened into flight and cracked Beckham in the face, opening a cut above his eye. Beckham went for Ferguson and Giggs, Gary Neville and van Nistelrooy had to practically sit on him to restrain him.

I remember thinking, it was a good job Steve Staunton wasn't in the room, given his famouly low tolerance threshold for that kind of thing. He'd have had an aneurysm.

I heard about it from Roy. I was in the kitchen, tending to a bowl of mashed banana, when he started filling me in and I remember listening to the details with yellow-white pulp just spilling from the sides of my dumbfounded mouth.

'What were you doing while all this was happening?' I asked.

Roy shrugged. 'Just sitting there.'

I had to laugh. 'A fight in the dressing room and Roy Keane is an innocent bystander. So this is the new mellow you, is it?'

He laughed as well. We both enjoyed the gentle mocking that was always a feature of our relationship.

Anyway, Beckham went out to face the paparazzi with the hair swept back off his forehead and the newspapers – as they say in the trade – had a field day. And you knew from that moment that his days at the club were numbered.

A day or two later, Roy and I ran into him on a service station forecourt on Oxford Road, not far from Manchester Royal Infirmary. Roy had popped in for a Tracker Bar, which he was going to share with me, when we spotted Beckham filling up the Range Rover, with two strips of paper stitching crudely marking the point of the boot's impact like an X on a treasure map.

Roy told me to wait in the car. I stared across the forecourt and watched him, with a softly expression on his face, tell Beckham – no doubt – that he was a top, top player, possibly even world class, but he had to just put his head down now and work through this thing. Beckham listened with his bottom lip all stubborn-seeming. As we drove away – Roy forgot the Tracker, by the way – I watched Beckham replace the fuel gun. It was the last time I ever saw him.

On the field, Beckham's response to what happened was typical of him. He played some of the best football of his life. I'll never forget the image of him robbing Edgar Davids in the middle of the pitch to set up van Nistelrooy's winner against Juventus at Old Trafford just a few days later.

That was when it started, all the talk of a dream Champions League final. It was due to be played that May at Old Trafford and Roy gave me to believe that, if United made the final, he might bring me along as his guest. Or he'd at least ask the ground staff if there was any policy regarding animals as spectators.

Imagine, if you can, my excitement! My first football match! And though I had managed, over the course of my

life, to subjugate my selfish desires in the cause of serving
Roy, I must confess that my imagination ran a little away with
me. I kept thinking about the media reaction. The camera
zooming in on the VIP seats. Clive Tyldesley's disbelieving
voice wondering is that . . . no . . . surely it couldn't be . . .
could it? Is that Triggs? The Labrador who was at Roy Keane's
constant companion and, dare I say, sidekick throughout his
post-World Cup ordeal last summer? The animal described
by no less a wit than Frank Skinner as 'Greater Manchester's
fittest dog'? And there I'd be, looking dignified and, yes,
even quite beautiful in the blue glow of the downlights – it
hasn't escaped my attention that I have a certain something
– shampooed and primped for the occasion, no doubt, in one
of Manchester's finest dog-grooming parlours, with Sir Bobby
Charlton on one side of me – 'Tremendous sense of occasion,
Triggs!' – and Victoria Beckham on the other, provided she
didn't turn up wearing the same colour as me and demand
that I be moved.

And the front pages the following day. 'Roy Keane's Wag!'
they were all bound to say.

Yes, it was a beautiful dream, which lasted until the morning
Roy arrived home from training and told me they'd drawn
Real Madrid in the quarter-finals.

I'm not and never have been a defeatist dog. Check out
the Discovery Channel. You'll hear stories about Labradors
continuing to sniff through earthquake rubble days after most
humans have abandoned hope of finding anyone else alive.
That's what we're like. We don't give up. And neither did I
buy into this Team of the Century rubbish about Real Madrid.
Yes, they had Zinedine Zidane, Luis Figo, Ronaldo, Raul and
Roberto Carlos, but, as a team, they were top heavy and
far less than the sum of their parts. They didn't win a single
Champions League game between the middle of September
and the middle of February. Roma beat them. So did AC

Milan. AEK Athens managed to score five goals against them in their two group games.

They weren't unbeatable. I just doubted whether United had the personnel to do it over the course of two matches.

I shared one or two ideas I had with Roy a few days before the first leg in Madrid. He was clearing old paint tins out of the shed ahead of a skip arriving that afternoon. The approach of spring always brought out this urge in Roy to dejunk his life. 'Jesus,' he was saying, 'I don't even recognise half these colours. Saffron. Obviously taupe . . .'

*Tauuupe.*

The previous day, United had beaten Liverpool 4–0 and there was a lot of talk afterwards about them having to fear no team.

'I don't think Real have anyone as bad as Sami Hyypia,' I said. Hyypia had been sent off after five minutes for pulling van Nistelrooy down like a steer.

'At the same time, they're not unbeatable,' he said. 'Yeah, they've got obviously players who can punish you. But I think I'm on the record as saying that they've got their weaknesses, same as any other team.'

'As you know,' I said, 'I've been watching quite a bit of La Liga this season.'

'You have actually.'

'And I've noticed that the teams who've had the most success against Real are the ones who've attacked them down their right flank.'

'You don't rate the lad Salgado?'

'He's good. But he doesn't get a lot of defensive cover from Figo. Doesn't get any, in fact.'

'You might have a point there.'

'And you've watched them with me. We know that Claude Makelele will run the match from the middle of the field if he's allowed. But if he's harried and closed down quickly, you can disrupt the tempo that's so important to Real's game. And Beckham needs to push forward more than he's been doing lately because the way to blunt the attacking threat of Roberto Carlos is to keep him inundated with defensive work.'

'You've always said that, in fairness.'

'So plenty of width. The full-backs need to show a bit of courage. Forget Conceição – you and Paul Scholes have to make sure that Makelele always has someone nipping at him. When he gets the ball, four out of five times, he looks for Zidane. Remember that. And in the centre of defence, Fernando Hierro is slow. And Ivan Helguerra is a converted midfielder who can be a bit sloppy with his challenges in and round the box.'

Roy laughed. 'Okay, point taken, Triggs.'

He ran me over to Cheadle that night.

There was an unusual atmosphere between Idina and Hugh that I sensed on the night of the match. It wasn't unpleasant. It was a more of a stiffness of manner. I was lying on my front on the carpet, following the early exchanges, and Hugh was just watching me, as he usually did. He was genuinely fascinated by me.

'Esther Rantzen,' he said. 'That's who'd love her.'

'You've said that before,' Idina said, through a miasma of John Player smoke.

'Well, happen I'm saying it again. What were it that other dog used to say? Sausages, I think it were.'

'Triggs doesn't say anything. She just barks . . .'

'Every time she sees *him* ont screen.'

'That's not the same as saying sausages.'

'It's better than saying sausages. I'm telling you, Dina, she's followingt play!'

Yes, I was as it happened. And I wished they'd bloody well leave me to it.

I mentioned that Real Madrid weren't unbeatable, though I didn't think United had the players to do it over two legs. And it gave me no pleasure to discover that I was right. They did a competent enough job of keeping the score down. But Real had too many players who forced you to concentrate too hard. There was Zidane and his unending scheming and his reverse passes that could give you brain cramp. Figo could make a ball bend to his whims like no player I had ever seen. You had Roberto Carlos going up and down the wing like a crash cart. And Raul had better positional sense than any centre-forward I'd seen before.

And there was something else that I was forced to admit. Roy wasn't the same swashbuckling presence that he was before his hip operation. It hadn't been so apparent in the Premier League, but it was here.

In the first half, Real played like they had no intention of ever giving up the ball. And the requirement on United to focus so hard meant there were always going to be mistakes. Figo lobbed Barthez from out wide to put Real ahead. Then Scholes lost the ball to Zidane, who slipped it through to Raul to put Real 2–0 ahead.

Idina and Hugh were talking. With more urgency this time. God, it was distracting.

'I don't see why not,' he was saying.

'Because,' she said.

'*Because* int an answer.'

'I told you last night. I don't think of you in . . . that way.'

'What way?'

'*That* way.'

'I don't think of you in *that* way either.'

'So why do you want to marry me?'

'There's more to marriage than that, Dina. There's, you know . . .'

'What?'

'Companionship and that. We could be a comfort for each other.'

'I'm too old for that, Hugh. Too set in me ways.'

'There's nowt wrong with having someone to look out for you, Dina.'

This conversation continued, with occasional silences, for most of the match. Figo cut a neat swathe through the United midfield. Idina said what was wrong with things the way they were? Zidane danced passed Roy. Hugh said they could be even better – he could stay over, they could go on holidays, without folk gossiping. Raul was left unattended on the edge of the eighteen-yard box and made it 3–0. Idina said let folk gossip, she didn't care – she was allowed to have friends. Scholes got booked and would miss the second leg. Hugh said he wanted to look after her. Gary Neville got booked and would miss the second leg. Idina said they didn't have to be married for that. Van Nistelrooy pulled a goal back. Clive Tyldesley referred to it as a 'vital' away goal, but I had my doubts about that. Hugh told Idina she'd never been married before so she didn't know what a wonderful thing it was to have someone by your side who cares about you and is devoted to you and who considers you their whole world . . .

I stood up and walked with glum effort towards the door, ready for bed. I could feel the weight of them looking at me.

Have you ever had the feeling that you're suddenly the unwitting Quod Erat Demonstrandum of a conversation?

I heard Idina softly sob. Someone who cares about you and is devoted to you and considers you their whole world. Just in case you happened to miss it, that was me in that moment. An unknowing demonstration of true love. And through her sobs I heard Idina say, 'Yes . . . Okay, Hugh . . . Yes.'

I was pleased for them. And I could recommend the whole life companion thing to them.

There was no such happy ending for United. Look, I had

one or two ideas about stopping Zidane from getting the ball in the second leg, which may or may not have worked – doesn't matter now. I couldn't believe it when Ferguson dropped Beckham for the second game in favour of Veron, who hadn't played for weeks. It was over. I knew it before a ball was kicked.

But they did win the Premier League. They ruthlessly chased down Arsenal, who were without Vieira for the run-in and seemed to lose some vital part of their essence in much the same way that United did when Roy was missing. From nine points behind, United found themselves suddenly eight points clear and Arsenal's nerve failed them in a home match against Leeds United that they had to win but didn't.

Roy and I celebrated in our own quiet way by doing what else but taking the air together. The night cast a spritz of stars across a deepening navy sky as we wandered down Bankhall Lane and onto Ashley Road, the two of us conducting a silent audit of the ten months passed. Was he happy? Of course not. No European Cup. No nearer to it either, in my opinion, whatever that was worth. Me? Yes, I think I was. To my relief, two worrying theories had been repudiated – the first that the Manchester United era had given way to the Arsenal era, the second that a less mobile Roy Keane meant a less influential one. And all of that at the end of a season that began with us being coursed by a hungry pack along these same roads.

A thought occurred to me like a muscle memory. I was into my seventh year now. If I was to live to an average age for a Labrador, I was more than halfway through my time. I wondered was Roy thinking about the same thing – his ever-lengthening past and his ever-shortening future. How many more seasons? How much more time?

Watching him heave that Premiership trophy over his head, at the end of the year we'd just come through, gave me as much pleasure as anything in my life. I had no idea, of course, how few genuinely great days remained for us in football. If you don't count the FA Cup – and you might remember that 'bollocks' is how he'd dismissed it in the pages of *Keane* – it was the last thing of any importance I ever saw him win.

# 15.

# One Horse Race

BY NOW, I EXPECT MOST OF YOU WILL KNOW THE story of how Alex Ferguson thought he was the owner of a rare thoroughbred that was going to deliver him untold riches, but was forced into an embarrassing climbdown. Yes, Juan Sebastian Veron was finally packed off to Chelsea!

Okay, let it go, Triggs. Let it go.

Funnily enough, that's what Roy found himself having to tell me with increasing frequency as the 2003/4 season unravelled and my frustration with Ferguson grew. I wondered was I going through some kind of cranky middle life thing, which can happen with dogs as they age. Or was it just the final realisation that the opportunity to build on what we'd all achieved in 1999 had passed?

Around the club there was a real sense that the momentum was lost. I know Roy felt it. There wasn't another European Cup in this group of players. I knew that as surely as I knew there wasn't an astrophysicist among them, or a major poet, or — if I was being nasty — a world-class centre-half.

It was too late in the day for Roy to think about going somewhere else. He had his various war wounds. The knee that still ached. The hip that would eventually have to be replaced. On the television they talked about his 'decreased mobility', like he was some doddering member of the Royal household who everyone agreed was 'marvellous' for his age.

He was still only thirty-two. Old for a box to box midfielder, but young for a man in whom the fires of desire still raged.

'*Age wrinkles the body,*' as he was heard to say from time to time, quoting I'm not sure who. '*Quitting wrinkles the soul.*'

Our best days were all behind us, nevertheless. The truth dawned much more slowly on Roy, but I knew it then. And I worried about him. I thought about the European Cup final of 1999 and the World Cup of 2002 and the great European teams that had coveted him back in the days when he was in his physical prime, and I wondered would he come to look back on his career as one defined essentially by opportunities missed. Crazy, I know. But like I told you, Roy was a glass half-empty kind of fellow. Isn't that what made him the competitor he was?

Anyway, that was all for the future. In the meantime we still had to get up every morning and go to work.

For me, the 2003/4 season is memorable for two things – and neither of them involves United beating Millwall in an FA Cup final that was so stultifyingly dull, I could have sworn I watched my nails grow. No, the first was Rio Ferdinand being banned for eight months for missing a drug test. The second was Ferguson suing the club's major shareholder over the ownership of a racehorse. And as the season wore on, all of us – Roy and I included – found ourselves talking more and more about those things and less and less about football.

Roy liked Rio, although I guessed that Rio's admission that he did ballet as a teenager may have placed something of a constraint between them. I was rather fond of Rio myself – certainly based on the two or three occasions I met him: once, at Carrington, when he was wandering around the car park of the training ground asking if anyone had a battery for a Nokia 8800; once, briefly, at traffic lights outside the Dunham Forest Golf and County Club, when he lifted his Aviator shades to get a better look at me, strapped into the back of Roy's car, and said, 'Ah, the famous Triggs. Proper legend. It's an honour and a privilege!', and appeared to mean every word of it; and once, stepping out of the Hugo Boss shop on King Street and acting – *I* thought – a bit embarrassed about the number of shopping bags he had, with one of Roy's recent jeremiads about players growing fat and complacent on the spoils of their success no doubt still echoing in his ears.

Or maybe I imagined that. He was quite in awe of Roy. But then, weren't they all? I knew that on his first day of training at United, Rio had got the usual lick of love from Roy, who you can bet was thinking about that £30m transfer fee.

'Pass the fucking ball forward,' he told him. 'It's fucking easy going sideways; pass it forward.'

Subtext – you're not at the fucking ballet barre now, Billy Elliot. The dynamic between them I don't think ever changed.

Anyway, I was watching a History Channel documentary about the Battle for Mount Longdon, one of the defining moments in the 1982 Falklands War, when Roy arrived home one lunchtime that autumn and told me about Rio's missed drug test and the inevitable field day that the newspapers were expected to have with the story.

'Says he forgot,' Roy said.

I could buy that. God knows, he forgot about the rudiments of defending often enough.

Rio's account was that, despite being told twice that the testers were waiting for him after training, it just clear slipped his mind and he went off to buy bed linen in Harvey Nichols, then stuck his mobile phone on silent while he ate a lunch of quail's egg sandwiches with Eyal Berkovic.

It was my view – vindicated, I think, by later events – that United should have told him to, pardon the pun, take his medicine and bought a world-class centre-half to fill in for the duration of his suspension. Or permanently. Instead, the story – or rather more the whole sense of victimhood that the club tried to claim for itself with its talk of 'trial by media' and Ferdinand being 'hung out to dry', whatever that meant – overshadowed the entire season.

As did, although more insidiously, the Rock of Gibraltar business. If you're looking for my opinion on that, it was a stupid waste of everyone's time and energy, the club's most important employee suing its biggest shareholder over the ownership of – let's speak plainly here – a big, dumb and overly precious beast, who, unlike another four-legged but far lower maintenance animal whose name I'm too modest to mention here, wasn't going to win you Premier Leagues or European Cups!

I tried once or twice to bring it up with Roy. The sense I got was that he felt the same way about it as I did. But to say it would have implied criticism of the manager and Roy was still at that point of his life where he considered Alex Ferguson his friend rather than his employer.

He was fixing his breakfast one morning, frying eggs as it happened, when I threw my front paws up on the kitchen counter and said, 'You'd have to wonder what Ferguson's playing at, wouldn't you?'

It had been all over the news that morning. I remember him staring at the egg whites as they blistered in the pan. The oil was too hot. 'I don't know,' he said. 'I just don't know.' Then he ran his hand over the crown of my head and said, 'Imagine what kind of money *your* pups would fetch!', which was one of the nicest compliments he ever paid me. Motherhood was something I chose to sacrifice in the interests of his career. To hear him acknowledge it in the form of a compliment brought me to the verge of tears.

David Beckham, by the way, was gone and the halogen heat he drew on the club shifted to Madrid. Veron, as I mentioned, was gone too. By a barely believable stroke of good fortune, a Russian billionaire called Roman Abramovich bought Chelsea and offered United £15m for him. And Ferguson sold him in accordance with that great economic theory that somewhere out there in the world there is always a greater fool than you. Those Russians, I thought, would get the hang of capitalism eventually.

Not for the first time in my life, I started to get excited about how United might spend this new money they had. Ronaldinho was supposedly coming and they were also chasing Harry Kewell, who I'd admired for years. In the end – be still, my beating heart – they got Jose Kleberson, David Bellion, Tim Howard and, a blast from the past, Eric Djemba-Djemba!

'So bad they named him twice,' I used to say when the man touted as the next Roy Keane turned out to be, well, nothing of the sort. Roy thought I was unduly hard on him. On all of them. But come on! What's *your* standout David Bellion moment? Which of the twenty – twenty! – matches that Jose Kleberson played during his two years at Old Trafford was the most vital, in *your* opinion?

You couldn't say that the summer's business had improved the team any. A Basenji could have seen it, and dogs don't come any more stupid than that.

There was, as it happens, one happy exception. One day, in August 2003, I was in the carpark of Sainsbury's in Altringham. Roy was doing a light shop and had left me in the car with the window cracked open an inch or two, thinking about the new season. I noticed a teenage boy hanging about near the car, rawboned and gaunt-faced, with blond-streaked spaghetti hair and a constellation of zits splashed across his beardline. I hoped Roy remembered to lock the car. And that's not intended as a slur on anyone. It was just a conditioned reflex of mine to the sight of teenage boys, which was down to a combination of Pavlov's theory and growing up in Manchester.

Anyway, a moment later, Roy was walking across the tarmacadam with two full shopping bags distending from either arm and I noticed the boy step up to him, although not in any threatening way. He'll be an autograph-hunter, I thought. This kind of thing happened a lot more often than perhaps I've given the impression in these pages. Roy was unfailingly polite to strangers and unstinting with his time. Personally, I thought this kid outstayed his welcome by a good five minutes, but Roy eventually returned to the car and threw the shopping on the front passenger seat with a benign smile playing on his lips.

'You still enjoy it, don't you?' I said. 'Chatting to the fans.'

'Fans?' he said. 'Triggs, that's Cristiano Ronaldo.'

'Who?'

He laughed. 'The lad I was telling you about. The manager's just paid £12m for him – from, as I said before, Sporting Lisbon.'

'*That's* him?'

'Yeah, no, he's a smashing lad as well. Good natural ability. You're on about good in the air. Good footwork – that's documented. The manager thinks he's going to be a player. Although, I think I said it before, he's still obviously young and he's proved absolutely nothing in the game.'

And to think, I would live long enough to see that limp-haired kid with the moonscape complexion inspire United to three Premier League titles and a European Cup.

But not that year. There was a very perceptible sense of the ground having shifted. Of course there was. Chelsea were now in the ownership of a man who could afford to bid for players like they were works of the Great Masters – even if the players were, frankly, less than that. (Fifteen million for Veron! I've got be careful here I don't twist my stomach like poor Marley.)

But Arsenal were the team that really concerned me, and why wouldn't they? They had Thierry Henry. But there was also a defiance about them, a meanness that reminded me of the way United used to be. This first struck me towards the end of September, when the two teams played out a scoreless draw on one of those typically splenetic afternoons they used to share together. Patrick Vieira was sent off for kicking out at Ruud van Nistelrooy, although I always felt it was one of those kicks – like Beckham's at the World Cup in France – that never really believed in itself. But van Nistelrooy jumped backwards like a car had almost taken his toes and Vieira had to go.

The atmosphere turned horrible – or more horrible than it had already been. In the final act of the game, van Nistelrooy crashed a penalty kick off the crossbar and Arsenal's celebrations gave way to a prolonged bout of pushing and shoving between the two sets of players that would have been rightly described as a fracas but became known as The Battle of Old Trafford. We English do love our war imagery.

Anyway, I stared at the television, at that rolling, red and yellow maul of snarling humanity, and a thought struck me. Where was Roy? Instinct told me he was right in the eye of it – trying to land a clean punch on Martin Keown's ample chin, no doubt. But he wasn't there. And then I saw him. He had an arm around van Nistelrooy's shoulder and he was steering him away from the trouble. The sensible thing to do. United had enough problems with injuries at the time and they didn't need him missing for another month.

He was like Dylan forty years earlier, I thought, freeing himself from the expectations of his audience. But then, I was probably overthinking things. I did that occasionally. But I did have to seriously wonder whether this mellower, more commonsensical Roy would be less effective as a footballer. Of course I did. Everyone was wondering.

Roy and I had a conversation about it. Like we talked about everything. It was the morning after the Arsenal match and we were passing the little stationers opposite Costa on Ashley Road. Two men were in the process of wrestling a steel filing cabinet into the back of a white van when they noticed us pass.

'Alright, Keano,' one of them said.

Neither of us knew him.

'Yeah,' Roy said, without turning around, 'not too bad.'

'I'll tell you what, you could have punched that fucking Keown's jaw loose yesterday and no one would have blamed you. They'd have thanked you.'

Roy demurred somehow and we continued walking.

'Trigger,' I heard the other man say. 'I were trying to think of his fucking name. Would have bothered me all day that.'

When we'd walked a short distance, I said, 'I was quite surprised myself that you didn't get involved.'

He threw his shoulders. 'What would the point have been, Triggs?'

'I don't know – to let Arsenal know that you weren't going to be a pushover this season. Let them see there's a lot more fight left in this United team.'

I was playing the devil's advocate, just regurgitating the kind of thoughts I usually heard from him at this time of year.

'No sense in getting involved, Triggs. Maybe throwing a dig, getting sent off, obviously banned for three, four matches. Paul Scholes is already out with a hernia. One or two others. Ole – *your* friend. I think I've said it in the past, Triggs, that there comes a time in your life when you've got to maybe get wise.'

No one, in all good conscience, could argue that Roy was a lesser player that season. In the first few months, in fact, I thought he played some of the best football of his life, buoyed, as ever, by my little contributions. He scored an outstanding goal against Leicester – his first in forty-one matches, no less – egged on by some good-natured teasing from me as we cut across the golf course the previous day. I told him it was that long since he scored that most of his goals on YouTube were in the old black-and-white Pathé news format.

The old chemistry between us was still there. There was no doubt about it.

'I'll score one tomorrow night,' he laughed. 'Obviously just to spite you.'

Of course, I also happened to mention a flaw I'd spotted in Leicester's offside trap, which proved to be extraordinarily prescient.

He could still be unsparingly hard on himself. It was Roy's misplaced pass that led to Kevin Kuranyi's winner when United lost to Stuttgart in the Champions League that October. He was furious with himself. The same when he cut down Joe Cole to hand Chelsea a penalty winner in the league. But then he was the same old brilliantly decisive Roy against Leeds and Portsmouth and Blackburn, and against Glasgow Rangers in Europe.

I must confess, I was also very excited by Cristiano Ronaldo's by now regular cameos, even setting aside an infuriating tendency he had to throw himself on the ground as if shot by a hidden sniper. Plus all the unnecessary step-overs.

I remember mentioning him to Roy one Sunday morning that winter. We were in the back garden. Roy had a black refuse bag in one hand and a rubber glove on the other and was picking up my week's droppings. I was wandering around the grass with my nose down, pointing them out as I remembered them. Bomb squad duty, Roy and I used to call it.

'I think Ronaldo might end up being the find of the season,' I said. 'If he can add a few pounds of muscle to his frame and, well, cut out some of the indulgences, I think he could become a great player.'

And Roy said, in that way of his: 'The time to judge him, Triggs, is in maybe two or three years, when he's obviously won something.'

And wasn't he right?

United finished 2003 on top of the league. Four points clear. Better goal difference than any other team. Still in the

Champions League and still in the FA Cup. We made a decent start to 2004 as well. But then it all started to go away from us because we were suddenly required to think about all these other extraneous things. Well, two specifically: Rio Ferdinand and that idiot horse.

*'Football news now and Ipswich Town were condemned to a sixth successive defeat this afternoon by bottom of the table Preston North End. With this report, Eric Allison . . .*

*"'Yes, a farewell goal from Iain Hulme for relegation strugglers Preston increased the pressure on under-fire Ipswich boss Roy Keane at Deepdale this afternoon. The former Manchester United star watched his team dominate the first half, with Grant Leadbetter particularly unfortunate to see his twenty-five-yard shot go narrowly wide.*

*'But the Tractor Boys paid the price for failing to make the breakthrough when Hulme – in the final game of his loan spell from Barnsley – signed off with a sublime side-footed finish to a neat passing move. So a parting gift, then, of three much-needed points for Preston manager Darren Ferguson, who is, ironically, the son of Keane's former mentor at United. What Keane wouldn't do for some of Sir Alex's inspiration now!*

*'The Irishman was offered a vote of confidence by Town chief executive Simon Clegg after last weekend's 3–1 defeat at home to Swansea. But this defeat – Ipswich's sixth on the bounce – is sure to increase the pressure on the increasingly beleaguered Tractors boss."*

I don't remember when I realised that Arsenal had yet to lose a match in the league that season. Maybe I was aware of it, maybe I wasn't. I had one or two health issues that winter that I was keeping from Roy. Somehow I got it into my head that I had a posterior polar subcapsular cataract and was going progressively blind. So you could say I had my own distractions.

The Invincibles, they came to call that Arsenal team. I don't know. I could be wrong, but I don't remember them exactly shooting out the lights every week. I do remember a lot of draws. And them looking, well, very vincible indeed at times. But then again, that might have been my eye thing.

There was, I'm sure I mentioned, a truculence about them, which a lot of the United players thought had its roots in that bit of business at Old Trafford.

'We've unleashed a monster,' I remember Phil Neville saying. Roy and I were leaving the house one morning when Ryan Giggs's Bentley Continental GT pulled up alongside us. Inside were the faces of Giggs and Gary Neville, then squeezed together into the back, like jays on a branch, Phil Neville, Paul Scholes and Darren Fletcher, the latest player I'd heard described in a hopeful way as the next Roy Keane.

Gary and Phil were bickering. 'I'm in the front because I've said the word shotgun,' Gary was telling his brother. 'That's got to mean summat at the end of the day.'

'I've said shotgun *before* you,' Phil said.

'Well, *I've* not heard you.'

Roy bent down to their level. 'Alright, lads?' he said.

'Alright, Keaney?' came the chorus.

Scholes said, 'Alright, Triggs?' and Gary trailed his left arm out of the window and rubbed me behind the ears.

I hope I haven't given the impression in these pages that I didn't like Gary Neville, when in fact the opposite was the case. Yes, I mocked him unendingly, but he was a good bloke and – if you want my opinion – a far better full-back than he was ever given credit for. He was asked once what he thought would be written on his gravestone and he said, 'Six out of ten.'

I'd have said, 'Seven-and-a-half – but quite often a pain in the rear end with it.'

You may already know the story of how his father came to be called Neville Neville. The story has it that his grandmother was lying in the labour ward when a midwife came in and mistook the surname on her chart for the christian name she intended giving to her newborn boy. The midwife chuckled when she realised her mistake. 'Of course, you couldn't call your son Neville Neville.'

And Gary's nan said, 'I'm not having her or anyone else telling me what I can or can't call my own son. He's Neville Neville – that's it and all about it!'

If personality traits can be passed through DNA, that story would explain a lot about Gary. Like I said, I liked him. But I think even he'd agree that we were just two very different animals.

Anyway, Giggs, Scholes, Fletcher and the Nevilles were off to play eighteen holes in Hale Golf Club. It must have been the end of January because Ferdinand had just played his last game before his eight-month ban became a fact – a 1–0 defeat to Wolves, the bottom club in the division, which, though no one realised it at the time, would mark the beginning of the end of United's season.

'No disrespect to Wolves,' Gary said, 'but ninety-nine times out of a hundred, you're thinking, okay, that's three points. But they've not read the script, have they?'

'It's obviously galling,' Scholes piped up from the back seat. 'Overwhelmingly galling.'

You know by now how these conversations tended to go.

'Well, we've only got ourselves to blame,' said Giggs. 'For me, we've had opportunities to put the game beyond them and we've not taken them. Full credit to Wolves – they've just wanted it more on the day. And they've done ever so well to take the three points.'

'And now we've lost obviously Rio,' Gary said, 'which I, for one, am not happy about. For me – I think I'm on the record as saying it – he's been hung out to dry by obviously the media. If he's guilty of anything, it's being maybe daft and forgetful!'

Roy cut into the conversation. 'Listen,' he said, 'we can complain about it all we like, at the end of the day, it's not going to change anything. We've lost Rio and we just have to fucking get on with it.'

'Roy's right,' Gary said. 'We have to place it firmly to one side and move on. Show our quality.'

I gave a sharp bark – bored, if I'm being honest, and a bit impatient to be off.

'Hey,' Giggs said, 'have you seen obviously Sky Sports News this morning, Keaney?'

We hadn't. We were watching something on National Geographic – fascinating – about a catastrophic flood that happened 5,600 years BC and may or may not have been the historical origin for the bible story about Noah's Ark.

Roy just said, 'No,' because, well, it was simpler all round.

'The gaffer's bought Louis Saha from obviously Fulham.'

This was news to me. It was obviously news to Roy as well. I was sure he'd have mentioned it to me had he known.

'As a goalscorer,' I heard Scholes say, 'I think we all know the quality he's got. His record at Fulham – I think I've said it in the past – is downright amazing.'

'For me,' Phil Neville said, 'he's one of the most ruthless finishers in the game. Every team makes special precautions for him – not that it does them any good! I'm going to have to resort to cliché here . . .'

I thought, why the pre-announcement all of a sudden?

'. . . he does things that would literally take your breath away.'

'He's a tremendous acquisition,' Gary Neville agreed.

'He's the one player who – Phil said it and I think it's well documented elsewhere – every defender in the game doesn't relish playing against. I think it were Sheasy who's used the phrase *thorn in our side*, which is true. He's give me a torrid time once or twice – got obviously bags of pace, two good feet, always lurking with intent.'

I had to agree – although obviously in different words. Roy did too. I think he felt everyone needed a new focus. The Ferdinand business had been distracting. The Rock of Gibraltar thing was still dragging unconscionably on. United had taken one point from their last two games. And Arsenal's continuing quest to go through the entire league season unbeaten was suddenly becoming everyone's focus.

That's when Phil Neville said his thing about unleashing a monster. 'It were since we played them,' he said. 'What happened that day, it drew them closer together. A siege mentality, to be fair. They've just said, right, that's it, the minute we cross that white line we're just not going to be beat.'

He might have had a point. The media attention that fixed itself to Arsenal and their unbeaten run was like a gathering drumroll that threw everyone else off their rhythm. That was one of way of looking at it. The other was that it was all Rio Ferdinand's stupid fault. Look, I had some issues with his defending – never made any secret of it – but there was no question that they missed him. They lost 3–2 at home to Middlesbrough that February on a day when Juninho scored with two headers. Headers! Juninho! Jesus, I was nearly taller than him standing on the pads of my four feet.

That was the day, I think, that the belief went out of us like breath from a punctured lung. Arsenal finished the month nine points clear of United and Chelsea. And though we all soldiered ever on – pit bulls have nothing on Labradors when it comes to spirit – we all knew in our hearts that all we were doing was listening to those quickening drum beats and awaiting Arsenal's final ta-dah.

A year without winning the Premier League was, by definition, a bad year for United. That was the standard that we had set for ourselves. The base camp of our ambition. Every year. So I could almost hear the disillusionment in Roy gurgling to the boil. There were fresh attempts to, shall we say, conventionalise our relationship. Nothing like before. But when we returned from our walks, he insisted on stepping into the house ahead of me, which someone — it might have been Ruud van Nistelrooy, who had an Alsatian called Ari — told him was a way of reminding a dog of its station. I just played along with it for as long as it lasted, which, from memory, was only about three or four days.

It was that same week that I became convinced that I was losing my sight. There was a black border closing in from the periphery of my vision in my left eye and it came so bad that I decided to mention it to Roy while we were watching television one night. I know he had bigger fish to fry, but then, I was no good to him blind.

I remember him looking back at me, just incredulous. 'Say that again,' he said.

'A posterior polar subcapsular cataract,' I said.

He got up and, sighing, plucked the veterinary A to Z from the bookshelf, shaking his head in an I-can't-believe-we're-going-through-this-shit-again kind of a way. The book was full of folded-down pages, each dog-ear representing some injury or malady I was convinced I had, but, as it usually turned out, didn't. He kept the pages that way, I think, to make a point.

'Give it to me again,' he said.

Jesus, what part of posterior polar subcapsular cataract did he not understand?

I spelled out the first two words for him and he quickly

found the page and read the entry with – I couldn't fail to notice – a sceptical expression.

'Triggs,' he said, after a time, 'it doesn't even *cause* blindness.'

'It can in rare cases,' I said.

'Well, it doesn't fucking say that here.'

'Two per cent,' I said. 'It's also an inherited condition. Perhaps you could try to remember the name of the breeder you bought me from, phone them and ask if either of my parents had an autosomal dominant gene.'

He laughed. Actually, it sounded ridiculous as I was saying it. He shook his head wearily. 'Come on,' he said.

'Where?'

'The fucking vets, where do you think?'

An eye test confirmed what Roy suspected, which was that I didn't have a posterior polar subcapsular cataract. Or anything, in fact.

Okay, I might have had a lot of completely baseless anxieties about my health that to some people might have suggested hypochondria, but I was also, as you know, a highly intuitive animal. The black edging on my vision, I came to realise, was in reality a feeling of foreboding.

United had drawn Porto in the first knockout round of the Champions League. From what little I'd seen of them, Porto were a good side, but nothing special. They had a good and experienced midfield anchor in Maniche and a very fine playmaker in Deco, who nonetheless – and it was just an opinion – tended to shrink in a physical contest. But they weren't in United's class. I think everyone agreed with that.

Yet I couldn't get that image out of my mind of Juninho leaping off his little corgi legs to score two headers against United two weeks earlier. As Roy and I sat in front of the fire one night, our shadows dancing like phantasmagorical figures on the wall opposite, I had a word with him about Benni McCarthy. Admittedly, he wasn't the best striker in the world, but he was robust and springy and, I thought, might cause trouble for United's interim central defence of Wes Brown and Gary Neville.

Well, I might as well have not spoken at all. I watched the first leg in Oporto in what was now Hugh and Idina's house – they'd been married since a week before Christmas – worrying the Wilton with my agitated pacing.

'I'll tell you what,' Hugh said, 'I'd give nearly anything to know what's going through that dog's head.'

And I thought, 'No, you wouldn't, Hugh. No, you wouldn't.'

United had scored first, but then surrendered the initiative. First, McCarthy found enough space to equalise with a volley. Then, in the second half, he rose to meet a cross from Deco and even seemed to hang in the air, above Neville and Brown, for a whole conceited second before arcing a perfect header over Tim Howard and into the goal.

Shit. That's what I was thinking, Hugh. Apologies for the profanity.

I told myself to stay calm. A 2–1 defeat was far from a calamity, especially with an away goal banked. Then, with the minutes ebbing away, I realised just why I'd been feeling so unstrung for the past few days.

Roy went chasing a through-ball he had no hope of catching, as pointlessly as a Jack Russell chasing a Renault Mégane he has no hope of driving. The Porto keeper, Vitor Baia, threw himself down to smother the ball, requiring Roy, who was approaching at speed, to hurdle over him. Roy jumped alright, but then he did something so stupid that it could have only come as an expression of the same disenchantment that had been welling in me all year long. With a trailing leg, he trod on him.

Yes, so much for the new Roy.

Look, I know Baia made a one-act drama out of it, but Roy deserved his red card. He knew that as well as anyone.

I retired to my bed in Idina's kitchen, but didn't shut my

eyes once that night. He'd miss the second leg in Manchester and possibly both quarter-final legs if United made it past Porto, which looked far less a formality now.

What made it worse was that it hadn't come as a result of what they called the red mist descending. This sending-off was more in character with the one he got for clattering Jason McAteer – a result not so much of the rage in his heart than the turmoil in his head. I thought about all of the frustrations of the past few months. Watching Roy carry that team on his ageing shoulders. The disappointments of the Djemba-Djemba, Kleberson and Bellion signings – where the hell were they, were we permitted to ask? They weren't on the pitch, I knew that much. Ferdinand's dunderheadedness. I had my doubts about Ferdinand, as you know, but they were still a better team with him than without him. And then all the fuss over that idiot horse who at that moment was probably helping himself to the best females on a stud farm in southern Tipperary – like [name removed for legal reasons], blithely unaware of everything except a vague notion of where he was going to stick his penis next.

Roy was mad at himself for what happened. I'm sure I don't need to tell you that. 'Fucking stupid,' I was liable to hear him mutter at any time of the day, shaking his head and, mentally at least, adding another weal to his back.

I made sure he got plenty of walks. They were a good purgative for both of us, even if my insistence that the tie was still alive was nothing more than a white lie. They just weren't anything like the same team when Roy wasn't playing. That was inescapable.

The realisation of what that moment of madness probably cost him came in a kind of slow release. First there was the late equaliser in the second leg at Old Trafford that sent Porto through and Jose Mourinho hot stepping in celebration along the sideline in his chief mourner's coat.

And then, as the weeks fell away, it slowly dawned on us what could so easily have been. There was no Real Madrid barring their way. No Milan. No Barcelona. No Bayern Munich. No Juventus. Porto's route to winning the trophy that May was via Lyon, Deportivo la Coruña and Monaco, none of whom, if you want my opinion, would have presented any difficulty to United, even this United.

And that was it. Roy's best chance of ever playing in a Champions League final, gone.

'There'll be other years,' I told him one bleak, grey evening that June.

'Of course there'll be other years,' he agreed.

'And thirty-two,' I reminded him, 'isn't old.'

'Courage doesn't always roar,' he said. 'Sometimes courage is the little voice at the end of the day that says I'll try again tomorrow.'

We reached the level-crossing next to Hale railway station. The barrier was down. We both looked up at the slate-grey undersides of the clouds above us. It was the logical moment to turn for home.

'Will we keep going?' he asked, a smile splitting his face.

'Keep going,' I said. 'Let's do it.'

# 16.

# Never Another
# May Like This

I'VE LEFT OUT A PIECE OF THE STORY – A VITAL piece, as it happens, for it signalled, at least in my mind, the first clear shift in the dynamic between Roy and Alex Ferguson. And you know by now what an intuitive animal I was at that point of my life.

Some time early in 2004, Roy decided that he wanted to play for Ireland again. Actually, I can almost hear him correcting me. He never stopped wanting to play for his country, he'd tell me sharply, he just didn't want to play for Mick McCarthy. But now Mick was gone and Ireland had a new manager called Brian Kerr. I never had the pleasure myself, although Roy seemed to like him, based on the two or three times they spoke when Brian tried to persuade him out of international retirement in 2003.

Ferguson wasn't crazy about the idea. It came up at the time when he first started talking about using Roy's talents more judiciously, and returning to play for Ireland would mean more games for him and less rest. I wasn't asked for my opinion. But if I had been, I'd have told Roy to do whatever made him happy. That was all I ever really wanted, you see. Roy's happiness.

Ferguson and I had our differences of opinion over players

and tactics — nothing you wouldn't expect from two strong-willed individuals with their own views on football and how it should be played. But I had no real beef with the man, even after what happened later on. He wanted what was best for Manchester United and I wanted what was best for Roy Keane. And though for many years they amounted to the same thing, I think I understood better than Roy that they wouldn't always.

Initially, Roy told Brian maybe. Then he told him no. But — that heart and head thing, again — he didn't say no in a way that discouraged Brian from asking him again. They would text each other occasionally. And Brian clearly had a certain charm because Roy, I noticed, would read those messages — watching television, preparing our meals, enjoying one of our walks — with a slight smile towing at his lips.

Then, out of the blue one day — with all of the suddenness of Ferguson's realisation that Liam Miller wasn't the next Roy Keane either — he changed his mind.

'Unfinished business,' he called it.

We were climbing Rappax Road at the time. It was a beautiful spring morning, with only occasional scuds of cloud obscuring the sun. Roy had his lucky blue Diadora sweatshirt knotted around his waist.

'Oh?' I said. If there was a note of disapproval in my voice, it wasn't intentional.

'For me — we've spoke about it in the past — it's the biggest honour there is, to play for your country. And I wasn't happy with the way it obviously ended. But now there's a new manager. Obviously a new set-up . . .'

I stopped to scratch myself.

'What about the other players?'

'What other players?'

'The ones who heard you call Mick McCarthy a cunt.'

'I called him a wanker, didn't I?'

'I think you called him a cunt as well,' I said, 'going by the accounts I've read. And a bollocks.'

He laughed and shook his head. 'Jesus, I'd love to see a fucking transcript of what I actually did say. I must have been talking for hours if you believe half of what I'm supposed to have called him. The other players will be fine, Triggs.'

'Do you think so?'

'Listen, I think I've said it maybe once or twice in the past, it's not important that we're all friends. There's been one or two in the United dressing-room over the years who I haven't got on with. I think it's documented. There's been players who'd nearly cross the road to avoid me.'

I actually saw this happen once or twice, although we did it ourselves occasionally.

'The important thing,' he said – and it had a very familiar ring to it – 'is that we all want to go to the World Cup finals.'

'The World Cup?' I said. 'That came around quickly.'

'The qualifying starts in September, Triggs.'

I wanted to ask him what Alex Ferguson made of it, but I didn't. Maybe it was an assertion of independence rather than a small act of mutiny and I didn't want to turn it into an issue.

The season ended and gave way to summer. Then the summer slipped by and the promise of another new season was suddenly upon us. That was how it went. It was relentless.

There'd been some changes. Jose Mourinho was the new manager of Chelsea. He was a man who understood football and loved dogs. Draw whatever inferences you want from that. Later, you might remember, he even let the police arrest him rather than hand over Gullit, his Yorkshire terrier, who, it saddens me to say, I never got to meet. It remains one of my few life regrets.

There was a very palpable sense that summer that Chelsea's time was coming. It had to really. Think of the money they had. I remember getting a sense of how times had changed when I heard that Arjen Robben, whom Ferguson coveted, came to Manchester, had a look around the club and decided that what Mourinho was offering better suited his ambition. There would be a lot of that.

You can imagine, I'm sure, how this went down with Roy. Chelsea, would-be usurpers of Manchester United's position. Well, they were going to have to work for it. Because the competitive edge never died in Roy, even when his body complained to him to slow down. As the 2004/5 season approached there was the usual hardening in his attitude, which told in the enthusiasm with which he tackled the steeper roads on our morning and evening walks. It didn't escape my notice either that when we played with my pull rope now, he allowed me to win far fewer of our little tugging contests.

I was fine with that.

That spikiness, which was always a central plank of his personality remained, although the older he got, the more of a pantomime edge it assumed. I remember one afternoon, Gary Neville sent a text message around to say that he'd changed his mobile number. Roy, who didn't even have his old one, sent him a message back, saying, 'So what?' or 'Why the fuck are you telling me?' or something of that colour. But he was smiling as he did it. There was a kind of Roy Keane Tribute Act aspect to it, although I could imagine poor Gary enduring a sleepless night or two, wondering if he was serious.

Anyway, United had an early opportunity to test Chelsea's conviction that this was going to be their year when the fixtures schedule threw them together on the first day of the season.

Roy left for London his usual bullish self, but I was worried. With Rio Ferdinand still missing for a few weeks yet, Ferguson asked Roy to play in the centre of defence. Whatever charms he did possess, Roy wasn't the big, burly figure they needed to deal with the physicality of Chelsea's twin totems, Didier

Drogba and Eider Gudjohnsen. It gave me no pleasure at all to be proven right. But they combined to score the game's only goal and there could have been more.

Roy was livid.

'We're straight away playing catch-up,' he said. He was bathing me in the ensuite of the main bedroom with the hand-held shower-head, but he was still so distracted by the result a full twenty-four hours later that I had to keep following the stream of water up and down the bath in order to get clean.

He was right about playing catch-up, though. It was what defined that season. By the time Ferdinand returned from his eight-month ban, they'd dropped yet more points against Blackburn, Everton and Bolton. Tim Howard was dropped for Roy Carroll. When was Ferguson going to sort out the goalkeeping issue, I wondered? They lost to Portsmouth. Drew with Middlesbrough and Birmingham. By the end of October, they were nine points behind – the same nine points they'd still be trying to make up by the end of March.

Roy's frustration told in the usual old ways. The leash made a return. He tried to teach me, by a process known as allelomimetic reconditioning, to walk by his side rather than ten feet behind or ahead, as had become my habit. Humans have a natty little phrase about old dogs and new tricks that I considered rather apposite in the circumstances. But I indulged him for a day or two until he quickly abandoned the idea and the leash was never seen again.

I'm not saying the season was a dead loss. There were occasional small glories. Beating Liverpool always made us happy. And I was still earning my board by sharing my thoughts with Roy, whatever they were worth. It was me, for instance, who first drew his attention to Liverpool's difficulty in defending at set pieces – this was weeks before Mikaël Silvestre's two headers, both from corners, secured three more points for United.

And then there was the part I played in bringing to an end Arsenal's unbeaten run in the league, which I think we were all sick to the back molars hearing about. I just hoped they'd keep on winning until they came to Old Trafford that October. Which they did. By that stage the sequence was forty-nine games.

Roy didn't play that day, but I did pass on some of my technical observations to him, including one or two comments about Sol Campbell's defending that he felt may have crossed the line into vitriol and/or personal abuse.

Look, I was really up for this one.

Arsenal had had it their own way for too long, with their smooth passing and their liquid movement. But I'd noticed that they didn't much enjoy a physical contest. Even though they had a lot of big, athletic players, they were more of a cerebral team. Looking back, I still think Roy was a bit surprised to hear me talk like that.

'Triggs,' he said, smiling, 'you're not suggesting we kick them off the pitch, are you?'

We were passing The Railway pub at the time.

'No,' I said, 'I just think if everyone puts an extra, say, ten percent more meat into their challenges, Arsenal couldn't live with that kind of intensity. It's just a thought that occurs – do with it as you will.'

Now, I'm not saying that United took all of their cues from me that night. But I did specifically say that Gary Neville should make himself known to José Antonio Reyes, unwittingly setting in motion a chain of events that would lead to Alex Ferguson being hit in the face with a slice of stuffed crust, quattro fromaggi pizza – then, three months later, Roy jabbing his finger at Patrick Vieira and telling him, 'I'll see you out there on the fucking pitch.'

Everything Arsenal did that night was just that millisecond behind the beat of the match. Oh, they won the food fight in the tunnel afterwards, but United won the match. And the star of the show – as he always seemed to be these days – was Wayne Rooney.

The first time I saw Cristiano Ronaldo play, I thought, yes, two or three years of tough love from Roy will hew the rough edges off this kid and he'll be a great player. But the first time I ever saw Rooney play for Everton, at sixteen years of age, remember, it was clear that he was already there.

Persuading him to sign for Manchester United that September was the most important step that Ferguson took to prevent United becoming English football's third team. Watching his hat-trick on his debut against Fenerbahçe in the Champions League – so strong, so fast, so unfazed – you just knew you were witnessing the future of the club.

Only once did I meet him. We were in Manchester City Centre for a dental appointment – Roy rather than me for a change – and Wayne was attempting to parallel park his Aston Martin Vanquish on Hanover Street while simultaneously eating a Scotch egg. I remember his hands, like baseball mitts, one enwrapping the egg, the other gripping the leather steering wheel, his child's eyes set deep in his medicine ball head, his teeth like headstones, and his voice emerging like a little boy trapped down a well.

'Alright, Roy?'

'Alright, Wayne?'

I think all three of us were equally amused by his efforts to reverse that car to within the required six inches of the kerb. For all his ability with a ball, it reminded you that he was still a boy in a man's world. He was only eighteen. Roy was thirty-three. Old enough to be his father – certainly in Liverpool, where I knew that kind of thing wasn't unusual.

'Do you need a hand obviously parking that thing?' Roy asked, failing to suppress a smile.

'No, you're alright,' Wayne said. 'At the end of the day, it's something I'm obviously going to have to get used to.'

Wayne looked at me then. 'Arr-eh,' he said, 'that's, eh . . .'

'Triggs,' Roy said.

'Triggs, that's right. I remember him off the telly. Does he want some of me Scotch egg?'

'It's a she. And no, she's a vegetarian.'

Wayne started at him blankly. Was he really wondering what meat was contained in a Scotch egg?

'You played very well against Arsenal,' Roy told him. 'Won the penalty for obviously Ruud to score, then obviously got the second yourself.'

It might have been the day after the match.

'Arr-eh, that's great to hear, especially coming from someone who's done so magnificently well for the football club over the years and been so colossally influential. I think it's well documented, all you've done. Man U v Arsenal, I think we all know, can be tense affairs. Never much in them. The goal, obviously late on, was just a tap-in. And, yeah, no, it's always tremendous to score – I was ever so happy with it – but the most important thing is three more points and keeping up the pressure on obviously Chelsea.'

I remember, sitting outside the dental surgery waiting for Roy to re-emerge, feeling suddenly very old. God knows how Roy felt. It was true, though. We were becoming a part of Manchester United's past. Rooney. Ronaldo. Alan Smith. Darren Fletcher. Gabriel Heinze. John O'Shea. They were the future.

Don't get me wrong, the desire still raged in Roy like a kind of fever. Ireland drew 0–0 with France in Paris that October – a good result by most objective standards – but Roy returned home furious that they hadn't won.

'Had the chances,' he said to me in the car on the way home from Idina's. I'd watched the highlights myself. 'Just maybe lacked that bit of belief that we could go to somewhere like obviously the Stade de France and win.'

He was still influencing matches. Not with goals. His latest dry spell would run to fifty matches. But just with the simple intelligence of his passing and his unending and high volume demands for everyone to do better, to be better. And my help as well, of course.

Yet no one could play with the intensity that Roy did without it taking a toll on his body. The little tells became more and more noticeable. The dull snap of bones moving whenever he bent down to pick up after me. The low, involuntary groan whenever he reached for the television remote. There was talk of him becoming a player in the mould of Claude Makelele, dictating events from a position just in front of the back four and rarely, if ever, venturing into the opposition half. Ferguson thought he could play on for three or four more seasons like that.

But I knew Roy better than anyone. I was attuned to the sound of his body and I knew that, the longer he played, the more he was borrowing against his future fitness and mobility.

We were getting on. Both of us. In a few months time, I'd be facing into my ninth year. Old age was coming with the sad undeniability of winter.

*Roy picks through the morning post. Bank statements and bills. Fliers for car valet services and landscape architects and companies offering to consolidate your existing loans into a single loan. And one or two Christmas cards, more than a week after the event. He tuts disapprovingly. People still failing to prepare. He never changed. I never wanted him to.*

*I still get letters, presents, cards, the occasional play date invitation from other dog-owners, though nothing like the deluge that would arrive on a daily basis back in 2002. They come now in a slow but pleasant trickle. Letters asking me to mind Roy. Renderings of me in crayon by children familiar with us from television. Doggie coats and fleeces and bandanas in the colours of Manchester City – or, more recently, Norwich City – that arrive unfailingly every Christmastime.*

*'Why do people always think they're first to think of this?' Roy will say, at the same time laughing – laughing at the good of it.*

*Invitations to weddings. Invitations to civic receptions. Invitations to children's birthday parties, sweet sixteens, twenty-firsts, fortieths, fiftieths, eightieths. Valentine's cards and, tucked inside, photographs of male Labradors staring lasciviously at the camera with only one thing on their minds.*

*But it's nice that people still remember.*

*All in all, it hasn't been a bad Christmas. Ipswich broke the cycle of bad defeats by beating Leicester 3–0 at home. Then, on New Year's Day, they drew away to Coventry. And even though Coventry had a man sent off, at least it wasn't another defeat. One more point accumulated. Nineteenth in the table now. Eleven points off the play-off positions. I think about Alex Ferguson and how he used to gather everyone together at Christmastime to get them refocussed. An eleven-point differential isn't impossible to make up. Not in this division. Roy proved that before.*

*But there's a curious ease about him right now. Someone on the television said he seems resigned, like he did in his final weeks at Sunderland. His thought for the day today comes courtesy of Arthur Balfour – 'Nothing matters very much and few things matter at all' – and I noticed earlier that he'd put a big urgent circle around it.*

*The post, by the way, contained at least one piece of bad news, because I could read it in his face. There's no secret he can conceal from me. I know him too well.*

*When he disappears upstairs, I throw my front paws onto the countertop and use my nose to sift through the rubble of paper and torn envelopes until I find it. A piece of laminated card, small enough to fit inside a wallet, with something written in Welsh on one side, and on the other a photograph of Idina, just as I remember her – her black pompadour, her make-up a little on the overcooked side.*

*It says underneath that she died on Christmas Day. I presume it was her lungs in the end.*

*I think about Hugh. Poor Hugh. A widower twice over. The last time I saw them was back in 2008, during Roy's final days at Sunderland. She'd just finished feeding the dogs and was taking issue with the job he'd done of cleaning the windows. Streaks. That was the problem. Except it wasn't really a problem. Idina liked things just so. It was just the tension that comes from living your life alone, then deciding one day to open yourself up to being loved.*

*I'm happy that's my last memory of them together – 'It's only a few bloody streaks, Dina!' – and not something more cinematic. Hugh was right. They were a comfort to each other in the end.*

*Humans have a strange relationship with death. It's the one thing that unites us all. Higher consciousness and lower. The fish and the birds. Advanced and primitive. Carnivores and herbivores. Animals, plants and micro-organisms. Two legs, four legs, eight. We're all going to die – and I'm saying that, remember, as a dog who has recently read her own obituary.*

*Humans seem to live with the hope that a cure will be discovered before death turns its attention on them. But for all the advances in science you've made over the centuries, the best you've been able to do is forestall it. You might even find a cure for cancer one day, but you won't find a cure for death. The bad news is that there's never going to be one. But there is a palliative for grief. And that – as Hugh knew – was to have a consoler, a playmate, a partner in crime, a confidant, a protector and a best friend by your side.*

*I hear the front door open, then Roy calls my name from the hall.*

Alex Ferguson did something very stupid that winter. After watching United coast through their Champions League group, he threw on a weakened team against Fenerbahçe in Turkey, surrendering their place as winners of the group. It meant they got AC Milan – in my view, the best team in Europe – instead of Werder Bremen in the first knockout round.

There was no point in any of us carping about it, of course.

'Tough draws are never a valid excuse for not winning something,' was Roy's unsurprising response when I brought it up with him while we were taking the air on Mayor's Road a day or two after the draw. He never believed in the principle of the path of least resistance and he wasn't going to change now.

That was the thing about Roy. There was no lessening in his desire. Ever. Even as his body began its slow betrayal of him. And there were still some great days left. Look, the league was Chelsea's; by early February I think everyone had reached an accommodation with that fact. But Arsenal at Highbury was a game that always got our red cells humming, even with nothing at stake.

One morning, it must have been still January, I awoke from another of my nightmares – 'When I am shitting on the bench, I am thinking, "Jusht you wait until I get on that pitch – shoon ash I crosh that white line, I will domonshtrate for you what I can do!"' – and padded out to the kitchen to find Roy enjoying an early breakfast and reading a page torn from what turned out to be *The Observer*.

It was an article about Patrick Vieira's charity work in Senegal. It had been lying on the telephone table in the hall for a day or two, though I still had no idea who gave it to him. I was already smiling before he asked me the question.

'Where the fuck is Senegal, Triggs?'

'It's a small country in West Africa,' I said. 'An old French colony. I think Vieira was born there.'

'That's what I was thinking,' he said. He was sitting at the free-standing island. His hair, I noticed, was still mussed from his pillow. 'He was born there. Says it here. Dakar. So why doesn't he fucking play for them?'

'What?'

'You know, you're on about how much you love Senegal, obviously want to give something back – why don't you fucking play for them, if that's the country you were born in? That's the question *I'd* be asking. Why did you decide to play for obviously France?'

He stood up and carried his cereal bowl to the dishwasher.

I liked the way he was thinking, although I must confess I did keep one ear almost permanently cocked for the sound of Dylan's voice in the week before the game. Once, I thought I heard it, but it turned out to be just some stones trapped under the gate at the side of the house when Roy gave it a shove.

I've mentioned already the part I played in what happened that night. Vieira took issue with the literal marking job that Gary Neville had done on José Antonio Reyes in October, which had been my idea, remember. Vieira came in after the warm-up, told him to watch himself tonight and pushed him in the chest.

Neville reacted like any non-alpha would by – oh, dear – telling Roy.

'Summat's wound Vieira up,' he said. Or something like that. 'He's had a right go at me out there in the tunnel. He's pushed me! I'm literally gobsmacked!'

I was watching it at home in Hale. The first I knew of the trouble in the tunnel was when – probably like you – I heard Roy roaring, 'Why don't you pick on me? Why don't you pick on someone your own size?'

Roy, incidentally, was a whole inch shorter than Gary Neville.

He said other things as well that were audible only to a dog's ears. I could make out, 'You can't even look me in the eye! Look at you!' and 'Hard man! You're soft as shite, Vieira.'

There were lots of people shouting Roy's name in a reasoning way, trying to calm him down. Then Vieira emerged from the back of the tunnel, looking shaken, like a man who'd just been cut from a car wreck. Dennis Bergkamp had an arm around his shoulder and was whispering soothing words in his ear.

Roy wasn't finished. He came tearing through the press of bodies, his index finger already prodding the air. 'You're not a nice guy,' he said. I knew he was thinking about that piece in *The Observer.* I thought, this is great – provided he doesn't punch him in the face now. 'I'll fucking see you out there on the pitch.'

And didn't he just. I can remember every intimate detail of that match. Every move. Every pass. It was one of Roy's five greatest ever performances, to my mind, and proof that there was a lot more life in him yet. To see him relieve Robert Pires of the ball in midfield in the lead-up to the goal that put United ahead for the first time was about as exciting as anything I ever saw on a football field.

I thought maybe Ferguson was right – Roy might have years ahead of him after all.

It's easy to forget how good United were for most of that season. Either side of Christmas they put together an unbeaten sequence of nineteen games that included fourteen wins and five draws.

'Championship form,' as Paul Scholes pointed out when we ran into him in the car park of a garden centre in Failsworth. He was lifting ceramic pots into the boot of his Mercedes S Class and we stopped to give him a hand. Well, Roy did. I was clearly limited in the amount of heavy lifting I could do.

'I fully understand the fans' frustration,' Scholes said in that nasal way that always made me think of him as a boy. 'Two years would be a long time for them to go without winning obviously the Premier League. But alls we can do is keep grinding out results and hoping Chelsea maybe slip up, which they've not shown signs of doing. I mean, that's documented, isn't it?'

Roy pulled a face. 'I don't think you can say it's just down to Chelsea not having a bad patch. We gave ourselves too much to do. You're on about us showing obviously championship form. But we didn't in the first part of the season. We didn't play for the first two months! Threw away too many points, which in the old days – I've said it before – we could afford to maybe do. Not anymore. Chelsea and Arsenal, they've improved their squads, obviously brought in top, top players, who've proved their quality. It was up to us to lift our game. And we've not done it.'

Poor Paul, I thought. This was his day off.

Roy was right, though. You knew it was a bad year when you found yourself taking the domestic cups seriously. But the season wasn't a complete loss for United. There were the early stirrings of a relationship between Rooney and Ronaldo that would bring about the next era of success for the club. But would Roy and I be around to see it? That was the question that hung over us that entire dispiriting and ultimately fruitless spring.

I remember one afternoon we were driving somewhere and we spotted Ronaldo checking himself out in the window of the NatWest in Alderly Edge. 'Such a pity he doesn't have any confidence,' I said. 'If he had that, he might make a half decent winger one day.'

Roy laughed. He liked that.

'He's going to be a player,' he said. 'Might take another season or two, but he's going to be a top, top player, Triggs, who'll win things for the football club.'

Yes, there was a definite sense that a new era was a season or two away. But I feared it might come a season or two too late for us. I was right about that.

I was right about AC Milan, too. Not that I gave up and hid. No, I did my work on them as I always did, watched the Serie A highlights programme on Channel 4 and boned up on their strengths and weaknesses. After his performance against Arsenal, I was encouraged into thinking that Roy could do a job in reducing Andrea Pirlo's influence in the middle of the field. Beside him, Gennaro Gattuso was nothing more than a bag of wind, if you want my opinion. And any team with Jaap Stam in the centre of its defence, as Milan had, was immediately carrying a weight handicap, even with Paolo Maldini beside him.

I told Roy all of this, and I think he took it on board. He was as fired up by his performance against Vieira as I was. He kept saying, 'Milan are not a better team than us, Triggs. For me, if you have a real go at them, you can rattle them.'

He was right about that. Remember what Liverpool did to them in the second half of the Champions League final in Istanbul that May?

I wasn't blind to United's problems at that time. Ruud van Nistelrooy wouldn't be fit for the first leg, and you had to wonder where the goals were going to come from. Scholes hadn't scored in the Champions League all season. Rooney hadn't scored in five European games. Between them, Stam, Maldini and Cafu had lived over a century of human years. Rooney and Ronaldo were still teenagers. Guile generally trumped youthful promise on the big European nights.

I was right. In more than three hours of football, United barely caused the Milan defence an anxious moment. Ronaldo's step-overs were beginning to resemble a nervous tic more than a means of beating opponents. But what I found more frustrating than anything was that it was an old squeaking floorboard of a problem that was their undoing. Clarence Seedorf found the space to get off what was really a poor shot. The ball bounced off Roy Carroll's chest and straight to Hernan Crespo, who scored from a few yards out. Jesus, I thought, how long had I been talking about the need to sort out the goalkeeping problem once and for all? Yes, since Peter Schmeichel left! And that was, what, almost six years ago?

So now Carroll was out and Tim Howard was back in again. And United went off to Milan in search of two goals and a victory to take them through. But that AC Milan side were built to pick off teams on the counter-attack – they could break from one end of the field to the other in three quick movements. Crespo scored another. Yet sitting in the nicotine fogged atsmophere of Idina's living room, I still felt that if United could get one back, then Milan's self-belief might waver. And it might have happened, had van Nistelrooy – his confidence unusually low at that point – not taken an extra touch before dragging the ball wide from ten yards out.

You've heard it said before, I know, but it's only a cliché because it's true: football is a cruel game. A few months later, Roy and I sat down together, my chin on his lap, his hand on the back of my neck, shared a box of eight roasted nut Tracker bars and watched Djimi Traore win a European Cup medal.

Unless I dreamt that.

Did either of us realise in that moment that Roy's last chance of ever playing in a Champions League final had just passed? He didn't. He wouldn't. Because that wasn't in his nature. Unlike Dylan, he never ran out of will, even as we were running out of road. He would have fancied his chances of bringing any team to a Champions League final. Even Celtic. Oh, yes.

I, on the other hand, had an inkling that it was coming to an end. I could hear his joints creak like a house cooling. I was listening to his frustration at another nothing season. Beaten by Arsenal on penalties in the FA Cup final. Third in the league – the season bookended, appropriately enough, by two defeats to Chelsea, the coming power in English football.

'Losing is part of life,' he told me. We were stretching our legs one night on Ashley Road. 'We'll be back.'

But somehow I knew – I just knew – that there would never be another May like this.

## 17.

# Take a Bow, Son!

SO WHEN DID IT HAPPEN? WHEN DID HE STOP hearing me? When did our conversations become one-way transactions? Well, you can take it for granted that it was before he signed for Celtic. Because take it from me, had I been in his head, that never would have happened.

He'd occasionally talked about ending his career in Glasgow, but I never took it seriously. I'd always looked away for fear of laughing in his face and hurting his feelings. Look, I understood it was a boyhood dream of his. So, I presumed, was being a train driver. But sitting in a Tube cab pulling four or five carriages up and down the Jubilee Line all day would have been a sinful misuse of his talent – and so, frankly, was playing for Celtic.

I wondered did he realise how far beneath him it was until he arrived in Scotland. But I watched him from Hugh and Idina's sofa throughout that bleak winter, playing football in places with names that even sounded cold – Dunfermline, Inverness, Kilmarnock, West Lothian. It broke my heart. He looked like a man who'd just woken from a twenty-year coma and was going through the motions of life while trying to remember who he was. I became agitated watching him. Once or twice, Hugh had to take me by the collar and put me outside the back door.

But I'm jumping a few months ahead of myself here.

The disconnection between Roy and I wasn't something that occurred overnight. Much like the end of his relationship with Alex Ferguson, it was a slow severance that happened over time. I still talked to him, but gaps began to appear in his response times. Slowly, incrementally, through the summer of 2005, those gaps grew. Occasionally, I'd say something – 'I can't believe they're seriously considering paying Rio Ferdinand a hundred and twenty thousand pound a week! What the hell is happening to the world?!' – and there was no response at all. And I'd just presume he hadn't heard me. But then it began to happen more. Every second thing I said – 'Was that Kieran Richardson at that traffic light back there? I can't believe he's driving around in a Bentley. Has he even played twenty matches?' or, 'Where is John O'Shea's head at these days?' – would be met with a sad silence. Then it was two out of three things. Then, eventually – I can't pinpoint the exact day, but it was a few weeks into the new season – he couldn't hear me at all.

Yes, I was a silent witness to his final weeks as a Manchester United player and forever after.

All summer I sensed that some significant change was about to happen. That's not down to any supersensory powers I had. Everyone felt it. Since his falling out with Ferguson over that stupid racehorse, John Magnier had sold his shares in Manchester United and the club was now the concern of an American family called the Glazers. Not everyone was pleased by this development. I stayed largely out of it. Business wasn't my thing and anyway, I was suffering on and off that summer with an especially debilitating dose of diarrhoea, which, at first, I put down to either an intestinal worm or a viral infection, but was probably just something I ate.

There was a lot of uncertainty. Everyone was looking around them, wondering what was going to happen next.

I sensed a familiar agitation in Roy. There were more efforts to train me that summer. Some basic but pointless obedience task, I remember, that involved me having to sit on command. I went along with it for a week or two. I'd been around Roy enough years to know that it was about letting him think he'd established dominance, and there was no real harm being done.

Alex Ferguson bought another goalkeeper – Edwin van der Sar – a good one at last. But the only other money he spent that summer was £4m on Park Ji-Sung. I thought, How many more years can we keep doing this? I even said it to Roy, outside the Co-Op Food Store on Ashley Road one afternoon – those very same words. How much longer? He didn't answer me. It was the first inkling I had that something was wrong.

I began to feel suddenly removed from the centre of things. In a general sense, I think Roy had come to feel the same way. There had been a slow change in the essential chemistry of the United dressing-room. It was younger. More 'with it'. Gary Neville wasn't called Busy anymore – he was Gaz Nev.

But you looked around and you thought, Where are all the alphas? The team he joined in 1993 had Bryan Robson, Paul Ince, Steve Bruce, Eric Cantona, Gary Pallister, Mark Hughes. Men. Hard men. Where were today's equivalents? Darren Fletcher looked like a male nurse.

Yes, just as the character of the game had changed, so too had the character of the men who played it. Footballers growing soft on the spoils of success had long been a plaint of Roy's. And it happened. Not just at United. Everywhere. You'd bump into many familiar faces around Hale or Altringham or Alderly Edge. They were all nice lads, but – you could see it when you looked in their eyes – herbivorous by nature.

And money allowed them to remain adolescents forever. They played video games. I remember Roy entering into a kind of trance every time he tried to get his head around the idea of that. Grown men playing video games. But they did. They ribbed each other about their avatars on the newest

*FIFA Soccer.* They checked their hair before they went out to play. They paused to consider their options in the deodorant aisle of the supermarket.

I thought about the United dressing-room and – apart from Wayne Rooney, perhaps – I couldn't think of anyone capable of leading the team in the way that Roy had done. Listen, Labradors – along with sheepdogs, bloodhounds and possibly Brittany Spaniels – are known to have the lowest dominance rate of any dogs over their owners. And yet I wouldn't have taken orders from any of them. If Cristiano Ronaldo had told me to remove my muddy self from his Italian leather sofa, I would have rolled my eyes and laughed. And much as I liked John O'Shea, he could never have dissuaded me, with just a sharp word, from sticking my nose into a fresh piece of roadkill like Roy could. Kieran Richardson? Tch! I'd have bossed him around like I was a schnauzer and he was an old spinster.

But how much longer? That was the question as another season beckoned us on. I knew that Roy had dropped a hint about retiring in an interview the previous season. Ferguson sidled up behind him at training one morning and said something along the lines of, 'I'll be the one to decide when you retire.'

Roy was delighted with that. Although, given Ferguson's track record, it could have been construed as a threat.

The fact remained that he was now in the final year of his contract and there weren't going to be any more long and lucrative deals. The club's priority was no longer keeping him happy but sorting out a new arrangement for Rio Ferdinand. That's life. We grow old enough to outlive our usefulness – and that's if we're lucky. But what frustrated the hell out of me was the fact that Roy was still United's most influential player. You could see it in the first months of that season. They were half the team when he wasn't playing.

I can't say how prominent any of this was in his thinking

as the new season approached. I don't know if he was any more antsy than usual in the days before the team's pre-season training camp in Portugal. But, yes, I did hear Dylan's voice in the house the day before he left for the Algarve, painfully dragging five words across a line that required ten, then horning twelve into a line that could only accommodate six. The usual with Dylan. I think it was *The Times They Are a-Changin'*. I mentioned it to Roy in the car as he drove me to Hugh and Idina's the following day.

'Are you, er, bringing that CD with you?' I said. And Roy acted like I didn't speak at all.

Allow me to go on a short tangent here.

You may or may not know that dogs will avoid, if it's at all possible, expressing pain or sorrow. Yes, I know what you're thinking: a bit rich coming from an animal who's just spent a fair proportion of her autobiography detailing her medical history. But, believe me, I could have filled five books with the various illnesses and injuries that I suffered over the years.

There are very good evolutionary reasons for canine stoicism. Dogs are pack animals, predisposed by instinct to focus their attention on the weakest individual in a group – which, now that I think about it, might explain my fixation over the years with Mark Bosnich, Jaap Stam, Laurent Blanc, Diego Forlan, David Bellion, Juan Sebastian Veron, Massimo Taibi and Eric Djemba-Djemba, to name but a few. Did I mention Jaap Stam there? If I didn't, then Jaap Stam.

A demonstration of weakness, even within the pack, will alert a rival and trigger a change in the hierarchy. Which is why, hundreds of thousands of years before humans ever decided to domesticate the grey wolf, we learned to suppress signals of distress.

But there are times when we can't, when even our famous reserve fails us. That was me during the week that Roy spent in Portugal. Poor Idina and Hugh didn't know what to do with me. It was like Saipan all over again. I could hear myself panting, but I didn't know why. I felt tired – pure bone-tired – all the time. But when I lay down, I discovered that I couldn't settle, kept shifting position, couldn't get comfortable. At night, I shivered and trembled, even though the house in Cheadle was always unnaturally warm. Occasionally, overcome by tiredness, I would fall asleep and Ole Gunnar Solskjær would haunt my unconscious.

('Obvioushly, Ruud ish doing ever sho well – shtill shcoring goalsh for fun – and now the gaffor hash brought in Wayne Rooney and obvioushly Louis Shaha. Sho yesh I have poshibly fallen down the pecking order a bit! But there hash alwaysh been competition for plachesh at Mancheshter United. Right now I am not thinking about thash. My priority ish obvioushly to get my fitnesh back.')

I'd wake up yelping. Idina noticed that my eyes were dilated. I shrank from Hugh when he tried to place a consoling hand on me. They took me to the vet, who conducted a whole battery of tests and decided that – not for the first time in the experience of a veterinary surgeon in the Greater Manchester area – there was nothing physically wrong with me.

Which, if I could have spoken to them, I could have told them myself. It was my intuition at me. Something bad was happening in Portugal.

I spent most of that week sitting in Idina's hallway, staring at the front door. And when, after a wait of four or five days, a blurry shape through the frosted glass panel finally resolved into his face, I temporarily lost it. I jumped up at him so hard that I almost put him on the flat of his back.

'She were acting right strange,' I heard Idina tell him after he'd buckled me into the back of the car. 'Like she were upset about something. But we can't for the life of us work out what it could have been.'

Roy was good enough to fill me in during the drive back to

Hale. There'd been a row over the training facilities, which Roy described to me as 'just not good enough at this level'. And the fact that the players were permitted to take their wives and girlfriends to Portugal with them. This was at the height of that period when the women were being invited to share the stage. It was all part of the softness that had been allowed to seep into the bones of the club like arthritis. Angry words were spoken. Things were said.

Look, I was just happy to have him home.

But things were changing between Roy and I. Increasingly, our relationship was becoming characterised by the long periods of silence between our interactions. I remember complimenting him on how well he played against Everton on the first day of the season and receiving a vigorous petting by way of return. But when I said to him a few days later, 'If Rio Ferdinand is a £120,000-a-week footballer, then I'm a Bavarian mountain hound called Clive,' he didn't laugh like he usually would. Similarly, 'Phil Neville out, Park Ji-Sung in isn't the kind of business that wins teams Champions Leagues,' elicited not even a nod of acknowledgment.

I continued talking to him, but the responses became rarer and rarer, until I realised one day, a few weeks into the season, that he was completely deaf to me. And will I tell you the most heartbreaking fact of all? I don't remember the last words I ever spoke to him.

I know I was completely mute to his ears by the time he broke a bone in his foot at Anfield in the middle of September – a match that, trivia buffs will know, was the last he ever played for Manchester United. I wonder sometimes did he know that then. I watched him pick his way around the house on crutches and I tried to think of something suitably vitriolic to say about Luis Garcia, the girlish-looking Liverpool winger with the rhinoceros touch whose tackle had put Roy back in plaster. But what would have been the point? He wasn't going to hear me.

No, I was a dumbstruck bystander during those weeks when he moped around the house and must have been asking himself the same question that I had asked: how much longer can we keep doing this? And what was the point anymore?

In two years, all we'd won was one FA Cup and it was clear, within a few weeks of him injuring himself, that this season wasn't going to yield much either. They just weren't the same team without him. They couldn't impose their will on opponents. No one feared them. By the time the clocks went back, they were thirteen points behind Chelsea in the league and on their way out of the Champions League in the group phase. Wayne Rooney was sent off against Villareal. Paul Scholes was sent off against Lille. They struggled to even score a goal in an average group. And Ireland had lost to France in September, which meant there was going to be no World Cup for Roy next summer.

He must have thought, as I did, what are we hanging around for? To lift the Carling Cup in February?

*He notices that the front gate needs oiling. And that's when I know for sure. He pulls it back and forth in sharp little motions and it keens away on its hinges. Then he pushes back the arms of the Leyland Cypress that has been slowly colonising the driveway for months now and looks up at the windows, which could probably stand a coat of paint. He's identifying jobs for himself. Things to do to keep him busy.*

*I knew anyway. The night that Ipswich lost to Nottingham Forest had the undeniable feeling of an ending to it. A sending-off. An own goal. Roy bickering with fans sitting behind the dugout. I thought, yes, this thing has run its course.*

*I wasn't sure how much longer he could have stood it anyway. Not just failing for the first time in his professional life but failing week after wearying week. Asking players to do the kind of things that he used to do when they weren't capable or they weren't willing or they just weren't wired that way. Trying to come up with new formulas of words to say the same things.*

*He catches me staring at him from the kitchen with my front paws on the window sill and his smile is like a lance of sunlight struggling through a cloud. He can't get the key in the door fast enough.*

*We spend the afternoon in front of the television, me tucked into the crook of his armpit while his fingers worry lovingly at my coat. A montage of images plays in a loop. Roy stretching a blue and white scarf above his head on the day of his appointment and looking as uncomfortable as he always did with silly little ceremonies. Followed by two of the four goals conceded against Norwich. Then – one of my favourites – Roy's eyes searching the room for the reporter who let his phone ring during a press conference. ('That's lovely manners.'). Then Damien Delaney's own goal against Forest that confirmed the end. Then Roy driving away from the club within the last hour.*

*And alongside the pictures, a soundtrack of clichés. Upcoming cup games against Arsenal and Chelsea – how he'd have relished the chance to, uh, renew old acquaintances, as it were . . . Found it difficult to persuade players to come to the club and found it increasingly difficult to get the ones he had to do what he wanted them to do – there was talk of him losing the dressing-room, as they say . . . The famous, uh, vote of confidence from the chief executive of the club a week ago . . . Patience finally snapped . . .*

*I can feel myself slipping off to sleep here, while Roy quietly makes a list of his new priorities. WD40. A good garden shears. Paint.*

Events have a momentum that you can sometimes feel ushering you along. I felt it in those weeks. Roy had to go to Dubai for treatment one week that autumn. As he was stuffing clothes into a bag, I noticed the jewel case from *Highway 61* Revisited cast aside on the bedroom floor. I nosed it open when he bent down to open his underwear drawer and noticed that the CD was missing. I knew where his Discman was because I'd watched him put it into his hand luggage. I could have reached into that bag and extracted it with my mouth. But I didn't. I thought, No, Triggs – just leave it. What will be, will be.

Like you, I didn't hear Roy's denunciation of his teammates on MUTV immediately after his return from Dubai. I heard what he was reported to have said on Sky News and thought – also like you, I expect – well that's a pretty accurate summation of where United are right now, without a single word wasted. In fact, I recognised a line or two of mine – if not the words, then certainly the sentiments I expressed about Darren Fletcher, Alan Smith, Kieran Richardson and, of course, Rio Ferdinand. What did they expect? He'd just watched United concede four goals against Middlesbrough, then they sat him in a chair and asked him what he made of it. It was someone's fault, but it wasn't Roy's.

I saw the highlights of the game, by the way, and it wasn't possible to discuss that performance *except* in pejorative terms. They were a shambles.

But I was also a sensitive enough animal to realise that we were on old and familiar ground here. A furious row over the standard of the training facilities followed by an interview in which he implied criticism of the manager. Was he formulating an exit strategy for himself, whether he was conscious of it or not?

I didn't know what was in his head. Because for the first time in the eight years I'd known him, I no longer had access to his thoughts. So all I could do was offer him the consolation of my company and, through the long silences, try to fathom what he was feeling.

It's sad when things end. I got that much. His relationship with Manchester United had all the intensity of a love affair. But now it was over. They both knew it. So what were they going to be to each other from now on? Friends? No! That was something I'd noticed about humans – they often found it easier to walk away from relationships when there was ill feeling involved.

I'm only guessing here, of course. I'm just trying to think in human terms, which I know is as futile as you trying to see the world as I do. Dogs and humans. Doesn't matter how much we love you and you love us, there'll always be things about each other that we find unfathomable.

What *is* true, I know, is that Roy had been coming to the slow realisation that he was just another employee, like Stam, like Beckham, like Veron, like Nicky Butt, who was now playing for Newcastle. All that really mattered in football was whether or not you had a contract. And even contracts could be bought or exchanged. Or terminated.

There was, I gather, some effort at reconciliation. But then you know all of that. Ferguson called a meeting in his office. He gathered all of the players together, as he always did during times of crisis. This time, though, I wasn't a witness to it. But I could imagine the scene.

Twenty or twenty-five players squeezed into that room, sitting on chairs, on the edges of tables, standing. Ferguson, florid-faced and serious, looking at them over the top of his glasses and reminding them – but really Roy – that they were Manchester United players and Manchester United players have always stuck together.

I could see nice, well-meaning Gary Neville sitting there with that shop steward air of his.

'I know some people won't have relished hearing what's Roy's said in his controversial interview,' I could almost hear him saying, 'but he's still our talisman – I don't need to tell anyone here about obviously his quality – he's one of the main reasons we've done so tremendously well over the years.'

Ruud van Nistelrooy, saying nothing and everything, with his long, superior face. Darren Fletcher with his little jaw clenched, a bit hurt, but trying not to let it show. Paul Scholes and Park Ji-Sung, as inscrutable as each other. Wayne Rooncy wondering what the hell they're even doing here. Rio Ferdinand poised to add the rejoinder, 'Definitely!' or even, 'Wicked!' to any vaguely correct-sounding point he heard made. Cristiano Ronaldo wondering if he'd maybe overdone the pomade.

I was really going to miss those guys.

And Roy, his little features arranged into a defiant expression, looking each and every one of them in the eye and telling them, his voice rising, seeking its ceiling, that he didn't say a word that wasn't true — in fact, at the end of the day, he possibly didn't go far enough.

The week that followed passed more slowly than any I ever remember, even going back to Saipan. Experience suggested that Roy and the manager had finished the meeting not on speaking terms. I sat and watched Roy suffer. Do you know how difficult it is to love someone like I loved Roy and not be able to offer them so much as a single word of comfort? But then, what would I have said to him if he could have heard me speak? Nothing I couldn't have said by following him around the house, or by depositing my chin on his lap and sighing, or by inviting him to take the other end of my pull-rope.

We passed the afternoons and evenings watching television, just like we used to, except this time with no additional commentary from me. We watched documentaries about John Coltrane, the Spanish Civil War, Yuri Gagarin and the Battle of Saratoga, waiting for Roy, Alex Ferguson, someone, to put us all out of our misery.

Then one day, while Roy was at training, I noticed some figures appear outside the front gate, which was always a sign. I skittered into the living room. Sky News was reporting that Roy Keane's contract with Manchester United had been ended by mutual consent. I ran to the kitchen and stood on two legs, staring out the window, waiting for the sound of his car.

The little knot of people outside kept growing. An hour later, I watched the crowd part. The gates suddenly jolted to life, then opened slowly and through them came Roy, hunched over the wheel of the car, his face tight, his hands, as usual, at ten and two.

When he walked through the door, I was waiting for him in the hallway. The sight of me standing there triggered his reluctant smile. I loved him and he loved me. However you choose to audit your life, that's not a bad bottom line for a dog, you know?

I barked. Once. Twice. He laughed.

'Triggs,' he said, his foot on the bottom stair, 'I'm fucked. I need to obviously lie down.'

I barked again. He shook his head.

'Okay,' he said, grabbing the banister, 'just let me change my clothes.'

He went upstairs, then a couple of minutes later reappeared in the hallway, in a blue fleece sweater, jeans, trainers and a beanie hat.

'You know it's pissing rain out?' he said, then he opened the door. We walked towards the front gate under a hail of camera flashes and questions.

'What now, Roy?'

'Any regrets?'

Out through the gates we went, picking our way through the crowd, then out onto the road. The rain was really coming down now. A sneeze gathered in my nose. I hoped I wasn't developing a cold. Or an upper respiratory tract infection. We turned right. Then down Bankhall Lane we marched, our noses up, meeting every set of eyes, but saying nothing. The crowd followed as one, some of them with television cameras propped on their shoulders, running backwards, from their knees down to keep up with our lengthening step.

'Hello, Triggs!' someone said.

Our feet splashing on the wet road sounded like little lip smacks.

We looked great.